CONTENTS

		Page
Preface		7
Chapter		
1.	The Predecessors	11
2.	The Texts	21
3.	Cosmology	28
4.	Man	55
5.	Jesus Christ	70
6.	The Disciples	86
7.	The Practices	98
8.	The Sects	133
9.	The Gnostic Influence	161
10.	The Eleutherians	175
11.	The Moderns	181
12.	The Gnostic Paradox	188
	Bibliography	191
	General and Bible Index	213

PREFACE

This book surveys the gnostic religion from its beginnings, outlines the course of its expansion down the centuries, and indicates the extent of its continuing influence in modern times. Gnosticism has never died out, and in many ways remains a living creed, which is perhaps its chief claim on our interest today.

What is attempted here is a presentation of the broad flow of a major heretical movement that is both highly mystical and highly provocative. To deal with the vast quantity of data in limited compass has presented certain problems. Much of the material can only be abridged, and the difficult, and frequently discrepant versions, collated – a process that has obvious drawbacks, for not all the inconsistencies can be reconciled.

The main ideas and principles of the gnostics have been set down in the light of recent discoveries, and it is hoped that the basic strands have been separated from the ravelled skein and a pattern laid out as lucidly as the complex and often obscure facts permit.

I have outlined the teachings of the leading gnostic thinkers, together with the essential particulars of the more important sects, without going into the subtler theological distinctions between them. I believe that to the general reader the primary interest in the subject does not lie in these minutiae, but in the principles underlying the movement.

Gnostics were generally antagonistic to the Old Testament and all that it stood for, although they did not hesitate to cite its texts in a favourable light when it suited them. This hostility to the Law and the Prophets was one of the reasons why they appeared in an unfavourable light to the Church. Another was the often wildly antinomian ritualism of the more extreme

sexual

sects. Referring to some of their practices, St Paul wrote: 'It is shameful even to speak of those things which they do in secret' (Eph. 5:12). Quoting him, the fourth-century bishop Epiphanius of Salamis adds, 'I am truly ashamed to relate their foul actions, yet I will not shame to say what they do not shame to do, and I shall make all who hear me shudder at their disgusting practices.'

Although these features of libertine gnosticism might, with ample justification, be regarded as offensive even to modern sensibilities, I have decided, after much thought, to retain the passages dealing with them, as they have been discussed often enough in recent publications. In any event, there would be little point in omitting such material from a book that purports to give an all-round picture of the gnostic faith.

The fertility of their grotesque interpretations of holy writ, and their misrepresentation of the life and sayings of Jesus, should not blind us to the sometimes remarkable insights the gnostics have brought to certain aspects of the Christian message. They faced many moral questions without flinching, and came up with some most unusual answers.

Books on gnosticism are often replete with technical terms. I have not avoided the use of such terms where they are needed, though I have confined them to a minimum, and chiefly to those that constantly crop up in gnostic writings. In all cases they are defined or are clear from the context.

Except where specified, all foreign terms enclosed in brackets are Greek. These terms are transliterated without diacritical marks distinguishing epsilon from eta, or omicron from omega. For those who are interested, they are marked in the Index. Important Bible references will be found both in the text and index. All dates are AD, except where otherwise stated.

Writing a book on a recondite subject must at times place an author in a situation where his own resources are inadequate for all the material he might require for his research. On more than one occasion in the past I have had the pleasure of acknowledging the help received from the public library service in my area. I cannot let this opportunity pass without expressing once again my thanks to Derek Jones, MA, FLA, Borough Librarian of Richmond Upon Thames, and Philip Rayner, District Librarian, Teddington, and to the members of the staff, in particular Sheila Turner, Jane Anscomb, Jane Clement, Terence Daily and Richard Dennis. With the help of the excellent facilities provided by this library, I was able to consult books otherwise unavailable through the usual channels, many of which were obtained for me at short notice. I am most grateful for the courtesy of all concerned.

B.W.
Teddington

palestinial
& syrian adaptations
of Zoroastrian elements (Mesopotamian mystra)
anti semitic from start
ambiguous about Baal
(Adoni) Rakka (Ianna-Ishtar)
Anat-warrior spouse of Baal
Seth-Shamash-Mithra-sun Baal

1.

THE PREDECESSORS

It is not easy to find one's way through the complex labyrinth of gnostic teachings. To start with, there is much confusion about the precise definition of gnosticism. The Congress on 'The Origins of Gnosticism' held at Messina in 1966 tried to secure agreement on the significance and correct usage of such terms as gnostic, pre-gnostic and proto-gnostic, but without success.

Gnosticism embraces several religious doctrines of a secret character, embodying certain mysteries which, in a broad sense, are common to religious systems in many parts of the world. Dr. Günter Lanczkowski of Heidelberg, for example, finds gnostic elements in the religion of the Aztecs of ancient Mexico (Bianchi, 1970, p. 676).

But strictly speaking, gnosticism is a post-Christian phenomenon, and can only be understood in a Christian context, for Christ is fundamental to the gnostic doctrine of salvation. It is the name given to the beliefs and practices of a number of unorthodox sects that flourished in the Roman empire and western Asia in the first few centuries of the Christian era. Its chief diffusion centre was Alexandria. The gnostics salvaged much of the scrap from the wreckage of the pagan world around them, and added to it their own versions of the Christianity that was being propagated in their midst. Many elements of this eclectic system were borrowed indiscriminately, and taken together they represent an unassimilated miscellany of conflicting opinions. Their ideas are set forth in a wide variety of texts propounding teachings that are not consistently advanced.

There can, therefore, be no synoptic presentation of gnosticism, and any attempt to reconstruct it must be a patchwork made up of heterogeneous material culled from widely disparate sources. The few issues on which most gnostic schools are in general agreement may be set forth in broad outline as follows.

Fundamental to all is belief in a transcendent God, merciful and good. He is God the Father, who belongs to the upper world of light, but is utterly remote from our cosmos, and is indeed a stranger to it. Associated with him is his Son, the Logos. The cosmos itself is intrinsically evil, and is not the work of the true God, but of an opposing entity known as the demiurge, or 'creator'. There is a pantheon of sorts, a hierarchy of celestial beings, roughly divided into two classes: good angels, working for the upper world of light, and evil archons, working for the inferior world in which we live.

Man is involved in the primordial duality that pervades the universe. He fell from the world of light where he had his origin, and is now entrapped in matter and in the clutches of the demiurge. Salvation from this predicament has nothing to do with morality, good works or faith, but depends on a kind of transcendent knowledge (gnosis) of God's redemptive purpose through the Logos. The world and its laws, religious, moral and social, are of little relevance to the plan of salvation.

Each gnostic sect filled in the bare bones of this theology in its own way, depending on the particular background from which it emerged.

Gnosticism was born at the crossroads of many ancient cultures, at a time in history that marked the end of pagan antiquity. It owed its strength to the fusion of past and present, old and new, east and west. It became heir both to the rational tradition of the classical world and the mysticism of the oriental cults of antiquity.

The sources of gnosticism are therefore to be sought deep in the past. They are fed by many diverse streams of the ancient world, and influences from many religions are discernible in the broad flow of the gnostic faith. Among these sources we find Egyptian mythology, Hellenistic speculation, Zoroastrian dualism and Jewish apocalypticism, while certain of its practices are directly traceable to Chaldean astrology, Phrygian sensuality and the baptizing sects of Palestine. Some of these may be briefly mentioned.

The influence of Egypt on gnostic thought through Hellenistic channels is now well established, especially since the recent discoveries of about fifty texts at Nag Hammadi in

Upper Egypt, which we shall consider later.

Such ideas as the 'emanation' or emergence of gods one from the other, as Khepera from Nun, and Ra from Khepera; the pairing, or syzygy, of the gods; the arrangement of deities in groups, like the triad at Thebes, the ennead at Heliopolis, and the duodecad at Heracleopolis, were taken by the gnostics from Egyptian tradition.

Several of the greater Egyptian deities also figured in their writings and were engraved on their gems. These included: the artisan god Ptah; the ibis-headed Thoth, the scribe of the gods (known to the gnostics as Hermes Trismegistus); the ram-headed Khnemu (the Khnubis of the gnostics); the cow-headed Hathor; and the supreme trinity of Isis, Osiris and Horus.

Isis has been called the mother of all mysteries. According to the Greek philosopher and historian Plutarch, the base of her statue at the temple of Sais in the Nile Delta bore the inscription, 'I am everything that was, and is, and shall be, nor has any mortal ever uncovered my veil'. The gnostics held that the Egyptians were among the earliest nations to understand the 'holy and venerable mysteries relating to the rites and orgies of the gods', which they sedulously withheld from the uninitiated.

Furthermore, the Egyptians had a deep awareness of the importance of the asomatic or non-physical elements that make up the human being, such as the etheric double (Egyptian *khaibit*), the astral body (Egyptian *ka*), the soul (Egyptian *ba*), and other refinements, for which they had a large and varied vocabulary. This, and their tendency to personify the different attributes and powers of the gods, were taken over and adapted to their own needs by the gnostics. Such were the concepts of Fate (Egyptian *shoy*), Reason (Egyptian *ab*, 'heart', the seat of reason), the Word (Egyptian *hu*), the Name (Egyptian *ren*), the Power (Egyptian *heka*), Wisdom (Egyptian *sia*). According to Professor C. Jouco Bleeker, the latter personification 'shows resemblance to the gnostic Ennoia', or First Thought (Bianchi, 1970, p. 235).

The protective spells found in the *Book of the Dead* are analogous to the gnostic phonemes learned by initiates to guard against danger during the post-mortem journey of the soul.

In considering, among other matters, the Egyptian beliefs on death and resurrection, and the idea of a divine trinity, Dr

Pahor Labib says, 'There are many other Egyptian survivals in the Nag Hammadi library, a wide field of future research' (Wilson, 1978, p. 151).

An earlier generation of scholars, like Sir Grafton Elliot Smith and Professor Williams James Perry, were of the opinion that Egypt was the grandam of all civilizations, and that the similarity of early cultures was due to their common origin in Egypt, from where they were diffused around the globe. This theory has now been discounted, but there is still general agreement about the profound influence that this great civilization had on the cultures of the Mediterranean lands and the Middle East.

Like Egypt, Babylon too had its champions, who claimed priority for her in the cultural field. Scholars like Hugo Winckler formulated, and Friedrich Delitzsch developed, a pan-Babylonian theory, which assumed that most of the oriental peoples of antiquity were indebted to the Babylonians for their religion, their social organization and their cultural forms. More specifically, the New Testament scholar Wilhelm Bousset traced several gnostic elements to ancient Babylon.

From the Babylonian and Chaldean civilizations of Mesopotamia (the name by which the Greeks referred to the land 'between the rivers' Tigris and Euphrates), came the star-lore and number-lore that were to play a prominent part in gnostic thinking. Also, the legend of the love of the beautiful goddess Ishtar, known to the Philistines as Ashtaroth, for the young Tammuz, and of her descent to the underworld to seek him after his death. Associated with her worship was a rite of sacred marriage, or hierogamy, that used to be celebrated in her temples, and mimetically enacted by the chief priest and priestess in a small inner sanctuary called the bridal chamber, to dramatize a divine act taking place in the realm of the gods. This too was to assume a central role in gnosticism.

Another significant figure was a Babylonian culture-hero of great antiquity, the man-fish Oannes, who appeared out of the Persian Gulf during the first year of the creation of the world. This mythical association of Oannes with water is said to be the source of all baptizing cults. Some scholars believe that his name is the ultimate origin of such names as Jonah, Ion, Ian, Johann and John.

Turning now further north, it has been said that Iran's major contribution to the religious philosophy of the west, and to gnosticism in particular, was the idea of a fundamental dualism underlying the universe. This was expressed by Zoroaster (c. 700 BC) the prophet of ancient Persia, in terms of a continuing struggle between two cosmic powers: Ormazd the ruler of light, representing the principle of good, and Ahriman ruler of darkness, representing the principle of evil. Subordinate to these two principles were ranged the good and evil spirits, whose hostile and opposing ranks bequeathed many features of angelology and demonology to the religious tradition of the ancient world.

Certain other Zoroastrian concepts were also adopted by gnosticism. Thus, the Iranian figure of Gayomart, a gigantic primordial Adam, is thought to be the prototype of the gnostic Anthropos. The Zoroastrian notion of Zurvan, 'time', and its two divisions into 'infinite time' and 'time of long duration', provided the basis for the gnostic concept of the timeless sphere of the Godhead, and the limited time-duration of the universe made by the demiurge or 'creator'. The idea of lesser 'times', with their ruling deities, may have been responsible for the gnostic concept of the 'aeons'.

Associated with Ormazd in his struggle against Ahriman was Mithra, also a deity of light, who became prominent from the third century BC. Having completed his redemptive labours, which included slaying a Bull, Mithra celebrated a last supper with the companions of his toils and then ascended to heaven. An important Mithraic rite was a ceremony of death and resurrection. The candidate was laid on the ground as if dead, and the hierophant with his right hand grasped the right hand of the recumbent man and raised him up. He was thenceforth spoken of as one of the *syndexi*, united by the right hand. Another rite was that of baptism, in which the candidate was made to stand naked in a pit beneath a grating, and a ram or goat, or more rarely, a bull, was sacrificially slaughtered above. The blood fell through the grating onto the body of the neophyte who sipped it and rubbed it over himself. After the ceremony he partook of a sacramental meal of bread and wine.

In the west, the Greeks in their turn garnered a rich harvest from the beliefs, mythology and ceremonial practices of the earlier inhabitants of the Mediterranean regions and the Near East, which in time was inherited, through Greek writings, by the gnostics. The most famous of the Greek cults, from which the gnostics derived much of their ritualism, was linked with the great Eleusinian mysteries (see below).

Another cult, said to have come down unchanged from pre-historic times, was centred on the Aegean island of Samothrace. The details are not clear, but fragmentary descriptions survive of certain strange idols that adorned their sanctuaries. The Greek historian Herodotus relates that when the Persian king Cambyses (d. 522 BC) entered one of their temples he was unable to restrain his laughter on seeing a statue of a man standing erect opposite the statue of a woman standing on her head.

In imitation of the Samothracian figures was a sculptured work on the gates of Philius in north-eastern Greece, showing a woman fleeing from an old man with wings and erect phallus. Hippolytus, who wrote on the gnostics, also refers to Samo-thracian temple statues, among them the representation of two ithyphallic men with arms stretched up to heaven.

These Samothracian figures were well known in the mythology of esoteric art, and were used by the Roman architect Vitruvius and others to illustrate the ideal canons of proportion. During the Renaissance two such human models were portrayed to symbolize the two extreme forms of religious dedication: asceticism and licentiousness, both of which were exemplified in the gnostic sects.

Each figure was drawn in the form of a cross. One in the shape of a T (the tau cross, from the Greek letter *tau*), legs together, arms horizontally out at the sides, penis flaccid. The other in the shape of an X (the chi cross, from the Greek letter *chi*), arms up to form a V, legs spread out to form an inverted V, phallus erect. It was said that the candidates at the Samothracian mysteries assumed these positions before and after initiation.

One of the most important of the Grecian cults was Orphism, named after Orpheus, a semi-legendary prophet, poet and musician of Thrace, who was said to have descended into Hades in an attempt to bring back his deceased wife Eurydice. A number of the poems attributed to Orpheus were connected with the theme of the soul and its immortality. Man is half celestial and half infernal, and there is a constant struggle going on between the Uranian (heavenly) and Titanic (diabolic) elements within him. A basic Orphic doctrine was enshrined in the phrase: 'The body (*soma*) is the tomb (*sema*) of the soul', the implication being that the demands and desires of the physical body are a hindrance to the higher spiritual life.

The religious concepts and philosophical schools of the Greeks had a profound influence on gnosticism. The Simonians, Naassenes and other gnostic sects, devoted a good deal of attention to exegeses on the great Greek poets, especially Homer. Among their favoured philosophers were Pythagoras, Plato and the Stoics. The British scholar Arthur Darby Nock called gnosticism a kind of 'Platonism run wild', and the German authority Adolf Harnack described it as 'the acute hellenizing of Christianity', a Christian theology under the influence of the Greek philosophical tradition.

Gnosticism having reached its fruition in a Christian milieu, it was inevitable that it should take much from Judaism. Some of the early gnostic schools had distinct Jewish roots, and many prominent gnostics were Jews who had turned away from their own faith, denying Jehovah, the Old Testament and the Mosaic law, and propounding an inverse form of Judaism. R. M. Grant says: 'For all practical purposes the gnostics must have been ex-Jews, renegades from their religion.' Gnosticism evolved out of a disaffected and heterodox Judaism and perhaps expressed the failure of Jewish apocalyptic hopes.

A transition from Judaism to gnosticism is found in some of the nonconformist sects that flourished immediately before and after the Christian era. Chief among these were the Essenes (70 BC – AD 70), who dwelt in the wilderness west of the Dead Sea and numbered about 4000 at the time when Philo of Alexandria (d. AD 50) wrote about them. They worshipped Jehovah and observed the ritual laws of the Torah, but also paid adoration to the sun and followed a form of dualistic faith (taken from Zoroastrianism, based on the sempiternal conflict between good and evil, light and darkness. Their rites included a bath of initiation and a ceremonial supper.

In the opinion of many scholars, the evidence provided by the Dead Sea Scrolls, discovered from 1947 on, suggests that the material relates to the Essene community. The Scrolls speak of a Messiah-like figure, the Teacher of Righteousness, who was persecuted and probably executed in 88 BC at the instigation of a wicked priest. The sect barely survived the destruction of their monastery at Qumran in AD 68, and they finally vanished after the Romans destroyed the second temple two years later. It has been suggested that both John the Baptist and Jesus were Essenes.

In contrast to the active and nationalist Essenes, were the

contemplative and universalist Therapeutae (AD 20–80), who
lived around Lake Mareotis, south of Alexandria. According to
Philo, the community consisted of both men and women who
lived in separate cells where they meditated and read the
scriptures, which were interpreted allegorically. They claimed
the goddess Isis among their patrons. It is said that their ascetic
practices had an influence on the gnostic communities of the
Thebaid. Their origin and final fate are both unknown.

The Mysteries

The outer observances of the great religions of bygone times
often took the form of popular festivities open to all. At the
same time there were certain other rites of a grave and solemn
nature known as the mysteries, reserved only for those specially
prepared to receive them. In contrast to the public festivals,
which were celebrated for the welfare of the state, the inner
mysteries were meant for the individual and were conducted in
secret.

In one form or another, religious mysteries were practised in
ancient Egypt, Mesopotamia, Thrace, Macedonia, Greece,
Rome, Armenia, and various other parts of the world, from
Gaul to the Pre-Columbian civilizations of America.

Several theories have been put forward regarding their
purpose: they were ceremonies of initiation into the social laws
and customs of a community; they were rites in which the
traditional knowledge of healing, hunting, mining, metallurgy
or some other science or skill was communicated to suitable
candidates; they were puberty, fertility and phallic rites; they
were agricultural ceremonies connected with seedtime and
harvest; they offered a mystical experience of some sort; they
provided an actual foretaste of death and resurrection.

There is much uncertainty about the exact details relating to
most of the inner mysteries; the accounts we have of them are
not consistent, and in some particulars confused. Many
elements have been forgotten since they were never put down
in writing, but some idea of their character can be pieced
together from scattered hints in extant texts.

No one has ever betrayed the mysteries. Although sceptical
and even cynical about many things, the Greeks and Romans
took them very seriously. The Greek dramatist Aeschylus (d.
456 BC), who was initiated into the Eleusinian rites, dedicated
one of his eighty tragedies (only seven still exist) to his native

town of Eleusis, after which these famous mysteries are named. Certain of his writings were alleged to have been so full of the spirit of the mysteries that he was charged by the Areopagus, the supreme court of Athens, with divulging the secrets, and banished from Athens. Some think that his missing plays were deliberately suppressed or destroyed. It was generally thought that he received his just deserts when an eagle dropped a tortoise on his bald head and killed him.

The mysteries were conducted with the greatest secrecy, the candidate taking a solemn oath (Gk. *horkos*; Lat. *sacramentum*) that he would never reveal anything of what he saw or of what was imparted to him. The word mystery is said to be derived from the Greek word meaning 'to shut' (*myein*), that is, to seal the lips in secret, and the initiate himself was called *mystes,* the one instructed in the secrets.

Death held the key to all the greater mysteries. The candidate for the highest grades appears to have been given a form of god-experience through the death experience, which was often very convincingly enacted. He participated, as it were, in a rehearsal of his own death. Hence initiation was known as *telete*, a word related to *teleute,* meaning 'death'. The experience in some cases was apparently communicated with such realism that it is thought likely that the candidate, after his long vigils and fasts, may have been put into a hypnotic sleep or other xenophrenic state, and his subtle body was then helped to exteriorize in full astral consciousness.

The most important part of the rite took place in a section of the shrine especially designed for the purpose. The candidate was brought into an antechamber, his mouth was bound, he was blindfolded, his head further encased in a hood, and his hands tied behind his back. This symbolized his state of dumbness, blindness, ignorance and general benightedness. He was then led into the main chamber and laid down on the ground as if dead, and his obsequies conducted. After that he was made to stand up and was placed in the charge of a mystagogue representing the god Hermes, who is the 'conductor of souls' (*psychopompos*) responsible for guiding the dead through the underworld.

The ensuing journey entailed a descent (*kathodos*) into a subterranean chamber echoing to harsh and threatening voices, then turnings and gropings through perilous labyrinthine passages which, according to Plutarch, 'create amazement, trembling and terror'. Origen, quoting an earlier account, speaks of a terrifying 'masque of phantoms', perhaps representing the denizens of the underworld.

Then, following an ascent (*anodos*) to an upper chamber, his hands were untied and the blindfold suddenly removed, and he found himself in a brilliantly lit and richly decorated hall, filled with his fellows. All voices swelled in the great Eleusinian cry: 'Give rain! Give life!' (*Hue! Cue!*). Plutarch describes his own experience: 'A wonderful light burst forth, friendly landscapes received us, and by song and dance the splendour of sacred things was revealed to us.' The neophyte to whom these final revelations were made was now known as the witness (*epoptes*), and welcomed as one fully initiated into the mysteries.

In some places religious mysteries were also presented for popular entertainment and instruction in the form of a colourful spectacle (*thea*), with a great deal of dramatic display. Herodotus and other Greek writers have described the midnight pantomime beside the lake in Sais in Egypt that told the story of the god Osiris. There were scenes of the birth of the god, his struggle (*agon*) against an adversary, his death (*teleute*) and burial (*entaphiosis*), the search (*zetesis*) for his body, its discovery (*heuresis*), and its resurrection (*anastasis*).

St Paul used the symbolism of the ancients when he spoke in a Christian context of the purpose of the hallowed revelation that transcends the rites of seedtime and harvest, of fertility and the phallus – that of death and resurrection: 'Behold', he exclaims, 'I shew you a mystery... For this corruption must put on incorruption, and this mortal must put on immortality' (I Cor. 15:51–53).

2.

THE TEXTS

There is no gnostic canon, although gnostics accepted the
broad outlines of the Bible, with their own curious qualifica-
tions. They regarded the Old Testament as a set of writings
largely inspired by the Jewish god, and hence to be interpreted
with care. The New Testament, they said, was written by Jews
who had seen the light, but their work still retained certain
Jewish elements, and here again caution was advised.

Apelles, a disciple of the gnostic Marcion, said that in
interpreting the Bible it was necessary to distinguish between
those parts inspired by Christ and those by Jehovah. He quotes
a saying recorded in an apocryphal gospel: 'Be you tried money-
changers', meaning, learn to distinguish between the genuine
and the counterfeit.

Because of this conviction gnostics tended to comment on
the Bible in their own way, offering, as they chose, literal,
allegorical, symbolical or secret meanings to scriptural texts.
Where a given text was felt to be erroneous they rejected it, or
tampered with it as they thought fit. Where they believed
something was missing they invented an appropriate verse,
chapter or even book. Such indeed was the view of Irenaeus,
Hippolytus and other Church Fathers, who wrote scathingly of
their inventions and the innumerable spurious writings they
forged.

'They do not speak with one voice', the theologians declared,
'nor do they say the same thing about important events, but
express contrary opinions. They call identical things by different
names and so cause further confusion in the minds of simple-
tons. But even intelligent people can make little sense of some
of their utterances, for they are meaningless and incoherent.
On many issues there is great dispute among them, and their

teaching is divided accordingly. There is no outrageous interpretation of the Bible that has not been made by them. They
invent newfangled theories and concoct scriptures, transfer
scattered words and phrases from their proper place to another
context. By their shameless interpolations, amendments and
manipulations, they quite pervert the original sense. To confirm
their fictions they pollute the holy works with their shameless
lies, and do not even refrain from mishandling the words of our
Lord.'

Some of the earliest texts in gnostic literature are to be dated
not many decades after the first Christian writings, so it would
seem that 'heresy' did not take long to raise its head. These
early writings included many works referred to as *apocrypha,* a
word originally implying that they were too sacred and secret to
be in the hands of everyone, but were to be reserved for the
initiates or inner circle of believers. The ecclesiastical writers,
following the lead of St Jerome, regarded all apocryphal works,
whether gnostic or not, as false and to be rejected.

The gnostics were extremely prolific in their literary output,
and were responsible for a bewildering profusion of texts
comprising a pastiche of doctrines characterized by variety and
novelty. 'Every day', Irenaeus complains, 'one of them invents
something new'. Some of these texts were ascribed by their
authors to the patriarchs and other characters of the Old
Testament, such as Adam, Eve, Seth, Enoch and others. There
were also apocalypses, acts, epistles and gospels associated with
the names of John, James, Peter, Thomas and other apostles,
and also with Mary Magdalene, Herod and Pilate.

In addition to their written expositions, it is believed that
much of their spiritual teaching remained on principle
unwritten. Professor Morton Smith speaks of a long history of
gnostic secret gospels of which we know little more than their
names. Many of their doctrines, alleged to be the esoteric
teachings given to select disciples by the risen Jesus, were never
committed to writing.

Until the recent discoveries at Nag Hammadi (see below),
much of what was known about the gnostics was confined to
what had been preserved in the writings of the Church Fathers.
The Christian writers tended to regard the gnostics not as
heathens but as heretics or 'faction-makers', who imported
false teachings into the community of Christians and whose
doctrines warranted rebuke as well as refutation.

Though at times scandalized by their practices, and driven to use intemperate language, they did try to understand them, and on the whole passed on with commendable accuracy the basic precepts of gnosticism, as recent studies confirm. They also made faithful excerpts from the works of the gnostic teachers, and thus preserved what would otherwise have been irretrievably lost. Listed below are the names of some of the Church Fathers who wrote about the gnostics.

Justin Martyr (d. 165), born of pagan parents in Samaria, taught at Ephesus. He turned from the Stoics to the Peripatetic philosophers of ancient Greece, then to the Pythagoreans and Platonists, and finally to Christianity. He held that an awareness of Christ as the divine Logos (Reason) was already sown in the hearts of the pre-Christian patriarchs and philosophers, 'so that even if they are accounted atheists, those who have lived with Reason are Christians'. He wrote about the gnostic teachers Simon Magus and Marcion and their followers. Justin's pupil, the Assyrian scholar Tatian of Adiabene (d. 180), was the author of a famous 'harmony' of the four gospels, combining them into a single composite text, but became a gnostic himself after Justin's death, joining the ascetic Encratite sect.

Hegesippus (d. 180) a Palestinian Jewish convert whose extensive travels gave him first-hand knowledge of contemporary gnosticism. His *Memoirs* in five books are now lost, although some fragments were preserved by the Church historian Eusebius of Caesarea (d. 340). Hegesippus argued that the Church, originally a 'pure virgin', was corrupted by various forms of sectarian Judaism, which led to the development of the major gnostic schools.

Clement of Alexandria (d. 215), born a pagan in Athens, was well versed in Greek philosophy, lived mostly in Alexandria and was acquainted with Ammonius Saccus (d. 242), the founder of Neoplatonism. He was converted to Christianity by Pantaenus (who preached the gospel in India) to become, according to St Jerome, the most learned of the Church Fathers. In his *Stromateis*, or Miscellanies, Clement claimed to have been taught by wise men from Italy, Syria, Ionia, Egypt, Assyria, Palestine and the 'East'. Familiar with gnostic writings he reviewed a number of heresies, including non-gnostic ones. He believed that some gnostic sects possessed certain teachings of a secret tradition, but had interpolated many erroneous ideas and so corrupted them. He was aware of a secret gospel allegedly written by St Mark, and some even suggest that he was a gnostic himself. It may have been for this reason that in 1750 St Clement was decanonized by Pope Benedict XIV. One of Clement's pupils was Origen (see below).

Irenaeus (d. 202) native of Smyrna in Asia Minor, studied in Rome under the apostolic father Polycarp (d. 155) and became bishop of the Graeco-Gaulish church of Lugdunum (Lyons). He suffered martyrdom under the emperor Severus. Zealous in his opposition to the gnostics, his famous treatise *Adversus haereses,* 'Against Heresies', in five books, of which only a mutilated version survives, sets out to show the absurdities and inconsistencies of gnostic teachings, especially those of the Marcionite and Valentinian sects. The portions against Marcion were largely borrowed from the writings of Justin Martyr and a now lost treatise by Theophilus of Antioch (d. 117) a Christian bishop.

Tertullian (d. 230) born in Carthage, the son of a Roman officer, became a Christian, received holy orders, and lived for a time in Rome. He wrote a large number of controversial works directed against the Jews, against docetism and other heresies, especially against Marcion and the Valentinians, providing, in his words, 'a remedy for the scorpion sting of gnosticism'. He had a vigorous and glowing style and is regarded as the father of ecclesiastical Latin. His opposition to worldliness in the Church and his strong ascetic leanings culminated in his becoming leader of the Montanist sect some ten years after his conversion to Christianity.

Hippolytus (d. 236), a Greek-speaking Christian and pupil of Irenaeus, taught in Rome and was embroiled in conflict with several popes. In his mid-seventies he was exiled to Sardinia and died there the following year. His *Syntagma,* dealing with some thirty-two heresies, is lost; but his massive *Refutation of All Heresies* in ten books, written to expose the 'wicked blasphemies of gnostics and other heretics' is extant in part. In 1842 an incomplete fourteenth-century manuscript of the latter work came to light in the library at Mount Athos and was published in 1851 under the title of *Philosopheumena.* It is known that the second and third books contained detailed accounts of certain gnostic sects, but after Hippolytus's death these two books were removed by the orthodox Fathers and were subsequently lost. The portions discovered at Mount Athos shed no further light on the matter.

Origen (d. 254) Alexandrian theologian, and highly original thinker, was one of the most erudite of all the Church Fathers. His collection of ancient texts included one he 'found in Jerico in a jar'. As a student he attended the lectures of the Neo-platonist philosopher Ammonius Saccus. While still a young man he came under the influence of a wealthy lady gnostic to whose fashionable *salon* both gnostic and orthodox intellectuals flocked. But Origen did not favour gnosticism and was strongly critical of them in his works. He tended to the ascetic life, slept on the floor, ate no meat and drank no wine, possessed only one coat and no shoes. Feeling that sexuality was the one great impediment to a life of piety, he finally castrated himself. Origen's writings include a refutation of a certain Platonist named Celsus (d. 185) who was the first opponent of Christianity among the philosophers. Probably the most notable theory advanced by Origen was that of restitution (*apocatastasis*), according to which all souls, including those of the wicked dead, the denizens of hell, and Satan himself, will repent in the end and be converted and redeemed. Certain gnostic sects adopted this doctrine but warned that no one should imagine that this blissful outcome of universal redemption meant that they would escape the punishment due to all those who ignore the gift of salvation offered by Christ.

Epiphanius (d. 403) a Greek scholar and native of Palestine, became bishop of Constantia (Salamis), capital of Cyprus. In his youth Epiphanius had allowed himself to be seduced into the Syrian gnostic congregation of the Phibionites by certain women who, he confessed, were very beautiful in form and feature and ravishing to behold, but 'in the depths of their corruption' had the hideousness of the devil. He eventually reported their activities to his bishop, as a result of which some eighty members of the sect were expelled from the city. He wrote the *Panarion*, which is a descriptive catalogue of some sixty heresies current in his time, including a number of gnostic cults. He also preserved the entire text of a valuable gnostic document, Ptolemaeus's *Letter to Flora*.

The Nag Hammadi Texts

The intervening gap of fifteen centuries between the evidence provided by the Church Fathers and the recent finds at Nag Hammadi was filled in from time to time by further occasional discoveries of ancient documents bearing on the subject of gnosticism.

These documents were written mainly in Coptic and Greek. Coptic was the Egyptian vernacular current in the later Hellenistic period, a language descended from ancient Egyptian, with an admixture of Greek, and written for the most part in the Greek alphabet.

Thus, in 1769, the famous Scottish traveller James Bruce bought a Coptic manuscript near Luxor, which claimed to record the conversations of Jesus with his male and female disciples. In 1773 a collector rummaging in a London bookshop found a Coptic text recording a dialogue on 'mysteries' between Jesus and his disciples. In 1851 came the publication of a German translation, from Coptic, of one of the greatest gnostic texts, the *Pistis Sophia,* which had been discovered in Egypt in the previous century.

In 1884 during the excavations of a tomb at Akhmim in Upper Egypt, a small parchment codex was unearthed, consisting of fragments of apocryphal and gnostic texts, among them the *Apocalypse of Peter,* the *Gospel of Peter,* and the *Book of Enoch.* In 1896 an ancient manuscript of the *Gospel of Mary* (Magdalene) was bought in Cairo by a German Egyptologist. Between 1897 and 1907 three Greek papyrus fragments came to light at Oxyrhynchus in the Nile Valley, that contained sayings of Jesus written in Greek and derived from the *Gospel of Thomas.*

In 1909 Manichean writings (c. 800) in Uighur, Chinese, Persian and Turkish were found at the oasis of Turfan in Chinese Turkestan. In 1930 a small library of ancient Coptic works (c. 400) was discovered in the Egyptian Fayum comprising several papyrus volumes of Coptic translations from the Manichean canonical scriptures. Manichean writings have also gradually been revealed as a result of wider contact with Mandaean communities still in existence.

The first of the Dead Sea Scrolls was found in 1947 by an Arab shepherd while searching for a missing goat. These Scrolls were encased in leather and copper cylinders hidden in large clay jars in caves near the monastery of Qumran on the western shores of the Dead Sea. Indirectly, they shed much new light on gnosticism.

But the most remarkable of all such finds occurred at Nag Hammadi, a town about forty kilometres south of Cairo in the Jabal al-Tarif, a mountain honeycombed with caves, and used as a burial site some 4,300 years ago. In 1945, an Egyptian *fellah* in search of manure came upon a red earthenware jar about one

metre high, which held some old papyrus codices. He brought
them home to his mother who, according to one story, burned
many of them in her oven. The man later sold the remaining
thirteen volumes for a small sum. Twelve were eventually
acquired by the Coptic Museum in Cairo, while the thirteenth,
containing the famous *Gospel of Truth,* found its way to Zurich,
where it was bought for the Jung Institute and has since become
known as the Jung Codex. The Nag Hammadi documents are
sometimes referred to as the Chenoboskion manuscripts, after
an ancient Christian monastery in the neighbourhood.

The material salvaged from Nag Hammadi consists of fifty-
three texts in thirteen leather volumes, some fragmentary,
some almost intact, totalling about 1,000 papyrus pages in all.
For the most part they are Coptic translations made by a
gnostic sect about 1,500 years ago (c. 350) of still more ancient
manuscripts written in Greek (c. 130). They contain secret
gospels, philosophy, including ancient Greek writings such as
portions of Plato's *Republic,* cosmology, poems, mystical
exercises, sex mysticism, merkaba mysticism associated with
the heavenly chariot, and miscellaneous hermetic tractates.

3.

COSMOLOGY

The complexities of gnostic belief might at first sight appear to present insurmountable obstacles to any coherent interpretation of the subject. There are considerable problems in the way of integrating the various conflicting views in terms of one consistent doctrine.

The terminology used is often imprecise and confusing. A large number of basic concepts represent personifications of abstract qualities that are raised to divine or semi-divine status, and in themselves make up a sizable nomenclature. Says G. R. S. Mead: 'He who makes a concordance of names merely, in gnosticism, may think himself lucky to escape a lunatic asylum' (1960, p. 309).

Yet a way must be found through the confusion, and within broad boundaries it should be possible to indicate the main features common to most gnostic schools and so present what is distinctive about gnosticism. There will inevitably have to be simplifications and generalizations in respect of the many abstruse and often contradictory teachings, if some of the wilder theories are to be reconciled with those that are more moderate. *the whole - the above*

We begin with the outlines of gnostic theology and cosmology, for as the gnostic states, Alpha and Omega are one (Rev. 22:13); origin (*arche*) and end (*telos*) are linked, and it is not possible to understand the destiny of things if one does not understand their beginning. *Man doesn't ⊙ the same*

The Godhead
Gnostic sects trace the origin of all things to a first principle, a pure, perfect and supreme power, which is eternal, infinite and absolute. These terms merely attempt to set out our under- *one-ness*

hi dya totality

standing of this being, for whatever we say of him would have to be denied. The way of negation (Lat. *via negativa*) is one way of setting forth what he might be.

To begin with, the Godhead is ineffable, not to be described or named, for he is beyond every name and category, beyond definition, utterance, conception and comprehension, and beyond all terms we may apply to him. He is nameless, secret, concealed, holy beyond holiness, and outside the range of all thought. He is a hidden deity (Lat. *deus absconditus*), utterly unknown and unknowable, and his ways are past finding out. Of him no words can tell. Silence (*sige*) can best express him.

Yet men have ever attempted to speculate about him, and to find terms to describe what he might be. Thus, the Godhead is said to be the forebeginning, antecedent to all origins and events, being self-existent, unbegotten and uncreated. As he is without origin, so he is without end. To these privative and negative attributes the gnostics add another, taken from Greek metaphysics, namely, that the divine nature is impassible, incapable of suffering, injury or emotion. Nor is the Godhead to be considered in terms of any moral quality, since he is morally neutral, and beyond good and evil.

Again, he is formless, boundless, indivisible, incorporeal, beyond measure, quality, quantity, and not subject to classification. To him can be applied no concepts of time, space, matter, or substance. He is immutable, stable and motionless, undergoes no change, has no history.

Even the concept of existence as we understand it, is so remote from existence as it might be applied to him, that it would be true to say that the Godhead does not exist. He is Nothingness rather than Existence. According to the Basilidean gnosis, these were the secret words of the Saviour: that in the beginning there was Nothing, and even that Nothing was not anything we know in this world as nothing. There was no matter, no non-matter; no mind, no non-mind. There was not even the One. Nothing existed even in the state of being. There was simply non-being; a non-existent Godhead, and non-existence over all.

Speaking in our terms we may say that through innumerable eternities, the unoriginated Godhead, undifferentiated, unitary, alone within himself, remained in profound repose, the king of pure light, immersed in a world of unmixed light.

God

The gnostic order of origination attempts to reconcile a non-existent Godhead and a non-existent cosmos, with the emergence of the universe.

An undisclosed process was initiated in which there arose within the Godhead those qualities we associate with will (*boule*), as a result of which the divine world-order came into being. The reason for this is unknown, but several theories have been put forward: that the Godhead wished that his divinity should be made manifest; that he wished to become known; that he made the universe for his own glory; that he desired to be many; that he acted on a creative impulse. The leading theory is that the Godhead is infinite and eternal light and love. Love demands expression and needs an object to love. So the Godhead provided the necessary conditions for the emergence of other beings who could receive his love and partake of his bliss.

Theologians make a distinction between the Godhead, and God as commonly understood. The latter is the revealed God (Lat. *deus manifestus*). The first stirrings of the unknown Godhead resulted in the showing forth of the divine self, who is conceived of as an active principle. He is the uncaused cause, the unmoved mover, the sourceless source. Invisible to all, he sees all. Uncontainable, he contains all. He has need of nothing, but all things stand in need of him.

Yet it must not be thought that even this revealed God can be comprehended in his pure and unitary essence. He can only be understood in terms of the fundamental divine aspects. Hence some gnostic cosmogonies begin with a trinity, for within the unitary essence are three Persons. This is gnostically stated somewhat as follows. The Godhead reflected, calling forth himself from within himself, and thus it was. And what was, was threefold: *Nous*, 'mind', *Ennoia*, 'thought' or 'idea', and *Logos*, 'word' or 'reason'. In the writings of the Christian theologians, Nous, Ennoia and Logos are equated with God the Father, God the Holy Spirit, and God the Son. The divine essence is to be regarded as indivisible and undifferentiated, so that together the three form a oneness. Each aspect of the divine essence is distinct but not separate within the unity.

The Naassene gnostic sect say, 'He who believes that the universe proceeds from unity is mistaken. He who believes that it is from three believes the truth.' The *Megale Apophasis,* a semi-gnostic text, states, 'There are three that stand, and without the three that stand, there is no order.' The *Apocryphon of John* relates that in a vision the apostle John had after the crucifixion, he 'beheld a likeness with three forms which said, "I am the Father, I am the Mother, I am the Son".'

In general the qualities of the Supreme Being are associated primarily with God the Father, who proceeds from the Godhead, and is thus pre-existent and self-begotten. In the Christian view God the Father is the creator of the world, the maker of heaven and earth, and of all things visible and invisible.

The Holy Spirit represents the presence of God, and is said to be the divine thought (*ennoia*), the wisdom of God, the tongue of the Father, and the exhorter and comforter (*paracletos*). In gnosticism the Holy Spirit is often given a female personification. In the apocryphal *Gospel of the Hebrews* Jesus speaks of 'My Mother the Holy Spirit'.

The Son of God is the Logos or 'Word', who shares in the qualities of both Father and Holy Spirit. As the Holy Spirit is the tongue of God, so the Logos is the Word of God, or his revealed expression. As the Holy Spirit manifests the wisdom of the Father, so the Son proclaims the name of the Father.

Although the Son is sometimes said to be co-eternal with the Father, and co-equal with him, a distinction is made between God the Father and his luminous first-born Son. Indeed, certain gnostic sects, classed by their opponents as Alogoi, denied that the Logos was divine, and attributed divinity only to God the Father. But most gnostics laid great emphasis on the divinity of the Logos who, they said, proceeded from the Nous as his Son.

At the same time it was generally held that the Son, though divine, uncreated and of one substance with the Father, is not self-begotten, but begotten of the Father before all worlds. He is the beginning (*arche*), and precedent to all else. According to the *Megale Apophasis* the Logos is an infinite power who came into being before the aeons, and 'stands, took his stand, and will stand'. The term only-begotten (*monogenes*) sometimes used to describe the Son (see John 1:14) means primarily the only one of his kind, or unique.

Later Judaism, too, was familiar with the Word as the medium of divine revelation. Philo of Alexandria (d. AD 50) calls the Logos the intermediate figure between God and man, and describes him as the Son of God, the first-born, the 'second cause', and 'second God' (*deuteros theos*).

In gnosticism the Father's name is unspoken and unknown, but is apparent only through the divine agent, his Son. It is through the Logos that God is involved with the world, and men may experience the love of God only through the Son. The Logos was manifested in the world as the Lord's anointed, the Christ.

Aeons

A fundamental concept of many gnostic schools relating to existence is that of a projecting forth (*probole*) or out-raying of qualities from the divine unity, commonly known as emanation. God generates or causes existence, not through the intermediary of another or an opposite, not by creation, reproduction or evolution, but by a unique manifestation that brings into existence a complex and at times paradoxical chain of being, forming a descending hierarchy of spiritual entities.

The divine attributes of God, that is, the virtues and powers associated with the Father, the abstract qualities, mental states, spiritual concepts and metaphysical ideas, like Love, Power, Will, Understanding, Mercy, Truth, constituted the Father's thoughts and designs, which lay hidden within the Father, known to him, but unknown to themselves. Then the Father gave them existence, and they flowed forth from the divine source.

At first these abstract qualities were unconscious, like unborn children, but when they became manifest and received names, they assumed identity, passed into separate existence, and were personified (hypostatized) as independent beings. They were then able to think and speak and gain some knowledge of the Father through the divine Logos. In gnosticism the externalization of the divine attributes in this manner constitutes the first stage of a long process resulting from the overflow or outpouring of the fullness (*pleroma*) of God.

The entities that emerge from this process are known as *aeons,* a class of celestial beings of varying attributes and powers. Their own qualities, the regions they occupy, the dimensions in which they function, and the time-span of their operations, all likewise become actualized, take on independent existence, and form links in the chain of emanation.

The aeons representing the divine qualities, their appearance, form and powers are referred to by their generic name of *angels,* a term which means 'messenger'; hence, they are often spoken of as courier spirits. But they have different powers and functions. Every manifestation of God is in fact an angel. A sincere prayer calls an angel into being. A prophet may experience a celestial vision through the intermediary of an angelic visitor. Angels have no perceptible form and cannot eat or drink, but when they visit men they take on docetic or apparent physical bodies, so that they might be thought human and not cause alarm.

Since, in the view of some gnostics, the angels played a contributory role in the messianic work of salvation, a cult of angel-worship developed among certain early groups. St Paul expressly warned against such misguided pursuits (Col. 2:18). But most gnostic sects regarded angels as part of the aeonic hierarchy and therefore not to be worshipped.

The heavenly hierarchy includes a great host of angelic entities: archangels, cherubim, seraphim, amens, voices, virtues, marks, guardians, splendours (*augai*), reasons (*logoi,* not to be confused with the Logos), authentics and others. In the Bible some are grouped as principalities (*archai,* literally 'ancient ones'), powers (*dynameis*), thrones (*thronoi*), dominions (*kuriotetes*), authorities (*exousiai*), lesser gods (*theoi*), and rulers (*archontes*). Among these, again, several were later degraded.

These divine virtues and agents, making up the angelic aeons, occupy and officiate over the management of the various heavens, constituting the 'many mansions' mentioned by Jesus (John 14:2). The highest heaven is an eternal and holy kingdom concealed from all but a few, in which only the 'angels of the presence', the 'angels of the throne', and the 'angels of the chariot' are allowed to serve. Though it is sometimes spoken of as the seventh or highest heaven, it lies beyond all the heavens and is the true heaven, the supercelestial heaven, the heaven beyond the heavens.

The Logos in his Christ manifestation came from the seventh heaven. Adamel, the prototype of Adam, was formed in the fourth (or third) heaven. St Paul was granted an experience of the third heaven (2 Cor. 12:2). Enoch and Elijah were translated to the second heaven and from there are said to attend the destinies of the righteous on earth. The archons or rulers came from the first or lowest heaven.

The heavens and their inhabitants comprised the earliest and

purest manifestation of the emanatory process. The entities
that emerged then were part of the divine perfection.

The Boundary

Gnostic cosmology speaks of two distinct and irreconcilable
worlds. One is the eternal world of God the Father and the
heavenly hierarchy, the world of fullness (*pleroma*), of reality
and of perfection, the noumenal world of things in their true
form. The other is the world in which we live, the world of
deficiency (*hysterema*), of illusion and imperfection, the
phenomenal world of time and flux.

Within and forming part of the heavenly region, though
sometimes treated as lying between these two worlds, the
spiritual and the material, there is an intermediate region,
referred to as the boundary (*horos*), which prevents entry into
the higher realm, conceals what occurs there, and admits only
those who are elected to pass. The horos lies outside the
manifest cosmic system; it is a realm of paradox that is
everywhere and no-'where'. Here we bid farewell to time and
space. In gnosticism the horos is closely associated with the
Logos.

Guarding the horos is the great aeon known variously as the
Limit-Setter (Horothetes), the Across-Taker (Metagogeus),
the Emancipator (Karpistes), the Guide or Leader (Kathegetes),
the Redeemer (Lutrotes). He is sometimes identified with
Christ (Jung, 1968, p. 65).

Across the horos there stretches a great veil or curtain
(*katapetasma*), which bears the secret patterns (*paradeigmata*) of
all things. These are the original concepts in the mind of the
Logos, and their distorted reflections abide as shadows in the
world below. The shining images on this curtain are neither
Platonic 'ideas', nor the abstract 'universals' of the medieval
schoolmen, but actual archetypal images. For this reason the
whole panorama limned on the curtain is spoken of as the
ontological world of really existing things, depicting innumerable multitudes of creatures in all their diversity, and through
all their vicissitudes.

The picture of himself that a man is familiar with on earth is
nothing compared with what is drawn upon the changing
tapestry above. In the *Gospel of Thomas* Jesus remarks, 'When
you see your likeness, you rejoice. But when you will see your
image (*eikon*) which came into existence before you, which

neither dies nor is manifested, how much will you endure?'

Although it is beyond human comprehension or conception, the horos is referred to by various descriptive names suggestive of its purpose. It is described as a wall, a pallisade, a turnstile, a portal (*thura*). The Logos himself is also spoken of as the door (John 10:9). Because it is believed to form the environs of the heavenly region it is known as the suburbs (*proasteion*), the frontier (*horion*), the barrier (*phragmos*), the partition (*dia-phragmos*), demarcating the bourn between the worlds.

Bounded by a circular embankment of dazzling white luminosity known as the Flaming Walls, it serves as a barricade against trespass, and is thus called the Ring-pass-not. A long narrow bridge, the Rope of the Angels, provides a way for the angelic couriers as they carry messages from the divine realms to mortals below.

Perhaps the most significant of all the descriptive analogies used for this mystical boundary is that of the cross (*stauros*), a symbol of world-wide diffusion. The Welsh mystic Thomas Vaughan (d. 1666) referred to the stauros as 'a thing appointed to a most secret and mysterious office'. Progress across this area separating the two disparate worlds involves an experience of terrifying magnitude.

The stauros is sometimes represented as a crossbeam or yoke (*zygos*) because that is what the Logos took upon himself, and calls upon his followers to bear (Matt. 11:29). But it can also mean a stake for transfixing, or crossed beams for punishment. In gnosticism the stauros signified salvation through suffering, redemption through affliction.

The concept of a turning, spiralling or cruciform figure, betokening the transit or crisis point between two worlds, is common to many mystical systems. The stauros is the cross-point of the world (Lat. *axis mundi*), marking the zone between the Real and the unreal. In the *Timaeus* Plato refers to the soul-stuff of the universe in terms of two circular strips joined together like the Greek letter *chi* (X). Similarly, *tau*, the last letter of the Phoenician and Old Hebrew alphabets, is shaped like a cross, and was popularly held to be a protective emblem of supernatural power. The enigmatic nature of the cross is also said to be hinted at in the 'line of confusion' (Heb. *kau-tohu*) mentioned in the Old Testament (Isa. 34:11), suggesting the unfordable divide that is drawn 'crosswise' and that separates the temporal and eternal worlds.

There is a more direct reference in the Old Testament (Isa. 28:13) to the stauros in the phrase, 'line upon line' (Heb. *kaulakau*), which is supposed to have been one of the three secret words spoken by Jesus to Thomas. It is believed to refer through the symbolism of the cross to the 'Being who is on high', that is, the Redeemer. The followers of the gnostic Basilides taught that the Redeemer descended 'in the name of Kaulakau' (Bruce, 1974, p. 119). In the New Testament the invisible cross is represented as bestriding the cosmos in terms of 'the breadth, and length, and depth, and height' of the love of Christ, which surpasses gnosis (Eph. 3:19).

Only through the stauros can souls enter into life eternal. Without it men are held in thrall by time, subject to Satan, to fate and to reincarnation. The stauros is the axis of a mighty spiral that reverses the order of the cosmos, and takes man from the emptiness (*kenoma*) of the lower world, to the fullness (*pleroma*) of the upper, from the flux to the changeless, from becoming to being, from imperfection to perfection, from reincarnation to redemption, from phenomena to noumena, from the world of illusion to the world of Reality.

The Place

In some gnostic systems it is thought that the phenomenal world lying on our side of the horos emerged as a continuation of the emanatory process that brought the aeons into being. As the process continued, elements of degeneration began to manifest themselves, and the aeons became progressively less and less perfect expressions of God. Between the inhabitants of the heavenly and the material realms there thus exist a graded series of beings, each one declining in goodness and spirituality as it recedes from the divine source.

In another theory the phenomenal world and the evil aeons who control it did not arise as a consequence of any decline in the virtues of the emanations, but resulted from a Fall that followed the exercise of free will. According to this theory, God the Father created the aeons out of love. It is within God's power to make perfect beings, but such beings would be devoid of will. Puppets could not experience bliss, earned out of understanding and effort. As long as creatures are devoid of their own will, freely exercised, they are automatons and not autonomous.

In order to make sense out of his desire to create independent

entities God had to give the aeons the power of free choice, even if it meant that they might choose to move out of the area of his love, and disobey him.

It is said that as a final gesture therefore, God withdrew the operation of his will (*thelema*) over the aeons, and bestowed upon them the gift of free will, letting them determine their own destiny. This is expressed in gnostic writings by saying that there was a contraction (*pyknosis*) of the divine will at this stage.

As God is one and unitary, the removal of his will was naturally accompanied by the withdrawal of the divine 'presence' from that area. The process of emptying (*kenosis*) left a vacant place (*topos*) for what was to become the natural universe we know. In gnostic writings a cognate word (*kenoma*), signifying 'emptiness', describes the illusive, phenomenal world of space and time in which we live. It is to be noted that by obscuring himself in this way God made the place where the world occurs, but he is not that place.

The exercise of free will requires an area for its operation, and this resulted in certain catastrophic consequences. Where the will of the Father was withdrawn, the will of the opposing archons prevailed. Where the writ of his goodness did not run, evil emerged. Where his spirit was removed, matter came forth. Where his light was withdrawn, darkness supervened. Instead of love and providence, there was now law and fatality. And where there had been life, there was now death.

Yet it must be remembered that nothing can have existence without God, and even when God is apparently absent, his erstwhile presence has left its permanent impress. The *Gospel of Truth* speaks of this residual presence of God even after his withdrawal, as the footprint-trace (*ichnos*) of the Father's will. Basilides too emphasized the essential presence of God in all circumstances and situations, when he said that the empty place resulting from God's withdrawal did not ever cease to show traces of the divine brightness. The vacated place retained the 'flavour' of the Father, just as a bowl containing sweet-smelling unguent retains the fragrance even after the bowl has been completely emptied.

No place is therefore quite devoid of the divine flavour, and the empty topos might be spoken of as a mixture of good and evil, light and darkness. It is because of this residue of God's presence that the demiurge was able to fashion this world.

The Archons

The withdrawal of his will by God and the exercise of free will by the aeons resulted in the dramatic situations recorded in many ancient mythologies. In the gnostic view, a number of aeons rebelled against the divine authority and a conflict of cosmic dimensions ensued.

Certain members of the celestial host play a special role in the subsequent drama. Among these is Sophia, a female aeon of wide significance in gnosticism. Another is Satanel (the *el* denoting his archangelic status), once a mighty aeon and chief of the angelic host, who was to become the demiurge or creator of the material world. And all-important for the human race is the figure of yet another aeon, Adamel. The story of the decline and fall of these three beings, who are among the aeons of the descent, figures prominently in gnosticism.

In contrast to the good aeons or angels, the wicked, evil and disobedient aeons are designated by the generic term, archons. In the Bible, words like 'chief', 'ruler', 'magistrate' or 'prince', are often used to translate the word 'archon'. But here too, in some contexts the usage is confined to an evil being, such as when Jesus speaks of the prince (*archon*) of this world, meaning Satan (John 12:31).

The various archons or hostile aeons, their origins, and their complex interrelationships are described in great detail in the gnostic writings. Irenaeus remarks scornfully that 'they recount all their ludicrous genealogy as confidently as if they had been midwives at their birth'. Not surprisingly, there is considerable variance of gnostic opinion about the archons, their names, numbers, their order of emanation, their place and priority in the hierarchy, their powers, their characteristics and destinies, which are not consistently given in the different accounts. Their numbers range from dozens to hundreds. The Valentinian system mentions 360 aeons and archons, and that of Basilides 365. On the other hand, according to the Nag Hammadi *Tripartite Tractate,* they are infinite in number.

These beings have their respective spheres of influence and their respective habitations or heavens. Like Irenaeus, Tertullian ridiculed the elaborate cosmology of the gnostic schools, with their multifarious paradises, like apartment houses for the elect. The universe, he adds contemptuously, has been turned into rooms for rent.

These paradises are said to be the lower heavens, and not to be confused with the heavens of the divine realms. They include the stellar and planetary spheres, the Elysian Fields, the Fortunate Isles and other traditional paradises of the pagan mythologies, which symbolize the passing pleasures offered by the archons to human beings in exchange for homage and worship. At the end of time, all these lower heavens are destined to be rolled up like a scroll (Isa. 34:4).

The leader of the archons is the demiurge, the creator and builder of the world, and he has subordinate archons to help in his government. In his *Laws* Plato writes that the ruler of the universe 'has appointed ministers to preside over the various functions of the cosmos down to the last fraction of them with infinitesimal exactness'. These subordinate administrators include the principalities, powers and other world-ruling dark aeons mentioned by St Paul (Eph. 6:12). They are the self-willed (*authades*) or arrogant ones, who as spirits of the opposition are regarded as antigods (*antitheoi*).

Some are collectively named after the places and things they rule: the abyss (*bythos*), unorganized matter (*chaos*), the place (*topos*). Those ruling the lesser localities are called toparchs. Each evil is likewise personified (hypostatized) as an archon. Time and its divisions and space and its dimensions are separately under the control of archons. Some supervise the workings of the heavenly bodies, such as the thirty-six *decans,* each responsible for ten degrees of the zodiac, and the 'liturgists' or public workers (*leitourgi*) who look after the pathways of the stars.

The elemental powers (*stoicheia*) referred to in the Bible (Gal. 4:3) are concerned with various aspects of nature and natural phenomena, and by their aid they plague mankind. Plutarch and other Greek writers frequently speak of local nature deities, like Pan, as 'spirits' (*daimones*), some good and some evil. There are also those who exercise control over the human body and its functions. One version of the *Apocryphon of John* lists the names of the archons who created each separate part and organ of the body.

All the lesser archons are treated as later and therefore more decadent phases of the emanatory process.

Sophia
One of the archetypal figures of gnostic mythology, Sophia, is an ambivalent character, with both a mystical and meretricious

side, both good and evil. She is treated in different contexts as one of the aeons, usually the thirteenth emanation, or as the mother of the aeons, including the demiurge and Ialdabaoth (see below).

A famous gnostic work called *Pistis Sophia,* 'faith-wisdom', (c. 250) which purports to record some of the revelations of the risen Jesus, also relates the circumstances attending the banishment of Sophia to the material sphere, and the sufferings she underwent as a result.

Various reasons are put forward for the fall of Sophia from the upper spheres and her plunge into the world of matter. In one view she craved for complete knowledge of the light of the Absolute, which is denied to all. This rash curiosity (*tolma*) led to her downfall and exile. In another view, the tragedy of Sophia occurred when she mistook the false light she saw below for the 'light of lights' for which she aspired, leapt forth after it and fell like a sparkling drop into the black waters of chaos in the plane of matter.

In another text she desired to create alone, like the Absolute, without the aid of a male counterpart. In the *Hypostasis of the Archons* it is said that Sophia 'wished to accomplish a work by herself, without a consort', and in this way to become independent of the aeons. She therefore ceased to perform with the aeons the profound mystery of sexual union, and strove to break away from their influence. Consequently, she was expelled from their company and forced to plunge downwards.

Because she had attempted to be better than the aeons they vented their animosity on her by punishing and humiliating her, and preventing her from reascending to the higher realm from which she came. In some texts she represents the doleful earth, and on earth the stricken city of Jerusalem for whom Jesus wept (Luke 19:41). The afflictions of Sophia are vividly portrayed.

She was imprisoned in a material body and made to transmigrate into different female bodies, in each of which she had to undergo various indignities. The gnostic *Exegesis on the Soul* speaks of her as falling among ruffians who repeatedly assault and rape her. On one occasion she even stood for hire in a brothel. The *Second Treatise of the Great Seth* refers to 'our sister Sophia, who is a whore'.

In this aspect as the lower Sophia she is the lewd and lustful one (*Prouneikos*), the keeper of corrupt and profane knowledge.

In contrast to Christ who is He of the Right Hand, Sophia is She of the Left Hand. Because she is banished from the realm of the aeons she is the 'exiled one', and in this respect shares the qualities of the Jewish Shekina.

The trials and tribulations of the suffering Sophia finally lead to remorse and repentance, a change of mind (*metanoia*), and in the end, redemption. Her love for the light of lights (the Logos) is restored and through it she acquires a new faith (*pistis*) in the light. As a result of her conversion she is permitted to return to the upper realm, rising to a height superior to that of the other aeons.

In some texts Sophia is spoken of as the sister and in others as the bride of Christ, and on her ascent she enters the Pleroma and is clothed by Christ in his light-vesture. Together they enter the bridal chamber, Saviour and Sophia, the Lamb and the Lamb's bride (Rev. 21:9), and together they rejoice in the mystical marriage. It is this same bridal chamber that is to be the scene of the nuptials of other redeemed souls.

Sophia has many transcendent and divine attributes. She is sometimes equated with the Holy Spirit; she is also the merciful one, with the title of Perfect Mercy. Because she was 'summoned forth' from the abyss into which she had descended, she is sometimes referred to as the Church (*Ecclesia*). Again, she is regarded as a manifestation of the thought (*ennoia*) of the supreme deity. In this respect she functions in accordance with her own name, Sophia, which means wisdom. Elsewhere she is referred to as Achamoth (from the Hebrew *chokma,* 'wisdom'). Achamoth as the Sophia above, is distinguished from the lower Sophia of death (Heb. *moth*).

Her paradoxical nature is brought out in a text discovered at Nag Hammadi and curiously entitled *Thunder, Perfect Mind,* in which the feminine divine power describes herself as: 'The first and the last, the honoured and despised, the whore and the holy one, wife and virgin, barren and fertile'.

The Demiurge

One of the fundamental beliefs of the gnostics is that the creator of this world and ruler of the cosmos is not the same as the supreme deity and loving Father ruling in the highest heaven.

The creator god, originally called Satanel and now known as Satan, was the chief of the aeons, and occupied a privileged

position within the pleroma or heavenly abode. He was so
highly esteemed that he was spoken of as the viceregent of God
the Father, and as Lucifer the bearer of light. In some accounts
he was the elder brother of Jesuel (the heavenly Jesus).

At some stage within the pleroma there occurred a fall, a
matter shrouded in great mystery. Satan was the chief exemplar
of the fall, but he was not the only one among the aeons to
suffer such a decline, and each such fall occurred because of
adherence to a primordial evil. Satan fell through pride (*hyper-
ephania*), Sophia fell through rash curiosity (*tolma*), the nephilim
or giants (Gen. 6:4) fell through concupiscence (*epithymia*), and
Adam fell through disobedience (*apeitheia*).

In Satan's case the exercise of his free will led to arrogance
and abuse, which created envy and ambition in his heart. In one
account he desired to emulate the Father and exalt himself
above God (Isa. 14:13). In another, satiety (*koros*) with his
happy state caused him to rebel. In yet others, he became
jealous of the importance accorded to Adam. The self-willed
Satan revolted, was joined by a number of other aeons, was
overcome and expelled from the heavenly abode. Christ, who
witnessed the event said, 'I beheld Satan as lightning fall from
heaven' (Luke 10:18).

Satan, the fallen angel, has a number of names and descriptive
titles. He is first and foremost the creator (*demiourgos*), a word
derived from a Greek word meaning 'craftsman', and used in
the sense of a creator-god by many early writers from Plato to
Philo, as well as by the gnostics. The demiurge is the ruler of all
(*omniarch*), meaning, of the whole temporal sphere of material
existence.

He is also the one possessing world power (*cosmocrator*). In the
New Testament he is described as lord of the universe with the
power to dispose of this world's goods (Luke 4:6). He is the
prince of this world (John 12:31), and the god of this world (2
Cor. 4:4). The Christian interpretation of 'world' in these
contexts is 'age', so that the demiurge or Satan is god of the
present epoch.

The Bible speaks of Satan as the old serpent (Rev. 12:9), and
among gnostics too a frequent epithet used for him is 'serpent-
shaped' (*ophiomorphus*). As such he received special veneration
from the Ophite sect.

Because he vilifies God the Father and the angels he is known
as the slanderer (*diabolos*), from which word comes the English

devil, and the Arabic name for Satan, Iblis. He is the monarch of demons (*demoniarch*), embodying all evil (*kakia*) and wickedness (*poneria*), and full of hidden plots and secret conspiracies to enslave mankind.

Satan is a fiery archon, but his fire is a dark element, for he is the prince of darkness. Among his chief agents are Death (*thanatos*) and Hell (*hades*), both of whom are mentioned in some texts as primordial beings or archons hostile to mankind. The Bible describes Death astride a pale horse, with Hell following close behind (Rev. 6:8).

virtue - law

Jehovah   *one-sided "righteousness" (wrath)*

Probably the most striking and, to many, the most objectionable assertion made by the gnostics about the demiurge is that he is identical with Jehovah, the god of the Old Testament. This Hebrew deity, they maintain, is to be distinguished from God the Father. Jehovah in fact is hostile to the Supreme Being.

Gnostic teachers were consistently unremitting in their harshness towards Jehovah, towards Moses and the Law, towards the prophets, and in general towards the whole of the Old Testament. Some critics have therefore tended to dismiss gnosticism as 'metaphysical anti-Semitism'.

Unlike the heavenly Father who is a loving God, Jehovah by his own admission is jealous, wrathful and full of vengeance, exacting retribution to the third and fourth generation. He is described as just (*dikaios*), in a sense implying legal severity and the imposition of the full rigour of the law unmitigated by any element of clemency or love.

This merciless and irascible god drowned the whole world in a flood. He burned the cities of Sodom and Gomorrah even though Abraham pleaded with him to spare them. Jehovah's chief spokesmen, in the gnostic view, were no better. Moses, immediately after receiving the commandment not to kill, came down from Mount Sinai and ordered the execution of three thousand persons (Exod. 32:28). A similar exhibition of callousness was shown by Elijah when he slew the 450 priests of Baal at the brook Kishon (1 Kings 18:40), and again by Elisha when in a rage he cursed some mischievous children in the name of Jehovah, whereupon two she-bears appeared out of the wood and tore forty-two of the innocents to pieces (2 Kings 2:24).

This, they declared, did not take into account the thousands of men, women and children slain by the chosen people of this partisan deity. In the Old Testament these chosen people, for whom Jehovah reserves his blessings, are promised possession of a land that does not belong to them and that is already occupied by other settled tribes. But with Jehovah's blessing, and by his aid, they set out to conquer and subdue the rightful owners, and acquire their territories by usurpation, bloodshed and treachery.

The gnostics condemned the Old Testament as promulgating a Jewish monopoly on God, and containing few elements of any value to non-Jews. They maintained that only the early chapters of Genesis, before the pagan Abram became the Hebrew Abraham, embodied some valid material, if allegorically interpreted. Heracleon, disciple of Valentinus, commenting on the remark made by the Samaritan woman about the well from which Jacob had drawn water in patriarchal times (John 4:12), said that Jacob's well represented the Old Testament, whose waters do not quench the thirst of the spirit.

The Psalms too were criticized as a mixed bag, some of the hymns being partly Jehovah-inspired and therefore Jewish, but the majority being no more than Hebrew renderings of hymns plagiarized from non-Jewish peoples. Likewise, the books of the prophets were for the most part revealed by world-ruling archons, including Satan, and taken down by 'ignorant fools speaking for a foolish God' (Jonas, 1963, p. 192).

The laws of Moses came in for similar rough treatment at their hands. Injunctions against adultery, murder and bearing false witness were common to most races of mankind in early times, and were not exclusively of Jewish provenance. The gnostic Ptolemaeus in his *Letter to Flora* pointed out that some of the basic principles of the Hebrew law, such as, 'Eye for eye, tooth for tooth' (Exod. 21:24) were obsolete. The statutes relating to animal sacrifices, fundamental to Judaism, ceased to be relevant with the destruction of the Temple. And as for sabbath observance, circumcision, fasting, dietary regulations, ritual cleanliness, phylacterism and other vain observances with which the Pentateuch abounded, they were the ordinances of the demiurge and were to be rejected.

The bulk of the Pentateuch was regarded as trivial and of tribal interest primarily to the Jews, and as having little if anything to offer to the rest of mankind. The dispensation outlined in it was restrictive, devoted mainly to materialistic ritualism and social observances that had nothing to do with the superior world. The law of Moses was blind to any spiritual dimension. According to the apocryphal *Book of John the Evangelist,* the Mosaic law was the work of the devil.

Some of its teachings were contrary to moral principles, and much of its élitist hocus-pocus. Wicked archons led by Satan inspired Moses to compile the Pentateuch and so imposed upon the Jews the complicated obligations of the Law. According to the *Gospel of Thomas* Jesus spoke three secret words to Thomas, which have been the subject of much gnostic speculation. The first of these words, *saulasau*, translated 'precept upon precept', was said to refer to the condition of that class of men here below who are subject to the law of Moses.

In the gnostic view the antiquated proclamation embodied in the Pentateuch was deliberately imposed on the Jewish tribes in order to multiply law-breaking (Rom. 5:20), so that the Jews, by a deluded compulsion to obey the law, might remain subject to the law-maker, Jehovah. Its aim was the enslavement of mankind.

The apocryphal *Gospel of Peter* states that the Jews were under the delusion that they knew God, but they were ignorant of him, and knew only a false god, an impostor, whose true nature was unknown to them. One of the titles used by the rabbis for their god was ha-Makom, 'the Place', whereas the gnostics speak of the Place (Topos) as the area vacated by God the Father to make room for the non-divine world, and thus implying a deficiency. According to the gnostic Valentinus, the Topos is the abode of the demiurge.

In the *Apocryphon of John,* and certain other gnostic texts, Jehovah is referred to by many names, and in some he takes on animal form. Among his names are: Yahveh, Elohim, Adonaeus, Sabaoth (bull-shaped), El Shaddai, Elilaeus, Iao, Iaoth (serpent), Oreus, Astaphaeus, Esaldaeus, Ialdabaoth (lion), Thauthabaoth, Erathaoth, Eloaios (eagle), Satan, and Thartharaoth (ass).

In the gnostic *Birth of Mary,* no longer extant but quoted by Epiphanius, it is stated that Zacharias, the father of John the Baptist, saw in the Jewish temple a vision of a man standing 'having the form of an ass'. And Zacharias went out and tried to tell the Jews, 'Alas for you, who is it that you worship?' But the creature that appeared to him in the temple stopped his mouth. And when his mouth was opened he revealed to the people what he had seen. And they put him to death (James, 1924, p. 19; Richards, 1977, p. 69).

Gnostics further point out that when Jesus reproached the Jews he said to them in plain words, 'Ye are of your father the devil' (John 8:44), because he knew the true nature of the god to whom they gave their allegiance. It is interesting to note that Jesus never refers to God the Father as Jehovah, and in fact the name Jehovah is never used in the New Testament.

Evil

In the mythology of gnosticism evil is to be distinguished in its origin, purpose and end from the principle of good.

Basically, there are two main theories about the origin of evil. The first is traditionally regarded as the oriental, or as Basilides put it, the barbarian (Persian, Zoroastrian, Manichean) view. It states that in the beginning there were two supreme, absolute and coeternal powers, one good, ruler of light, the other evil, ruling over darkness. These two primordial principles, separate and distinct, are in everlasting opposition. In this view evil has always existed, along with and independently of God, and will continue so to exist for all eternity.

In the occidental (Alexandrian, Palestinian, Syrian) theory, which is the one commonly held by gnostics, it is believed that evil is not an intrinsic or absolute quality in itself. On the contrary, it is a privative condition, arising out of the absence or attenuation of the divine qualities. Thus, evil is the natural consequence of the descent of the emanations, so that as the emanations recede from the primary divine source there is a progressive diminution in their goodness and light. Again, when God withdrew his presence to make room for the world, Satan was free to exercise his own will in opposition to the divine, as a consequence of which evil arose.

Further, the withdrawal of God meant that the light of his knowledge was likewise withdrawn, leaving the world in darkness (*scotos*), error (*plane*) and ignorance (*agnosia*). Through ignorance come delusion, defect, distress, bewilderment (*aporia*, 'roadlessness', or not knowing where to go), grief, shock (*ecplexis*), awe, consternation, anguish (*stenochoria*, 'constriction'), gloom (*zophos*) and terror (*phobos*), so that a man is as if lost in a fog and beset by horrifying nightmares.

According to Valentinus, the cosmos owes its creation and its continued existence to the presence of error and ignorance. If error were to be removed then all that has its existence by reason of it would be destroyed. Spiritual darkness is the condition of all things predestined for destruction. Salvation therefore lies not in faith but in knowledge. It is error and not wickedness that involves people in suffering. It is not unbelief but ignorance that sets the seal of doom on men and women.

Evil is not an abstraction or a passive condition, but a positive and violent force arising from the active operation of Satan and his archons. In gnosticism, the archons ruling the seven planetary zones of the hebdomad embody the great evils, which may be listed as follows.

Pride, under the archon of Jupiter, which is the evil most odious to God. It leads to such vices as insolence, arrogance (*hubris*), haughtiness, disobedience, boasting, ambition, vainglory, ostentation, obstinacy, vanity. Its opposite is humility or meekness.

Envy, under the archon of the Moon, leads to jealousy, covetousness, ill-will, bitterness, malice, hatred, mischiefmaking. Its opposite is love.

Wrath, under the archon of Mars, leads to violence, inordinate passion, force, strife, discord, tumult, agitation, rage, confusion, vengeance. Its opposite is long-suffering or patience.

Lust, under the archon of Venus, leads to wantonness, licentiousness, love of the body, concupiscence, lechery. It is the opposite of chastity.

Sloth, under the archon of Saturn, leads to non-caring (*acedia*), torpor, unconcern, indifference, tepidity. It is the opposite of well-doing.

Greed, under the archon of the Sun, leads to acquisitiveness, avarice, gluttony, drunkenness, love of money and the other sins of Mammon. It is the opposite of temperance.

Falsehood, under the archon of Mercury, leads to hypocrisy, lying, deceit, guile, cunning, scheming, gossip (idle or foolish talk), faithlessness. It is the opposite of truth.

In the gnostic view evil is not to be considered in terms of physical, social or moral ills. In religious terms, evil is sin. What we regard as crimes and other acts of a vile nature, are not the essential evils. They are what Basilides terms appendages (*prosartemata*). Jesus stated that publicans and harlots would enter the kingdom (Matt. 21:31); he forgave the adultress, and promised paradise to the thief and murderer on the cross. In the list of the seven deadly sins we do not find fornication, killing or theft. The evil is lust, the outcome adultery. The sin is wrath, the result murder. Caesar's authority can punish the crime. Repentance and restitution can mitigate its effects. But only divine grace can purge the underlying sin.

Evil is the reality behind foul deeds and sinful thoughts. Satan and his archons embody all the evils. The conflicts and antagonisms between the powers of good and evil in the invisible world precede earthly crimes and all unrighteousness. Evil has a transcendent character, and is to be treated in terms of what is inherently, intrinsically and ontologically bad (*kakia*). Only by understanding this can we hope to comprehend the great 'mystery of iniquity' (2 Thess. 2:7).

Matter

In the Christian view, God the Father made the whole material world out of nothing (Lat. *ex nihilo*).

In some, generally eastern, gnostic schools, however, matter, like evil, is regarded as eternal – that is, coeternal with evil – and the world is fashioned out of this pre-existent substance, not by God the Father but by the demiurge. In other gnostic systems it is said that the demiurge created the world out of the substance that appeared in the place that God had vacated.

The removal of God's presence resulted in an abyss (*bythos;* Lat. *vorago*), which is described in terms of darkness, fire, evil and death. It is known by a variety of illustrative names: the swirl, the whirlpool (*dine;* Lat. *vortex*), the wheel (Heb. *galgal*), the profundity, the depths (*bathos*), the bosom (*kolpos*), the womb (*hystera;* Lat. *matrix*), the waters, the sea (*thalassa*), the navel (*omphalos*), the whirlwind (*thuella*). The abyss arose in the outer rim of the upper world and constituted a generative waste. In the abyss lay the whole cosmic potential of time and space, the building elements of the phenomenal world, which were to provide the raw material for the work of creation. Matter (*hyle*) was formed out of primordial space.

According to the biblical account of creation (Gen. 1:2), in the beginning the world was 'without form and void' (Heb. *tohu-bohu*), and it was out of this state of formlessness (*chaos*) and voidness (*kenotes*) that matter issued. In the teaching of the Jewish kabalists, the abyss, which is described as a husk or emptied shell, became filled with degenerate entities known as *klifot*, and it was their pollutions, abortions and afterbirths that actually constituted the basic ingredients of matter. The substance of this world is therefore to be regarded as inherently evil.

In the pagan-classical view, the cosmos is governed by divine beings, and both the cosmos and its rulers are superior in intelligence and purity to man. The Greek philosopher Thales (d. 550 BC) said, 'The world is full of gods'. Plato in his *Timaeus* took a more pantheistic view, and wrote of the cosmos as 'a god, and in very truth a living creature endowed with soul and reason'.

In gnostic writings, too, the view is held that the world is governed by spiritual beings, and these are not necessarily inimical, but represent, as it were, the residual spark of God that abides in all things. The *Corpus Hermeticum* says, 'There is no part of the cosmos empty of spirits.' The Naassene gnostics said, 'Even the stars have souls.'

This often serves to emphasize the gnostic idea that nothing can have existence without God, and his 'presence', or that of a surrogate, is to be presumed in all things, even though he has withdrawn. In the *Gospel of Thomas* Christ the Logos says, 'Lift the stone and you will find me; cleave the wood and I am there.' God's light, or a reflection of his light, has been present in all things from the beginning (Gen. 1:3), so that the 'fragrance' of God abides even in his absence.

This is not to deny that the cosmos is evil, and governed by a malicious and tyrannical deity. All matter is part of the satanic darkness that emerged from the chaos. As the Bible has it, 'Darkness was upon the face of the deep' (Gen. 1:2). Darkness is the colour of chaos, and is an aboriginal evil. The demiurge wields darkness as substance. Darkness, say the Sethian gnostics, is not without intelligence, but cunning in all respects; it knows that if the light be totally removed from the darkness, the darkness will be without power, inert and feeble.

There is a profound mystery about this primordial darkness, and the whole subject remains an enigma, beyond human understanding. The *Pistis Sophia* says that at the dissolution of the world certain men will be given the secret concerning 'that mystery that knoweth why the darkness hath arisen, and why the light hath arisen; and that mystery that knoweth why the darkness of the darkness hath arisen, and why the light of the light hath arisen'.

The *Poimandres* speaks of 'darkness tending downwards, coiled like a snake, moist and confused, uttering an inexpressibly smouldering torch

doleful sound, and giving off smoke as from a fire'. To the Mandaeans the 'burning fire of the darkness' is one of the properties of matter. All matter is said to have emerged from the blaze (*aither*) or counterfeit light produced by the demiurge. This antithesis of light is actually a property of darkness. The Valentinians say that the topos or primordial place is fiery, fire being characteristic of the demiurge, who is the god of fire. In the gnostic document *Megale Apophasis* the origin of all things is said to be fire. Only the apparent aspect of this fire is visible, but the unseen aspect is diabolical and infernal.

From this fire emerged the elements of earth, air and water, which in gnosticism are closely associated with terror, ignorance, grief and bewilderment. The earth element is physical matter, the property of the demiurge. The source of the water element are the counterfeit lower waters, and not the upper waters of the divine realm (see Gen. 1:7). And as for the air element, St Paul says that Satan is the 'prince of the power of the air' (Eph. 2:2).

The demiurge has so arranged affairs that they all fall under the control of administrators appointed by Ialdabaoth, who was so named (Heb. *yalda,* 'child'; *bohu,* 'void') because he was born out of the primeval chaos; or, in another derivation, from Yahveh Elohe Sabaoth, 'Yahveh, God of Hosts'. Ialdabaoth, whom the gnostics call an archon of darkness, an ignorant god, and a cursed god, represents the 'fate' aspect of the cosmos, without any of the gentler features associated with providence (*pronoia*).

In the *Apocryphon of John* it is related that Ialdabaoth caused destiny (*heimarmene*) to come into being, and was thus able to control the workings of the cosmos and all things within it. Heimarmene was a concept taken over from ancient astrology. The active agents of heimarmene are the heavenly bodies, including the stars, constellations and planets, and fate and destiny are dispensed through them.

The archons of the planets, seven in number, report to Ialdabaoth, the representative of the demiurge, and are supposedly referred to in the biblical passage: 'These seven are the eyes of the Lord, which run to and fro through the whole earth' (Zech. 4:10). Professor Zaehner quotes an Iranian text that reads: 'The seven planets are said to be the seven commanders on the side of Ahriman', the latter being the Satan of Zoroastrianism.

Star spirits, demonic powers and the spirits of the elements (*stoicheia*) control all things, govern the elapse and division of time, look after temporal events and guide the forces of nature. But their rule is not providential; it is despotic and hostile. Man is shackled by heimarmene to the wheel of destiny. The exile, self-forgetfulness, sleep, intoxication, anxiety and ignorance of the human soul are all bound up with heimarmene.

But, say the gnostics, although the body is completely, and the mind partially, under the domination of heimarmene, the soul can be a completely free agent if only it can rid itself of the trammels of the flesh. Gnosis and a proper baptism can achieve this end and release man from the bondage of fate. Until baptism, say the Valentinians, fate is effective; but after baptism, the astrologer no longer speaks the truth, for the writ of Ialdabaoth ceases to run, and the individual is no longer subject to the iron law of the cosmic agencies. He who is sealed by the spirit is unassailable, immune to all evil influences. The soul moves beyond their jurisdiction.

The heavenly bodies of course continue to exercise their relative functions, but as far as the baptized soul is concerned these are now under the control of the higher powers. In this belief the gnostics regularly consulted the stars and drew lots in making appointments and arriving at important decisions, for the outcome was now thought to be determined by these sovereign powers.

Finally, it is to be remembered that when time ends the power of the demiurge and all his underlings will come to its appointed close.

Creation

Perfection abides exclusively in the world of light, the world of eternity, infinity and permanence, the world of archetypes and perfect forms. In the beginning the effulgence of God irradiated the heavenly spheres, and the reflected light from that effulgence illumined the darkness that, serpent-like, encompassed the region of the demiurge below.

In this reflected light that shone into the lower world was a pale image (*eidolon*) of the world above, so that only dim and distorted shadowings of the spiritual archetypes were mirrored on the surface of the dark waters. Since the fragrance of the divine presence is suffused everywhere, even these vague shadowings bore the impress of the heavenly spheres, and these the demiurge engulfed and took over as his own. But he was enamoured of the primal light; he coveted it, and longed to possess for himself the power and brilliance of the luminous realms, and to obtain custody of the archetypes. More than once he tried to invade the realm of light, but without success.

Enraged at being unable to obtain the originals and create a world like that of the Father, the demiurge attempted, as best he could, to fashion a world of his own. In the Talmud it is said that Jehovah actually made a number of worlds before the present one, and then destroyed them because they were unsatisfactory. According to the gnostics, the demiurge, using as models the reflected distortions that fell on his domain, sought to duplicate the divine originals. In this manner he fashioned the world of nature (*physis*), whose main elements are time (*chronos*), space (*kenos*) and change (*rheos*).

Out of space was formed matter (*hyle*), and from this the demiurge made the world and all living creatures, including man. These in turn assumed identity and brought into being a new hierarchy of entities on the material plane.

Time likewise was made in imitation of the evernow prevailing in heaven. In terms of Plato's *Timaeus,* the demiurge contrived time as 'a moving image of eternity', under the illusion that by piling up immense quantities of temporal units, days, seasons, and ages, he could achieve the eternity of the pleroma.

In short, the demiurge, wishing to copy the endlessness of eternity, the limitlessness of infinity, and the changelessness of permanence, only succeeded in making a world of time and its larger and smaller divisions, space and its larger and lesser dimensions, and flux, making for change and decay. Since his plan was the offspring of deficiency (*elleipsis*), his world is the world of kenoma or emptiness, as compared with the pleroma or fullness of the stauros and beyond.

The objects and creatures in the sphere of the demiurge are mere caricatures, like the impress of imperfect seals and the fruit of misshapen ideas. They are as illusive as shadows and as incomplete as mangled embryos. That is why the cosmos is spoken of as counterfeit (*antimimos*), and the demiurge called the 'ape of God' (Lat. *simia Dei*).

When the demiurge had completed his work of imitation (*mimesis*) he became blinded by arrogance. He announced to his creatures, 'Thou shalt worship no other god; for the Lord, whose name is Jealous, is a jealous God' (Exod. 34:14). This makes clear, say the gnostics, that there does exist another God, for if not, of whom has he any need to be jealous?

Again, because the demiurge had been able to fabricate a world, however spurious, he declared, 'There is no other; there is no god beside me' (NEB, Isa. 45:5). Several gnostic texts, notably the *Hypostasis of the Archons,* the *Apocryphon of John,* and the *Revelation of Adam to his Son Seth,* recount how this claim is rejected. A voice from above declares, 'You are mistaken, Samael', addressing him by a name said to mean either 'god of the blind', or 'god of the left side'. Likewise, another voice, that of Sophia, rebukes him saying, 'Do not lie. There is above thee, the Father of all'. And again, 'The Son of Man exists above thee, and so does Man'. And finally, 'The eternal angels are higher than the god who created the world'.

In gnostic writings the cosmos fashioned by the demiurge is described in many ways. In general, gnostic cosmology was based on geocentricity, the earth being the centre of the solar system, and indeed of the whole universe. Encompassing the earth like the coats of an onion were a series of eight transparent globes, each successive one enclosing the others. Immediately around the earth were the zones constituting the hebdomad or 'seven', comprising the Moon, Sun, Mercury, Venus, Mars, Jupiter and Saturn, which were the seven 'planets' of the ancient world.

Between the globe of the last planet and the outermost globe of the cosmos, lay the zone of the ogdoad or 'eight', containing the zodiac and all the other fixed stars. The powers exerted by the planets and the constellations are controlled by Ialdabaoth who dispenses fate (*heimarmene*). It has been pointed out that the idea of the ogdoad shows the influence of Egyptian astrology, and that of the hebdomad, of Babylonian astrology.

Enclosing the zone of the stars was the great firmament, known as the crystalline sphere, the poet's 'dome of many-coloured glass', and the fiery empyrean, making eight zones in all, encircled by the ouroboros or world serpent, with its tail in its mouth. The cosmos ends at the eighth sphere.

The cosmos includes the natural, physical dimension in which we live, as well as a dimension, invisible to us, of incorporeal beings. We share the cosmos not only with the material elements, with plants and animals, and the rest of the human race, but also with the etheric and astral entities in the non-material planes, with the klifot, with spirits and demons, and all the dark powers and principalities dwelling under the dominion of the 'god of this world' (2 Cor. 4:4).

The view that the world is made and governed by an evil principle and is entangled in darkness is one of the characteristic beliefs of the gnostics. In this they were opposed both to the pagan and Christian views. To the Stoics, for instance, the cosmos represented God's good order and the works of creation verified that a beneficent deity ruled over it.

Irenaeus expressed the Christian view when he wrote: 'To say that the world is a product of evil and ignorance is the greatest blasphemy'. The neoplatonist philosopher Plotinus says in his *Enneads,* 'One must instruct them [the gnostics], if they have the grace to accept instruction, that a divine providence has created this world and not an evil demiurge.'

4.

MAN

Anthropos or man plays a paramount role in the cosmic scheme. He is central to the designs both of God and the demiurge. Man was conceived in the divine mind and came forth in the upper world of light. In an apocryphal gospel Jesus says, 'Blessed is man since he existed before he was born. For all things were created, but man pre-existed.'

Man was formed in the fourth (in some accounts the third) heaven by the Logos, who made him in his own image. In the view of the Jewish philosopher Philo of Alexandria, nothing mortal can be made in the likeness of the most high, and when scripture says that God made man in his own image (Gen. 1:26) it means that he made him in the image of the 'second God', who is the Logos.

This pristine being, the archetypal progenitor of mankind, was an androgynous (male-female) figure, with a bright shining form, resplendent in his beauty. He was the pride of the Logos, who showed him to the angels and archangels. The beauty of his form and the power of his voice inspired envy and fear among many of the angelic host. He was given dominion over the whole heaven, and was called Adamas, 'invincible', or Adamel, and later Adam. He was the Adam Kadmon or primordial man of the Jewish kabala. Eve was created from him as his companion.

Satan grew angry at the important place assigned to Adam, and jealous of the glorious destiny promised to him. He rebelled against the most high, successfully recruited many angels to his side, and then tried to persuade Adam himself to join the rebellion. But Adam joined neither God nor Satan, preferring to remain neutral. Satan however, successfully tempted him to fall into disobedience. In the Christian view, the responsibility for the fall was Adam's alone; in the gnostic view it was Satan's.

As a punishment for his neutrality and disobedience, and Eve's complicity, the most high gave Adam and Eve fleshly bodies, or 'coats of skins' (Gen. 3:21) and banished them from heaven to the world ruled by the demiurge. In this view, the soul of man fell from its original high estate through error, and became entangled in the plane of matter.

In another version, the demiurge, desirous of creating a being in the glorious form of Anthropos, whose archetypal pattern had been reflected from the celestial curtain onto the world below, fashioned a physical image (*plasm*) of man from that distorted reflection, and gave him physical life by breathing upon him.

This primitive android or shapeless clod (Hebrew, *golem*), being a counterfeit creation, was unable to stand upright, but, says the gnostic Saturninus, lay crawling like a worm. It was necessary to provide it with a soul from the upper regions. Satan therefore lured down into his soulless universe a light-spark (*spinther*) from the heavenly realms and trapped it within the material sheath of Adam. According to Apelles, a disciple of Marcion, souls were enticed from their place in heaven by earthly delights, through the machinations of the fiery angel, the god of Israel, after which he bound them in sinful flesh.

In yet another version the Logos, seeing this parody, this misformed horror wriggling on the ground, out of compassion sent forth a spark of light from the celestial realm so that the man-plasm could stand upright. But even then the soul kept passing out of Adam through his anus or out of the big toe of his right foot in an attempt to escape from its bondage.

After much effort the demiurge was at last able to anchor the soul within the body, and this enabled the plasm to stand up and its limbs to develop. As generation succeeded generation and race succeeded race, the limbs became stronger and more perfect. This is the theory of the evolution of races taken over in part by the theosophists.

Both the cosmos and mankind are to be regarded as failures. As the demiurge has fashioned a world through imitation and error, so he has created a human race that has miscarried.

In the gnostic view the soul, coming as it does from the spiritual plane, cannot immediately be enshrined within a gross material body. It remembers its heavenly abode and is reluctant to remain entrapped in matter. Satan therefore ensures that each soul makes a gradual 'descent through the spheres' before it is finally incarnated in bodily form. First it passes through the sphere of the archons ruling the stars, where each archon engraves its seal (*sphragis*) upon it. The stamp (*charakter*) of these seals will determine the nature and disposition of the individual concerned. The soul then proceeds through the seven spheres of the archons governing the planets, who prepare a mask (Lat. *persona*) for it, so that it receives in varying degrees the torpor of Saturn, the wrath of Mars, the concupiscence of Venus, and so on.

In this way the soul is subjected to the authority of the stars and planets which thereafter rule its destiny. The memory of its heavenly abode is slowly effaced and it meekly submits to its captivity here. Man on earth is thus depicted as living in darkness, deafened by the noisy tumult of his senses, and blinded by greed, sensuality and ambition. He is bemused, intoxicated and sunk in sleep, his home forgotten, his glory renounced. In the gnostic *Gospel of Thomas* Jesus says, 'I manifested myself to men in the flesh. I found them drunk, I found them blind, and none athirst among them. When they have slept off their wine they will repent'.

The whole world-structure made by the demiurge depends on the sparks of light that lie hid in mankind, for the cosmos is nothing but darkness. The archons who watch over the world therefore have a vital interest in preventing the liberation of the spirit of man from its imprisonment in the body. They exert all their cunning and power to ensure that man remains drugged, intoxicated and asleep, so that they might retain their hold on the light.

Epiphanius writes that according to the gnostics, 'the soul is the food of the archons, without which they cannot live because it derives from the dew above and gives them strength'. If the light within men were to be liberated, the archons would be left famished, dark, inert and strengthless.

The Soul

Man is a dual being, possessing an immortal soul incarcerated within a physical body. The *Gospel of Thomas* points out how marvellous it is that such a treasure as the soul can find a habitation in such poverty, and can even exist in the body.

Man belongs to the abode of light and bliss, but is involved in the impurities of matter as a result of the fall. Since he is composed of a 'privileged mixture' of spirit and clay he is a great miracle (Lat. *magnum miraculum*) and can, as no other creature can, make himself familiar equally with the divine and the diabolical.

According to Severus, a disciple of Marcion, man is divine from the navel up, and the creature of the devil from the navel down. According to the Sethians, because of Eve's corrupt association with Satan, the whole human race represents the 'spawn of hell'; yet because of the light-spark within man, he is also a child of the most high.

Embedded in the Syriac version of the *Acts of Thomas* is a gnostic classic variously called the 'Hymn of the Pearl', the 'Hymn of the Soul', the 'Hymn of the Robe of Glory', or the 'Hymn of the Apostle Judas Thomas in the Land of India'. This mystical composition tells how a prince is sent on a mission to recover a precious pearl guarded by a serpent, how in the course of his travels he forgets his home and his mission, how his parents send him a letter reminding him of his royal origin and his important task. Reawakened, the prince recovers the pearl, returns home and is duly honoured for his successfully accomplished enterprise.

In this hymn the soul-spark is likened to a pearl immersed in darkness, but shining with its lustre undimmed. As a result of its involvement in matter the soul is encrusted with evil passions, much as a ship's hull gets covered with barnacles, shells and slime. Elsewhere the soul is described as 'gold in mud'. And just as gold will not lose its beauty but preserve its own nature even when sunk in the mire, so the soul's purity remains unsullied whatever the state into which it has been plunged. Only the light in the divine eyes of the soul can behold the light of the divine, but the eyes must first be cleansed and purified.

Besides the elemental spirits who rule the stars, planets and natural elements, say the gnostics, there are hosts of other unseen entities who try to influence man. Spirit beings are the constant companions (*paredroi*) of man, and dwell in him and struggle for possession of his soul. Some are good (*agathodaimon*), some evil (*cacodaimon*), while others simply record what is being thought, said and done by him.

Valentinus compared the human soul to an inn, where all comers lodge. Basilides calls man 'an encampment of many different spirits'. In the teachings of the neoplatonist Porphyry, 'the soul is a receptacle for either gods or demons'. The good spirits or guardian angels urge men to lead a life of faith, wisdom and virtue, and to be guided at all times by the monitoring light within. They dissuade from evil, admonish the wayward, strengthen the weak, and direct the soul along the right path. Isidore, the son and disciple of Basilides, writing in his *Expositions of the Prophet Parchor,* speaks of the secrets revealed to Socrates by his attendant spirit.

Evil spirits resent the human race. They seek to enter the heart and sow there the seeds of mischief and corruption, prompting all manner of wicked deeds. People are little aware how far they are motivated by these demons in their many symbolic guises: the serpent of lust, the dragon of wrath, the lion of arrogance. The Messalian sect speak of sarkic or carnal man as a man bedevilled, because he is incited by the spirits of sensual desire.

Man is deceived by the manifold allurements of the flesh. He is beguiled by sweet-smelling perfumes, the pleasures of food and drink, the possession of beautiful women. He abandons himself to his insatiable passions even while he cries out in his torment, 'I burn, I blaze, I am consumed, wretch that I am, by the evils that possess me.'

In the Nag Hammadi document, *Treatise on Resurrection,* which is a letter addressed by a gnostic teacher to his pupil Rheginos, the world is described as an illusion (*phantasia*), and involvement in it is said to bring spiritual death. Man is repeatedly warned in gnostic texts to place no trust in worldly things, which are deceiving shadows and images of clay that will dissolve and pass away as if they had never been. Physical entities are phantoms, matter is an illusion, and time will end.

Man must remember that he is rooted elsewhere, an exile from above, an alien who does not belong to this world, a stranger in a hostile environment. He is a wayfarer seeking lodging for the night, and not making here a permanent home. He is in bondage and must hasten to end his imprisonment. He is a warrior and must fight for victory so that he might return to his own country. He must therefore put on his spiritual armour, the whole armour (*panoplia*) of God, remembering that the archons are ever striving to weaken his armour and so capture the light. This concept of armour plays an important part in certain gnostic systems.

From time to time man receives intimations of his origins, for there comes to each person as he sojourns in the world, the sound of divine music, and a voice that calls out, 'Awake, thou that sleepest' (Eph. 5:14), 'Cast off the works of darkness and put on the armour of light' (Rom. 13:12). Those who have given themselves up to ignorance and error hear the voice but fail to recognize it, or to understand what is said to them. Some hear but do not always hearken, being torn between two worlds, and troubled by doubt, anxiety and dread, unable to make up their minds and give up what is so alluring.

But the voice breaks through the stupefaction and forgetfulness of the wise man, leading him to a recollection (*anamnesis*) of the higher world whence we have all come. He is reminded that, like all men, he is a king's heir with a spiritual origin, for whom a great destiny is reserved if he but pays heed. Like the prodigal son he 'comes to himself'. He is awakened, he sobers up, and is thereby restored to a knowledge of his true self. Filled with nostalgia, and yearning for the paradise he has lost, he experiences a change of mind (*metanoia*), repents, turns away from the world and resolutely keeps his mind on things divine, ready to assume his rightful robe of immortality.

When a man is motivated in this manner the light within him burns brightly. The demiurge is terrified of this light, especially if it is accompanied by prayer, for then the light rises up and is met and strengthened by a light from heaven that nothing can resist.

Man is the keystone of the whole cosmic arch, for among those who abide below he alone has been entrusted with possession of the divine light, which is the soul. In essence, man (*phos*), is light (*phos*). The soul is not made by the demiurge and is not native to this world. Its origin is the sphere of being, which is spiritual and enduring. It is the kingdom of God the Father hid in man.

Tertullian spoke of the soul as the luminous seed, the immortal spark, the divine light (*augeus*). In the *Megale Apophasis* it is written, 'Thou and I are but one'. And in the gnostic *Gospel of Eve,* the Great Being says, 'I am thou and thou art I, and where thou art, I am'. Men are the children of light, and their true citizenship is in heaven (Phil. 3:20).

The Three Types of Men

In the gnostic view all men are made up of three basic elements: body, mind and spirit. In each person the underlying essence of one or other of these three elements predominates, and this establishes the type of person he is, and to that degree also determines his destiny.

The body is formed by the demiurge from earth, clay or dust (*chous*), and hence is referred to as the choic element. Because it is composed of matter (*hyle*) it is also called the hylic element; and since matter has been fashioned into flesh (*sarkos*), the body is also described as sarkic or carnal. Finally, as this part of the human entity belongs to the works of nature (*physis*) it is referred to as the physical part of man. The body is regarded as the robe or coat (*chiton*) covering the psyche.

But man is not an inert substance, and he differs from a clod of earth. The material part of him is endowed with physical life (*zoe*) and physical consciousness (*dianoia*), which make up his etheric body. Man shares this non-rational instinctive element of himself, that is, this animal soul (Lat. *anima bruta*) with the whole animal kingdom.

The physical world, say the gnostics, lies on the edge of the nether regions, and since we live in the environs of hell, we are in a state perilously bordering on eternal perdition. The gnostics refer to mortal man as the stinking body, the fabric of pollution, the seed-bed of wickedness, the fount of corruption, ridden with the itch of greed and concupiscence, the living death, the walking grave.

Marcion speaks in brutal terms of the ignominy of man, created in loathsome matter, conceived in the filth of sexuality, born amid the unclean, excruciating and grotesque convulsions of labour, into a body that is a 'sack of excrement', until death turns it into carrion, a nameless corpse, a worm-filled cadaver.

The *sarkikos* or man of flesh is the one in whom the carnal elements are dominant. By his own default he has surrendered his will to Satan. He lives in a world of illusion and transience, that is, the present world of shadows. His soul, the incorporeal reality within, is shrouded in grave-clothes (*keiriai*), leaving him blind and bound. He is like a somnambulist, his body awake, his soul asleep.

He is the captive one (Luke 8:29), held down by the fetters of ignorance. He lacks even the awareness of his need for salvation. He is enslaved of the devil, and deaf to the call that comes to all from the realm of light. In his case, the light-seed scattered by the divine sower (Matt. 13:3) falls upon stony ground or is strewn by the wayside, and the birds of lechery, envy, gluttony and foolish desire devour the seed.

Sarkic man belongs to the left side, and there is little hope for him, for he is spiritually deaf and blind. The type of biblical man in this class is Cain.

education-doctrine

The mind (*psyche*) is the second constituent of man, and governs the mental, intellectual, thinking or rational side of the human being. The psyche is regarded as female. The mind-and-thought elements make up the astral body of man, and contribute to his ego or personality. Only man possesses the reasoning mind-and-thought element, which is therefore termed the human soul (Lat. *anima humana*) as opposed to the animal soul. The psyche is the vehicle (*okhema*) of the divine soul (see below), or in another metaphor, is its cloak (*himation*) or outer covering.

The *psychikos* or psychic man, in whom the psychic element predominates, operates in the sphere of becoming, for he is potential, and capable of evolving. He is self-determining in his actions, and responsible for what he does. As the psyche belongs to the middle (*mesos*) or intermediate realm, between left and right, overlapping, as it were, the carnal and the spiritual, psychic man can identify either with the upper realm and be transformed by it, or with the lower and perish as a result.

This type of man hears the call, but whether he listens and responds, or not, lies entirely within himself. He is capable of receiving the seed sown by the sower. But he is fertile ground for both tares and wheat (Matt. 13:25). He must take care that the thorns of intellectualism and disbelief do not grow and choke the seed. He has free will and tends both to good and evil, and must make up his own mind in which direction he will move. The type of biblical man in this category is Abel.

The soul (*nous*) or pure spirit (*pneuma*) is the third element in man. The nous is regarded as male, as compared with the female psyche. Being composed of divine essence (*ousia*) it is termed the divine soul (Lat. *anima divina*). In the course of its descent from the realm of light the soul is first clothed in the garment of the mind and then encased in the shroud of the flesh. And both these accoutrements are expendable (Matt. 5:40).

The body (life-and-consciousness) is produced through the sexual intercourse of its parents, but the soul is not the offspring of other souls. As St Jerome expressed it, 'God is daily making souls' for the bodies produced by the acts of human generation.

The *pneumatikos* or man in whom the spirit predominates (some gnostics preferred the Platonic term noetic to pneumatic or pneumic) is governed by the finest aspirations of the soul. He belongs to the company of saints; he possesses spiritual understanding (*noesis*), and responds to the divine element within him, recognizing the light and aspiring heavenward. 'The soul', said Tertullian, referring to the nous, 'is naturally Christian.' The seed scattered by the sower takes firm root in him and brings forth fruit in abundance. He belongs to the right. The type of biblical man in this category is Seth.

Eschatology

The gnostic doctrine on eschatology, or the destiny of man after death, ranges from certain salvation for the few, and hope for others, to hopelessness for many of the human race. Between the saved and the damned 'there is a great gulf fixed' (Luke 16:26). In the gnostic scheme not all men are saved, or even capable of attaining salvation. In certain schools the redemption of some and the damnation of others is already known to the omniscient God and in this sense is fore-ordained.

On death the characteristics associated with the physical body, such as outward form and feature, age and sex, all disappear. The body dissolves, and its physical constituents are returned to the elements of earth, air, fire and water. What happens to the non-physical parts depends on the individual.

All souls descend to hell, as did Christ himself. Christ went there for a redemptive purpose, but men must spend time there for chastisement, purification and self-realization.

According to the Valentinians, the sarkic or fleshly man 'perishes by nature', and has no hope of salvation. Blind to the world of spiritual realities, and lacking in faith, even his good works earn him no merit. On death, the light (soul) which he himself has kept hidden and untended (Matt. 25:3), is withdrawn, and his etheric body becomes the property of the demiurge. It is swallowed by a dragon-like archon, and after a period of digestion is voided into one of the lower hells, where it suffers torments with other damned souls. From time to time it is sent out as an evil spirit to afflict mankind.

In the psychic type of man, body and spirit are precariously balanced, and he determines his own ultimate destiny. If he is not successful he is sent to one of the milder hells, and may then be reincarnated for another chance. He is given three or four such chances in all. In the Basilidean view, the warning

appended to the second commandment about the sins of the
fathers being visited on the children to the third and fourth
generation (Exod. 20:5), actually refers to the sins of individuals
(called 'fathers' because they are responsible for their own
rebirth), being visited on these same individuals ('children'),
who may be reincarnated three or four times.

If he continues to fail he eventually suffers the fate of sarkic
man. But if he strengthens his faith, strives for true knowledge
and does good works, he will ascend through the spheres. He
then has to face the hazards of the return journey to the upper
realms.

The third type of man, the noetic, is 'saved by nature'. He is
spoken of as the 'elect' and 'perfect' by Basilides. Already
redeemed, he is counted among the privileged élite. He is free
from the influence of heimarmene or fate, and is beyond the
operations of the social and moral laws. After death he passes
through hell, only that he might be purged of the residue of his
physical state, before proceeding on his upward pilgrimage.

There are several stages to this journey, which must be
undertaken both by the successful psychic man and by noetic
man. At each stage the soul has to contend against the hostile
archons who guard the gates giving access to the next higher
sphere. They will try to restrain him as they do not want the
light-spark that he carries to pass out of their control.

He must first traverse the seven planetary spheres, where he
returns to the archon of each zone the corresponding evil
propensity with which he was endowed during his descent –
namely, pride, envy, wrath, lust, sloth, greed and falsehood.
After that he must pass through the stellar sphere, which
likewise has its hostile archons. He must be able to make the
correct signs, answer the questions put to him, and pronounce
the appropriate formulas. The true gnostic will have familiarized
himself with these matters in ritual practice during his lifetime.
But in any event he will receive help from his guardian angel, if
need be.

After these obstacles have been overcome, the individual
must confront the archon Sabaoth and trample upon his head
as a sign of triumph over him. By this time, too, the delusive
attributes of personality and ego will have been shed by the
individual and his psyche too will have been dissolved. The
soul, now like an aeon in its own right, stands freed of all earthly
encumbrances and is ready to pass into the timeless divine
spheres.

Referring to this long and arduous journey the *Corpus Hermeticum* says, 'You see, O child, through how many ranks of demons and through how many worlds we have to work our way in order to hasten to the one and only God.'

Some of these features in the ascent of the soul have been borrowed from pagan mythology, but the gnostic elements stand out. The end of man is inseparable from his beginning. In the *Gospel of Thomas* the disciples ask Jesus, 'Tell us how our end will be', and Jesus replies, saying, 'Have you discovered the beginning that you can ask about the end?'. Indeed, to know the mystery of the beginning is to understand the purpose and destiny of things, and so overcome death.

The noetic man is the chosen man, but this does not imply favouritism on the part of God. For God has given free will to all men. He calls to every soul, but he does not choose every soul, for the choice is not with God. It is for us to inscribe our own names on the list of the called, and be chosen on our own merits, for though many are called, few are chosen (Matt. 22:14). In the *Gospel of Truth* it is written, 'Those whose names are known in advance will be called at the end. He whose name has not been named is ignorant.' Knowing God is the best way of being known by God.

There is a reciprocal relationship between Saviour and saved. Jesus said that whoever acknowledged him before men, would in turn be acknowledged by him (Luke 12:8). The Logos promises, 'Who thinks of me, of him will I think. Who chooses me, him will I choose. Who calls my name, his name will I call.'

They are chosen to be saved, and they form the Church, who are thus 'called forth' (*ecclesia*). The early Christian view, expressed in the saying, 'Outside the Church there is no salvation', echoes the originally gnostic doctrine, that only the chosen are 'called forth', because they themselves have made the right choice in the first place. There is little hope for the rest.

The gnostic teacher Theodotus spoke of all members of the spiritual church as being saved and belonging to a 'chosen race'. Their salvation, he said, was exclusive, and it was certain. It was further believed that if a man did not attain resurrection while in the body, he could not receive it when his body perished and he became a phantom. In the *Gospel of Thomas,* when the disciples ask Jesus, 'On what day will the resting of the dead [resurrection] take place, and when will the new world come?'

Jesus answers, 'That which you await has come already, and you have not recognized it.'

Because the phenomenal world is an illusive creation, bound by time and space, it will come to an end when the times are fulfilled. There will then be no further chance of repentance, no scope for further delays, no interval for further opportunities during which things that were left undone might still be done, for 'there shall be time no longer' (Rev. 10:6).

The end of time will be marked by a period of tribulation, followed by the appearance of Antichrist, culminating in the battle of Armageddon. Then will come the last judgment, when the unregenerate will be subjected to the condition called 'the second death' (Rev. 2:11).

God the Father will then set about putting an end to all things. The heavens, as the Bible predicts, will be rolled up like a scroll (Isa. 34:4), which means the lesser heavens, the Elysian Fields, the Valhallas, and all the other post-mortem paradises of the pagan, heathen and other religious faiths. The fire that is latent in the world will blaze forth at Christ's command (Luke 12:49), and all matter will go up in flames. These flames will engulf the stygian gloom of hell, and both Death and Hades will be cast into the lake of fire (Rev. 20:14). This will mark the annihilation of these two dread servitors of evil (1 Cor. 15:55). Lastly, the fire will consume itself, leaving no trace behind.

Then he that sits upon the throne shall 'make all things new' (Rev. 21:5).

Existence

The gnostics were not alone in believing that salvation was for the favoured few. Accounts of the afterlife given in the ancient mythologies consistently reflect a condition of hopelessness and despair. And these are not accounts of the wicked being punished in hell for their misdeeds, but of ordinary men and women in their post-mortem existence. The next world is represented as a prolongation *ad infinitum* of the tedium and terror of this one.

The Egyptians reserved the benefits of the afterlife, such as they were, for a small and select minority. An Egyptian stela puts into the mouth of a dead woman the following lament addressed to her still living spouse: 'O my husband, the land of the dead is a land of the forgotten. Those who dwell here know nothing more of happiness. There is no way out, for they are here for ever, without hope and without joy. I yearn for the breeze on the river bank, the song of birds, the sound of cheerful voices.'

Mesopotamia had little more to offer people once they had passed the gloomy portals into the next world. Babylonian mythology relates what the legendary hero Gilgamish heard from his friend Enkidu when he journeyed to the land of the dead, and asked him about conditions there: 'Nay my friend I will not tell you. I will not tell you, my friend. I will not tell you. For you would sit down weeping. O, you would sit down weeping!'

From Greece, where one might expect a happier prospect, there is still further evidence of gloom and despair. The *Odyssey* tells of what happened when Ulysses visited the underworld. The scene is described in horrifying terms, with the unhappy spirits, including that of his mother, crowding around him, empty shadows, squeaking like bats. 'Why', he is asked, 'do you leave the realm of sunshine to visit the dolorous country of the dead?' He meets the great Achilles and tries to comfort him, and is told, 'Seek not to console me in death, noble Odysseus. Would that I were on earth, a slave of the soil; would that I were the servant of a master harsh and hard, some pauper whose living was scanty and scarce, than king of all the nations of the dead.'

Greek sepulchral inscriptions of later times, preserved in the Greek Anthology, reflect the beliefs about what people expected to find after death: despair, regret, bitterness, confusion, with scarcely a glimmer of hope. A characteristic epitaph reads: 'I was not. I was born. I lived. I am not. That is all.' Another reads: 'Here lie I, Dionysius of Tarsus, sixty years old, unwed. Would that my father had been the same.'

The Hebrew scriptures in general have little to say about the afterlife. No happy prospect exists beyond the grave. The word for 'grave' used in the Old Testament is often the same as for 'hell' (*sheol*), as if hell were the ultimate fate of the dead. The spirit of Samuel appears to the witch of En-dor 'out of the earth' (1 Sam. 28:13) and not from any celestial realm as would befit a prophet of God. There is no suggestion of resurrection in the Pentateuch. The Sadducees did not believe in the resurrection, neither did the Samaritans.

Existence itself was not universally seen as a blessing even by the Jews. The Hebrew *Mishna* records how for over two years the famous rival schools of Rabbi Hillel and Rabbi Shammai disputed the question whether it would have been better if man had not been created. When at the end the votes of the disputants were counted it was found that the majority agreed that it would have been better if man had not been created (Hausdorff, 1955, p. 232).

To the gnostic, too, the fact of earthly existence was a doubtful blessing, and indeed had overtones of terror. The soul, it is said, cries out in anguish, 'How long have I already endured? How much longer must I go on dwelling in the world?' The material world was seen as a necropolis, a place of the unresurrected dead. Since salvation was reserved for the few it was inevitable that the gnostics, like the rabbis, should debate whether it was a blessing to have been brought into existence. They reflected on the terrifying 'factness' of the world, and concluded that existence itself was a reality that held a frightening menace.

Man has been brought into existence without his knowledge or consent. He has emerged as a result of the lust of his parents. Once he has been created he is endowed with a soul and becomes irrecoverably immortal. Man is already in eternity. Whether he likes it or not he is destined to continue to exist for all time, probably in wretchedness and misery. There is no end to the dire future that stretches before him. There is no passing away, no final oblivion, no un-being.

The unborn are to be counted fortunate. Better than the living who are living in this world, better than the dead who are living in the next world, are those 'which hath not yet been' (Eccles. 4:3). Job cursed the day he was born (Job 3:3) and speaks of those unfortunates 'which long for death but it cometh not.' For there is no death. A man might think that his existence will end when his body dies. But bodily death does not terminate his existence. One of the principal aims of the gnostic, therefore, was 'no longer to remain in created existence', or as Valentinus put it, 'to make death die'.

Man is subject to all the adversities of chance and luck and the hazards of accident and circumstance. Through fate he becomes the puppet of the demiurge, the victim of malevolent spirits, and subject to the whims of the archons. In Greek terms he is the plaything of the immortals on Olympus; in Indian terms he is the sport (Sanskrit, *lila*) of the deities; in Islamic terms his fate (Arabic, *kismet*) is beyond his control. He is neglected and forsaken. In the words of a gnostic hymn, 'I lived in this world of darkness for myriads of years and no one ever knew that I was there' (Lacarrière, 1977, p. 41).

Into this weary world bereft of hope, say the gnostics, comes the message of Jesus. He awakens men from their slumber. He cleanses the eyes of the spiritually blind that they may see. Restores their limbs that they may move and touch. Heals the leprosy of their souls. He reminds men of their spiritual home and offers them a new birth in heaven. He provides the means for the soul's way out of this world. His purpose is to redeem, reconcile, justify, and sanctify. Irrespective of race, social status or sex, he saves us from sin, fate, demons, death and hell. But above all, he frees us from creation, from the terrors of being under the domination of the tyrannical god of this world.

The gnostic Marcion stated that Christ came from another realm with a wondrous message of deliverance. In ecstatic terms he wrote: 'O wonder upon wonder! Rapture, power, amazement! We can say nothing about the gospel message, not even compare it with anything else.' He was struck with astonishment, bowed down in awe before a revelation so utterly prodigious.

Clement of Alexandria felt equally exalted: 'Christ shines. He shines more brightly than the sun. Night flees before him, fire is afraid, death departs. He presents the believing soul to the Father to keep in heaven for all eternity. O true sacred mystery! O clear, pure light!'

5.

JESUS CHRIST

The phenomenon of Christ is a factor to be reckoned with in the history of the world. And the phenomenon in question is not so much the historical as the gnostic Christ.

There were many religious leaders and rebels in Palestine immediately before and after the advent of Jesus. There were also a number of sects: Pharisees, Sadducees, Herodians, Zealots. There was nothing so unusual in what Jesus had to offer, politically or socially, that sets him apart from the others. As has often been pointed out, there is no reason why the record of his life should not have been a mere footnote in the writings of the Jewish historian Josephus (d. 101).

The known facts of his life are meagre in the extreme. The English theologian and New Testament scholar Burnett Hillman Streeter calculated that apart from the forty days and nights in the wilderness, of which we are told virtually nothing, all that is reported to have been said and done by Jesus in all the four gospels, could not have occupied more than three weeks.

Yet such were the implications of his message that St John, with the extravagance of mystical fervour, ends his gospel by saying that Christ did and said many other things, which if they were all to be written down, 'I suppose that even the world itself could not contain the books that should be written' (John 21:25).

The records of his life are confused, and Bible critics are left with scores of unsolved problems, which have been the source of heresies that have racked Christendom from its beginnings. Scholars have been perplexed by the contradictions, inconsistencies and improbabilities in the canonical gospels alone, which they have never been able to reconcile.

The teachings of Christ are not even preserved in the

Aramaic language in which they were proclaimed. His sayings, or *logia,* delivered with great authority, were memorized, arranged under subject headings, and translated by Greek-speaking Jewish and Gentile converts. Certain sayings, called *agrapha,* or 'unwritten' pieces, were transmitted orally, and when finally put down in writing did not form part of the canon.

Along with his sayings, certain incidents of his life were also set down, and by the end of the first century there were several biographies of Jesus in circulation, some highly coloured, which were being used in the churches of Egypt, Syria, Asia Minor and Greece, written in Greek, Syriac and other languages. By the fourth century there were more than a hundred such records of his life, and over the centuries the flow has become a flood. More than sixty thousand works on Jesus are said to have been published in the nineteenth century alone (Stewart, 1981, p. 108).

Scholars make a distinction between the mythological Jesus, the historical Jesus, and the proclaimed or preached Jesus. At the same time critics are torn between a barely historical, an unknown, probably unknowable, perhaps even a non-existent, founder. Yet, in the terms of an earlier paradox, what is important is not so much whether his mission took place, as whether it took effect. The beliefs concerning his incarnation, crucifixion and resurrection are irrational in the sense that they are outside the scope of reason and inexplicable in terms of ordinary human understanding. Gnosticism is not rational.

It has been pointed out that the gospels do not present a biography, nor do they represent a doctrinal teaching (*didache*), but are a proclamation (*kerygma*) of a new dispensation relating to the kingdom of heaven. This is the 'myth' of Christianity. Not a fanciful tale, or a chronicle that can be verified in terms of history, but the living expression of a profound and eternal truth. Christ then becomes a figure as conceived by the gnostics, cosmic, archetypal, apocalyptic. He opens up the deeper significance of God's hidden mysteries. The completion of his mission was symbolized by the rending of the curtain (*katapetasma*) that concealed from all mankind the world of ultimate reality.

Paganism
The gnostics believed that the nations of the ancient world had been conditioned in advance for the Christian revelation. Jesus

himself had been prefigured in several cult heroes of antiquity, and the principal events of his life were a recapitulation (*anakephalaiosis*) of the spiritual evolution of the human race so far, summarizing and crowning, as it were, the experience and hope of mankind as expressed in primordial cycles of legend.

The teachings presented in a number of early pagan philosophies were regarded as rehearsals for the new revelation. The spirit of the Logos had been present among men before the Flood. Clement of Alexandria felt that Greek philosophy was divinely inspired, and it prepared the mind for the Christian message. St Ambrose wrote, 'All that is true, by whomsoever it has been spoken, is from the Holy Spirit.'

God had made the world receptive to Christ's dispensation by creating in the hearts of people of all nations an acceptance of similar beliefs in their own myths and symbols. Such foreshadowing confirmed the truth when it was at last made manifest. The wisdom of God fell like a shower from heaven to earth, and the particles fertilized the spirit of wise men, including some of those who wrote the Old Testament. In the *Gospel of Thomas* the disciples say to Jesus: 'Twenty-four prophets spoke in Israel, and all of them spoke concerning you.'

It was believed that with Christ's coming the decline of paganism was inevitable. One by one the ancient deities were overthrown, the mysteries connected with them were rendered obsolete, and the ancient oracles silenced. Already before the first century BC, the celebrated Eleusinian mysteries had begun to degenerate into a charade and few were any longer interested in them. Diodorus Siculus (d. 40 BC) called the temple of Eleusis 'a veritable brothel'. Philo of Alexandria (d. AD 50) reported that in his time it was becoming impossible to find honourable men for initiation, and they were compelled to fall back on vagabonds and courtesans (De Vesme, 1931, p. 129).

In about 40 BC the Roman poet Virgil wrote an eclogue, addressed to the consul Pollio, associating the arrival of a new epoch with the birth of a child, which was long regarded as a prophecy about Christ. He speaks of the child, 'dear offspring of the gods', and companion of divine beings, as descending from the celestial realms to usher in a new era on earth.

Plutarch (d. AD 120), in his *Cessation of the Oracles,* records a story he had heard from a reliable person who was present when it happened, about a mysterious voice loudly proclaiming, as their ship passed by a group of islands on the coast of Greece,

'The great god Pan is dead'. At this there came the sound of a mighty groaning and lamentation from countless throats. Rumours of this strange event reached the emperor Tiberius who sent for witnesses who corroborated the story. This too was interpreted by some scholars as a premonition of the end of paganism and the coming of a new dispensation. The apocryphal gospels relate that when the Virgin Mary and her child were in Egypt 'there was a trembling and quaking', and the power of the priesthood and their idols was brought to nought.

Some authorities, notably J. M. Robertson, hold that the gospel passion story is not originally a narrative but a mystery drama, and that this drama is 'inferrably an evolution from a Palestinian rite of human sacrifice'. The last supper is a re-interpretation of a sacrificial feast, and Christ's death conforms to the general pattern of past redeemer figures, Osiris, Adonis, Tammuz, Attis. Like other martyred saviours he was scourged, robed in purple, and sacrificed for the good of the community or the redemption of the world. He was like the son in the earlier trinities of the Babylonian Ea-Damkina-Marduk, the Egyptian Osiris-Isis-Horus, the Greek Zeus-Persephone-Zagreus.

The Church Father Justin Martyr argued that in their doctrine of the virgin birth of Jesus and his passion and ascension, the Christians were reaffirming in a new context what had anciently been alleged of the son of Zeus. Justin adds that if Christians called Jesus the Word of God, here was yet another point in common with the gentiles who called Hermes the Word of Zeus. Clement of Alexandria referred to Jesus as the Torch-bearer and the Hierophant, terms taken from the pagan mysteries. *Mithraism*

Like Orpheus, Jesus remained in the wilderness for forty days and forty nights, and neither the fierce beasts nor the venomous basilisk did him harm. Like other great culture heroes of the past Jesus had a contest (*agon*) with the adversary, when Satan tempted him. His cursing of the fig tree was a symbolic act, signifying his break with the licentious implications of the fig in paganism. His riding to Jerusalem on an ass was a symbol of his subjugation of the demiurge, one of whose forms is that of an ass. The brazen serpent being lifted up in the wilderness to counteract the poison of serpents (Num. 21:8) is a prefiguration of Christ being lifted up on the cross to counteract the poison of Satan (John 3:14).

Birth and Childhood

The genealogy of Jesus embraces all varieties and types of men. His progenitors included a Canaanitess of the line of Ham, progenitor of the black races; Terah a Chaldean, of Japhetic origin; Bath-sheba a 'Caucasian'. Jesus thus united in himself the three great races of mankind, black, yellow and white. Two of his ancestors were the offspring of incestuous unions: Moab son of Lot, and Pharez son of Judah.

In the New Testament, David was the forebear of both Joseph and Mary, and if Jesus's Davidic ancestry be accepted we find in his lineage four gentile women of dubious extraction: Rahab, a harlot of Jerico, Tamar a Canaanitess, Ruth a Moabitess, and Bath-sheba a Hittite, the last two named also being twice-married.

Jesus was born of a virgin, the term 'virgin' being in common usage among the Jews of the time for any young woman, married or unmarried. A talmudic text hints that the father of Jesus was a gentile named Panthera, thus making him a *mamzer* or bastard, an idea taken up by the Borborians.

Some gnostics held that Jesus was born in the natural way to Joseph and Mary. Also, that as the physical mother of Jesus, Mary was worthy of honour but not of special homage. In the *Gospel of Thomas* Jesus speaks of his earthly parents, Joseph and Mary, and compares them with his divine father, God, and his divine mother, the Holy Ghost.

Yet the body of the man Jesus was destined to be used as the vehicle of the cosmic Christ, and since gnostics regarded the body as corrupt and sinful, they tried to avoid any implication of contamination by often fanciful theories to preserve the supernatural character of Jesus's birth. Thus, Jesus passed through the body of Mary like water through a pipe, without receiving any taint from the womb.

Later, even the orthodox sought ways of denying normal conception. The Syrian churchman Ephraem Syrus (d. 378) said that Mary had been impregnated auricularly, based on the biblical text which states that the annunciation was delivered by the angel who 'came in unto her' (Luke 1:28), bearing the message of the Holy Spirit, and it was through the ear that the divine power passed into her womb.

Nestorius (d. 451), Patriarch of Constantinople, placed emphasis on the manhood of Christ, in contrast to those who stressed his divinity. The Nestorians referred to Mary as Christ-bearer (*Christotokos*), and taught that Jesus was a man who became divine, and not God who became a man. Their opponents among the Church theologians, on the other hand, referred to Mary as God-bearer (*Theotokos*), and taught that she was divinely maintained in a state of purity.

Faith in Mary's virginity and her unbroken hymen before birth (Lat. *ante partum*), during birth (*in partu*) and after birth (*post partum*), was to become official Christian doctrine many centuries later. References to the 'brothers' of Jesus in the gospel texts, was believed to apply to the children of Joseph by a former wife. Joseph died before the ministry of Jesus, and Jesus is therefore spoken of as the 'son of the widow', Joseph himself seldom being brought into a context suggesting his relationship with Jesus.

The virgin birth, in the mythology of the apocrypha, was one of several natural portents that heralded an event of unparalleled importance in the history of the universe. Another took place when the heavens declared through the star of Bethlehem that a New Man was born to whom the world would have to look for its deliverance from the dominion of sin and evil.

The star was seen by the three magi, three wise priest-kings of the east, descended from Shem, Ham and Japheth, representing the peoples of all the world. Balthasar belonged to the white race of Shem and brought the infant gold, symbol of the incarnation. Melchior belonged to the black race of Ham, and brought frankincense, symbol of the crucifixion. Caspar belonged to the yellow race of Japheth, and brought myrrh, symbol of the resurrection.

The gospels record only a single major instance from the childhood of Jesus, telling how, when he was twelve years old he went to the temple and discoursed with the doctors, and 'all that heard him were astonished at his understanding and answers' (Luke 2:47). But the apocryphal gospels of the infancy give numerous other stories of his supernatural power. Thus, he fashioned twelve sparrows out of soft clay, clapped his hands and they flew off. Again, he dipped several sheets of cloth into a vat of black dye, and when the dyer complained to Mary, Jesus took them out one by one, each dyed in a different colour as the dyer asked.

Another story relates that when he was being taught the alphabet, his teacher Zacchaeus said to him, as was the custom, 'Say *alpha*' (or in Hebrew, *alef,* the first letter of the alphabet), and Jesus said, 'Alpha'. When the teacher said, 'Say *beta*' (Hebrew, *beth,* the second letter), the child answered, 'First tell me what *alef* is and then I will tell you what *beth* is'. The child then proceeded to explain to Zacchaeus the construction and significance of *alef:* the diverging lines showing the relationship of what is above and what is below; the long middle stroke resembling the body of a man; the short descending stroke like an arm pointing down; the raising on high of the third stroke, like an arm uplifted; the dancing form as the lines come together; and the tension and balance of the whole composition that makes up the letter *alef.*

And when Zacchaeus heard the allegories of the first letter spoken by the child he cried out in perplexity, shame and rage, 'Woe is me, wretch that I am. I have brought disgrace to myself by agreeing to teach this young man. Take him away. He has confounded my senses. I cannot follow his meaning. I have been humiliated in my old age by a child. I am ready to faint and die in my disgrace. I cannot endure this hour for I have been brought to nought by a stripling.'

Docetism

The view held by certain gnostics was that Christ the Logos, being divine, eternal and perfect, could not assume material flesh, since matter was essentially impure and evil. According to Basilides, Christ could transform himself and make himself invisible at will (see John 8:59), because he was a bodiless power (Lat. *virtus incorporalis*).

He had a spiritual body, and although he consumed food like mortal men, there was no waste, and one could invoke the 'bowels of Christ' without impropriety. Valentinus wrote, 'Jesus ate and drank in a special manner, without evacuating the food. So great was the power of his continence that the food did not decay in him, for he himself was incorruptible and without decay.'

A fundamental belief of some schools was that Christ could not take on anything of human nature. He was impassible, that is, he could not suffer in any way, as this would imply deficiency, imperfection and mortality. Christ only seemed (*dokein,* 'to seem') to suffer, but did not undergo actual suffering. The docetists, or 'seemers', believed that Christ was wholly spirit and that his incarnate form was not real but was a phantasmal or apparent body, having only the appearance of being real, and that Christ only seemed to suffer and die on the cross.

It was not Christ who carried the cross, but someone else. According to Basilides, Christ changed places with Simon of Cyrene, who is mentioned in the Bible as bearing this burden (Mark 15:21). Christ then mingled with the crowd of onlookers, while Simon carried the cross, bore it to the hill, drank the gall and vinegar and was crucified and died.

In the *Apocalypse of Peter,* a Nag Hammadi text, Peter sees what appears to be Jesus being seized and prepared for the cross, and at the same time another figure above the cross who is 'glad and laughing'. On enquiry he is told that the happy person is the living Christ and the one being prepared for crucifixion is the substitute.

In this view the crucifixion of Christ was an illusion. The cross therefore has no significance, since Christ did not suffer on it. Furthermore, as an instrument of shame and punishment it should be treated as an object of detestation.

In another view, held by Cerinthus and others, the historical man Jesus, a good and holy person who had led a pure and unblemished life, was chosen as an instrument of the divine Christ, the Logos. Christ descended into the physical frame of the man Jesus and became incarnate in him. This incarnation took place at the river Jordan at the moment of the baptism of Jesus by John, at which time a light came out of the water, and the divine commission became manifest.

The Bible records that it was only at this time that the Holy Spirit hovered over Jesus, now Christ, and God the Father proclaimed, 'Thou art my beloved Son. This day have I begotten thee' (see NEB, Luke 3:22). Christ's mission of teaching and healing lasted till his betrayal by Judas, after which the Christ-force left the body of Jesus, and it was the man Jesus who suffered and was crucified. This explains the lament on the cross, 'My God, my God, why hast thou forsaken me?', which in the apocryphal *Gospel of Peter* reads, 'My power, my power, thou hast forsaken me' (James, 1924, p. 91). It is to be noted that the canonical gospels report no miracles performed by Jesus either before his baptism or after he was arrested and led out of Gethsemane.

Not all gnostics took a docetic view of the crucifixion. Many held that Christ's suffering was essential if any sense was to be made of his redemptive work. According to certain Valentinians,

Christ, though clothed with immortal life, accepted the endurance of suffering, and took death to himself as his portion in order that he might confront it and annihilate it utterly. The sect of the Melchizedekians likewise proclaimed the reality of Christ's physical body and passion.

The Church rejected the docetist doctrine as heretical, holding that the purpose of Christ's ministry was to identify with the human condition, know temptation, experience suffering, death and hell, in order that he might vanquish them.

Death and Resurrection

For those gnostics who did not take the docetic view, the problems connected with the death and resurrection of Jesus were: Did Jesus die on the cross? Or was a drug administered, perhaps by the skilled Essenes, that would only give the semblance of death (Schonfield, 1981, p. 110). The German scholar Karl Friedrich Bahrdt (d. 1792) suggested that Joseph of Arimathea and Nicodemus, who may have been members of the Essene brotherhood, prepared Jesus to face the ordeal of an apparent death. After removing his comatose body from the cross Joseph of Arimathea used secret remedies to revive him (Stewart, 1981, p. 155).

Again, was his resurrection a normal return to consciousness after a sudden collapse into a coma that was mistaken for death? If so the disciples may have bribed the Roman guards to let him go. It has further been suggested that Jesus went to the Essene community at Qumran, became an Essene monk, and then moved to Masada and perished with the other Jews when the Romans took the fortress in AD 74 (Joyce, 1973). Graves and Podro think Jesus may have been to Rome after his resurrection. There is also a legend that he travelled to India and died and was buried in Kashmir (Faber-Kaiser, 1977).

St Paul states that over 500 persons saw Jesus after the crucifixion (1 Cor. 15:6). But to his intimate disciples he usually appeared as a transfigured Jesus.

As the living exemplar of the divine light Jesus is frequently described as clothed in a brilliant robe of glory and with a dazzling countenance, especially when rapt in prayer and contemplation. The Bible records how on one occasion he took Peter, James and John to a high place, not named in the gospels but traditionally regarded as Mount Tabor southwest of the Sea of Galilee, and was transfigured before them as he spoke with Moses and Elias (Elijah). His raiment was white as snow and his face shone like the sun.

Just as gnostics make a mystery of the forty days in the wilderness, when Jesus was tempted, so they make a mystery of the forty days between the resurrection and the ascension. Several gnostic texts, notably the *Pistis Sophia,* as well as such Nag Hammadi documents as the *Apocryphon of John,* the *Wisdom of Jesus Christ* and the *Epistle of Peter to Philip,* give an account of Jesus after the resurrection, when he appears to his grieving disciples as the glorified Cosmic Christ, apparelled in a vesture of blinding light greater than the light of the sun, transcending the limitations of the earth and filling the heavens with his radiance. Then, reducing the effulgence of his glory, he makes a special revelation to his disciples, ending with a secret discourse on the Mount of Olives.

Christ in Hell
After the crucifixion Christ descended into hell. This phase of his mission is said to have been prefigured in the lives of several gods and semi-divine heroes of antiquity: Osiris, Horus, Isis, Ishtar, Demeter, Hercules, Theseus, Orpheus, all of whom descended into hell. Legends of the harrowing of hell often form part of the hero's descent into the nether regions.

In some of the apocryphal gospels Christ too is vividly described storming Hades and vanquishing the powers ruling there. His purpose is said to be threefold. First, he must redeem himself, for like other mortals he needs redemption, and therefore undergoes an experience of the lower planes. Secondly, he does so in order to save the souls of those who are there. And finally, and this will come at the end of time, he will assault and eventually overthrow Death and Hell.

St Paul says that Christ 'descended into the lower parts of the earth' (Eph. 4:9). St Peter writes that Christ 'preached unto the spirits in prison (1 Pet. 3:19), meaning hell; and also that 'the gospel was preached to them that are dead' (1 Pet. 4:6). The Apostles' Creed states explicitly that Christ 'descended into hell'. The apocryphal *Gospel of Nicodemus* (also known as the *Acts of Pilate*) speaks of Christ's decent into hell, and recounts certain dialogues that took place there.

In the gnostic view, Christ's redemptive mission did not begin on earth, nor is it confined to men. The mission of the Logos began when evil began. His work on earth is part of a

long drawn-out work of salvation. Christ has a function in every
region on our side of the Stauros. When he came down he came
to fulfil a specific mission for every form of creation: for the
fallen angels, the aeons, the archons, for man, and so on down
the hierarchy of beings. He goes to other worlds in the
remotest spheres of the universe.

In the Naassene Psalm, Christ says, 'All the worlds shall I
journey through, all the mysteries unlock.' In the Mandaean
Ginza the Redeemer says, 'I wandered through worlds and
generations.' The sage Silvanus speaks in his *Teachings* of the
many forms Christ assumed in his descent through the spheres,
each appropriate to the situation. According to the *Pseudo-
Clementines,* third-century texts wrongly attributed to the
apostolic father Clement of Rome (d. 100), 'The true Messenger
from the beginning of the world, altering his forms with his
names, courses through the ages until he shall have reached his
time, and, anointed by God's mercy for his labours, attained to
eternal rest.'

Christ the Logos

The gnostic conception of Christ as Logos was not far different
from that of the Church. Christ is the Light-Person, the Lord
(*Kyrios*), the image of the Most High, the Holy One of God,
'the same yesterday, and today, and for ever' (Heb. 13:8). As
God said, 'I am that I am' (Exod. 3:14), so the Logos declares,
'Before Abraham was, I am' (John 8:58).

Manifesting his self-giving love, God reveals himself in
Christ, who is the personification of the Logos and represents
the descent of the divine. Through the Logos made flesh (John
1:14) God enters history and the finite universe. He bridges the
gulf between God and man, and through him we meet God.

The Jewish philosopher Philo of Alexandria (d. AD 50), who
has been called the first of the Church Fathers because of his
almost Christian interpretation of the Logos, wrote, 'If there be
any as yet unfitted to be called a son of God, let him press to
take his place under God's first-born son, the Logos, who holds
the eldership among the angels, their ruler as it were, for the
Word is the eldest-born image of God.'

For mankind, Christ is not only the gracious and good one
(*chrestos*), but the anointed one (*christos*), anointed with the holy
chrism of God. He is the Good Shepherd, the Light, the Way,

the Truth, the Life. He is a unique being, who comes from the superior world, and we are not his equals. In the early gnostic texts Christ is spoken of as *Allogenes,* belonging to 'another race', that is, a divine personage, and not the 'brother of men'. Christ declared, 'I and my Father are one' (John 10:30).

The purpose of Christ's ministry was to enable man to establish a personal relationship with God, so that man's adoption by God might become possible. He taught a new prayer addressed to 'Our Father which art in heaven', distinguished from the 'father' of those who worship the god of this world. Without Christ, say the gnostics, man has no spiritual relationship with the divine world, no spiritual past and no spiritual future. The *Gospel of Philip* states that he who has not received Christ is an orphan, but when he becomes a Christian he acquires parents: God the Father, and the Holy Spirit.

Christ is the cosmic 'Son of man' seen in the vision of the prophet (Dan. 7:13). He shows the way by which man may ascend to heaven. In the words of the Bible, 'No man has ascended to heaven but he who came down from heaven' (John 3:13). Satan, Sophia and Adam indeed descended, but their descent was a fall. Christ alone descended voluntarily, and all things that were brought down can only ascend through him. Without Christ man cannot reach God. The biblical text commonly translated, 'Except a man be born again (*another*), he cannot see the kingdom of God' (John 3:3) should read, 'Except a man be born from above...', and this is how it is translated in the Jerusalem Bible.

Solely through Christ the Logos is such a rebirth possible.

Christ the Man

Certain gnostic texts speak of Christ the Logos as having come down to earth incognito, in order that Satan and the archons might not become aware of his presence on the physical plane. He therefore put on terrestrial garments, disguising himself in human shape, concealing his true form to escape recognition by the cosmic guards and archons.

But in another gnostic view the archons knew that Jesus was the Logos, and indeed Satan recognized and tempted him. The Syriac *Odes of Solomon* (c. AD 130), discovered at the beginning of this century, compare God's plan of salvation to a letter from on high, despatched like an arrow. The hands of many reached out to snatch the letter, but were afraid of the seal upon it, or lacked the power to break the seal.

Satan therefore was ignorant of the message. He was unaware of that hidden mystery that 'eye hath not seen, nor ear heard' (1 Cor. 2:9) concerning the destiny that God had in store for those about to be redeemed. Christ was bringing a messsage such as had never been heard, for, as he said, 'I will utter things which have been kept secret from the foundation of the world' (Matt. 13:35).

It was essential that Christ come to earth in the likeness of sinful flesh (Rom. 8:3). Just as God withdrew and 'made place' to provide an area for the world to come into existence, so Christ, according to the doctrine of 'emptying' (*kenosis*), emptied himself, and 'made himself nothing' (NEB, Phil. 2:7). The Prince of Glory had to take upon himself the misery of earthly existence, experience temptation and suffering, endure contempt and persecution. Though mighty, he humbled himself; though rich, he made himself poor (2 Cor. 8:9). His physical appearance was in keeping with his lowly estate. The Church Father Tertullian wrote that in the days of his flesh Jesus had an ugly countenance (see also Isa. 53:2).

The phrase St Paul applied to himself could with greater relevance be applied to Christ, that he was 'all things to all men' (1 Cor. 9:22). He was a source of universal interpretation and a projection of every human ideal. The gnostics were well aware of the diverse reactions to Jesus. 'He appears', it was said, 'different to each of the different sects who so contentiously seek him. Each responds differently to him, but he belongs to all.'

The Valentinian teacher Theodotus said, 'Each person will see the Lord in his own way, not all alike.' The *Gospel of Philip* states that Christ revealed himself in a manner in which all men would be able to see and understand him. To the great he appeared great, and to the small, small. To the immature he appeared as a youth, and to the mature as a man of wisdom. One of the gnostic gospels relates that when Jesus first called upon the brothers James and John to follow him, James saw Jesus as a boy, while John saw a handsome and cheerful young man, and thought that James's eyesight must be blurred and defective.

The ministry of Jesus was directed at all manner of people. He came to the despised Samaritans, the hated Romans and the detested tax-gatherers. His disciples carried on his work, so that Peter admitted to baptism the gentile proselytes (Cornelius and his household); and Philip the Evangelist the still more despised eunuch, a class barred by the Law from participating in the full privileges of the Jewish faith.

To some, Jesus was a pretender and a charlatan. To others he was prophet, priest and king. He was in turn stern lawgiver and implacable judge, as well as a champion of the poor and oppressed. He was the loving teacher and guide, and the rebel leader; the gentle preacher, and the reformer demanding social justice. He was a peacemaker who advocated turning the other cheek, and a radical declaring that he came to bring not peace but the sword. He was, in the words of Don Cupitt, 'a model for hermits, peasants, gentlemen, revolutionaries, pacifists, feudal lords, soldiers and others'.

His language was down to earth. He drew illustrations both from lilies in the field, and egesta in the privy (Mark 7: 15–19). Among the examples cited by Jesus of the everyday activities that would precede his second coming were: men working in the field, women grinding corn, and 'in that night there shall be two men in one bed' (Luke 17:34).

His attitude to loving relationships between people was often misconstrued. St Jerome mentions a verse in the *Gospel of the Hebrews* in which Jesus says to his disciples, 'Never be joyful save when you look upon your brother with love', a verse which became the subject of much free interpretation among the gnostics.

To certain of his detractors Jesus was an illegitimate half-caste, to others 'a man gluttonous and a wine-bibber, a friend of publicans and sinners' (Matt. 11:19). He was known to associate with delinquents and harlots, forgiving, if not condoning, adultery, and promising paradise to men of violence. In some gnostic sects he was seen as a homosexual, and in others there was a suggestion of more reprehensible practices.

A modern writer gives a few more examples of the individual interpretations to which the Christ figure has been subjected in our own times. He refers to 'the whimsical clown of *Godspell* and the strident social critic of *Jesus Christ Superstar*... the scheming Jesus of Schonfield, the mythical Jesus who is a phallic symbol of Allegro' (Bruns, 1976, p. 9).

In *L'Age d'Or,* a film made by the Spanish painter Luis Buñuel, Jesus appears as a 'master debauchee' who presides over the

Marquis de Sade's *120 Days of Sodom* (Tyler, 1971, p. 19). In the film *Theorem* of Pier Paolo Pasolini, Christ is in turn sexual and divine, the picture perhaps being intended to represent, among other things, 'faith as a phallic fantasy' (Weightman, 1973, p. 178).

Not many years ago another film producer, Jens Joergen Thorsen proposed making a film, with the financial backing of the Danish government, to be entitled *The Loves of Jesus Christ,* in which Jesus was to be presented as 'a warlord, love apostle, erotomaniac, drunkard, idealist and revolutionary', with some footage devoted to explicit portrayals of him in group sex scenes (Warner, 1976, p. 229).

In the gnostic view Christ's understanding and experience embraced all the evils. To fulfil his purpose he had not only to confront but identify with the Adversary. The temptations of Jesus are briefly recorded in the Bible (Matt. 4:1). Only three incidents are symbolically given, and we do not know the precise nature and full scope of the temptations.

To believe that man can know gentle love and violent lust, tender mercy and murderous hate, and that Christ cannot, is to believe that the range of human experience and knowledge is greater than that of the Logos. And it may have been in the wilderness, about which little else is recorded during the forty days and forty nights, that Christ became as much sin incarnate as he was God incarnate.

The gnostic denigration of Christ in this context was designed to reveal a degraded Saviour, who alone could understand the extent of their own degradation. In the words of the modern revivalist, Christ raises man 'from the guttermost to the uttermost'. But, the gnostic would ask, how could he save man from the abyss of sin, unless he entered the abyss himself?

This particular concept gave rise to the gnostic doctrine of the redeemed Redeemer, according to which Christ became incarnate as a man in order to fulfil in himself the process of purification and redemption. To do so he had to participate fully in the human condition. In this view redemption was necessary even for Christ (Foerster, 1974, p. 225).

He was born into the inheritance of Moses so that he could free mankind from the bondage of the law (Rom. 10:4). He was 'made to be sin' (2 Cor. 5:21) in order to remove from us our inheritance of sin. He was 'made a curse' (Gal. 3:13) to lift from us the curse of the Fall. He became man that we might become divine. He experienced death and hell that we might be ransomed and gain immortality.

6.

THE DISCIPLES

Jesus chose twelve of his closest disciples as his apostles to carry on his mission and spread the gospel, but it was the prevailing gnostic view that the majority of them remained under the influence of Jewish opinion and under the law of Moses. In the apocryphal *Acts of Peter* Jesus says, 'They that are with me have not understood me.'

The best known of the apostles is Simon Peter, and even he at a critical moment denied Christ three times. Another apostle, Thomas, doubted him. Judas betrayed him, though in the gnostic view he had a special mission to carry out. John wrote a life of Jesus that is highly gnostic in tone. Matthew wrote one of the three synoptic gospels, but the authors of the other two, Mark, the interpreter of Peter, and Luke, a physician and author of the *Acts of the Apostles,* were not Christ's apostles.

The gnostics derived many of their basic traditions from disciples who were outside the circle of the twelve. From James, the brother of Jesus; from Mary Magdalene and Salome; from Lazarus who was raised from the dead; from the secret disciple, the rabbi Nicodemus, who came to Jesus by night, and who later embalmed his body; and from Paul. According to Marcion, 'Christ's earliest apostles proved failures, but he raised up Paul after them' (Blackman, 1948, p. 48).

John
The son of Zebedee and brother of the apostle James (not to be confused with James the Just, the brother of Jesus), John was the 'beloved disciple', and the reputed author of the gospel and three epistles in the New Testament that bear his name. The adjective Johannine is sometimes used to distinguish his teachings from the Johannite teachings of John the Baptist.

It was concerning him that it was said, that he would not die (John 21:23). Tradition identifies him with St John the Divine, and says that he lived on in exile on the island of Patmos, where he wrote the *Apocalypse* (Revelation). From Patmos he went to Ephesus. Here, at a ripe old age, he entered a subterranean tomb, on the site of the famous temple of Diana of the Ephesians, at a spot that had been the last home of the Virgin Mary. And here, the story goes, awaiting the return of Jesus he still sleeps, and the ground heaves gently on his breast as he breathes.

In the view of Priscillian, the bridegroom at the wedding at Cana was none other than John, and the new wine that Christ miraculously created was a symbol of the new life of celibacy for which Jesus intended him (Chadwick, 1976, p. 105). Before the actual ceremony Jesus said to John, 'I have need of you', on hearing which John was suddenly taken ill and was compelled to postpone, and finally to cancel, the marriage (Bruns, 1976, p. 35).

From the very beginnings of the new Church there was a body of doctrine stemming from John to whom, it was said, the true secrets of Christianity had been communicated by Jesus. This teaching was strongly tinged with gnosticism. The *Apocryphon of John,* or the secret book of John, purports to reveal the 'mysteries concealed in silence' that Jesus taught him. The book was cited by Irenaeus, and a version of it was also found at Nag Hammadi.

Many gnostic schools claimed the canonical gospel of John as a work embodying their own doctrines, and used it as a primary source of their teachings. It differs so radically from the other gospels that a distinction is made between the three 'synoptic' gospels of Matthew, Mark and Luke, and the gospel according to John. It presents a mystical rather than a historical Jesus, with concepts derived from Alexandrian philosophy. Theologians like Rudolf Bultmann have suggested that the material in John's gospel is a demythologized and Christianized version of a pre-Christian gnostic source.

Epiphanius states that one of John's disciples, Leucius, was regarded as the author of the *Acts of John,* a gnostic work known to Clement of Alexandria. The Church tried to replace this work with a safer version purged of its unorthodoxy which came to be known as the *Acts of Prochorus,* and was still in circulation in the tenth century. In one tradition, Prochorus too was a disciple of John and the scribe to whom John dictated the gospel at Patmos.

Thomas

Didymus Judas Thomas, the doubting disciple of Jesus, was said to have carried the gospel message to India and Central Asia. The names Thomas and Didymus are derived respectively from the Aramaic and Greek words for 'twin'.

Thomas is the reputed author of the *Gospel of Thomas*, and the *Book of Thomas the Contender*. In the latter work Jesus tells Thomas, 'You are my twin and true companion. Know yourself and you will understand who you are.' The suggestion here may be that Jesus is the twin brother, the spiritual 'other self' of each person (Pagels, 1979, p. 18).

The fourth-century Coptic *Gospel of Thomas* formed part of the huge find of papyri at Nag Hammadi in 1945. Fragments of a Greek version had been discovered in the 1890s. The text of this gospel opens with the words: 'These are the secret words which the living Jesus spake and which the twin Didymus Judas Thomas took down.' The book has no connecting narrative and makes no reference to Jesus's work, but consists of 114 *logia* or sayings of Jesus after his resurrection, and probably embodies some genuine early material. It is thought to be a Coptic translation of a work of Greek origin dating from about AD 140.

Among the more curious verses in the *Gospel of Thomas* is one in which Jesus takes Thomas aside and says three words to him. When Thomas returns to his companions they ask him what Jesus said, Thomas replies, 'If I tell you one of the words which he spoke to me you will take up stones and throw them at me; and a fire will come out of the stones and burn you up.'

Some gnostics surmised that the three secret words spoken by Jesus were taken from the mysterious verse in the Bible (Isa. 28:10) translated: 'Precept upon precept [Heb. *tsav la-tsav*], line upon line [Heb. *kav la-kav*], there a little [Heb. *zeir sham*].' These three Hebrew phrases are usually transliterated: Saulasau, Kaulakau, Zeesar.

Hippolytus in his *Refutations* states that the Naassene sect have a curious commentary on this passage, and some indeed assert that the very existence of the world depends on these three words: *Saulasau* is thought to mean the law of Moses here below; *Kaulakau,* the Stauros or Cross, which is above; and *Zeesar,* the upflowing Jordan.

Judas

One of the twelve original disciples of Jesus and the treasurer of the group, Judas, like the others chosen by Jesus, obtained part of the ministry (Acts 1:17). The gnostic sect of the Judasites, a branch of the Cainites, assigned him a place above that of John the beloved disciple. They held that alone of all the disciples Judas had the true gnosis (Layton, 1981, p. 804). He was seen as the author of man's salvation, the chosen agent of the Atonement, and the one responsible for bringing the supreme blessing to the human race.

At the last supper Jesus washed the feet of all the disciples, including those of Judas. And it was to Judas alone that Jesus personally gave a morsel of bread after he had dipped it in a dish (John 13:26), something normally offered to a guest as a mark of honour. During the last supper Jesus authorized Judas to proceed with his allotted task, saying, 'That thou doest, do quickly' (John 13:27).

In the gnostic interpretation Judas 'betrayed' Jesus because he alone knew that Jesus had been sent by the true God. The demiurge and the world powers did not want Christ to suffer and die as he did, because they wished to prevent the salvation of the human race. Judas therefore helped to accomplish the mystery of the betrayal so that the designs of the demiurge might be frustrated (Bruns, 1976, p. 59). Thirty pieces of silver was a trifling sum, for which Judas would not have thought it worth his while to betray anyone, least of all his master. The kiss to identify Jesus was superfluous, since Jesus was already well known to all concerned, including the Pharisees. But all this was part of a great cosmic drama that had to be fulfilled.

Some derive Judas's surname Iscariot from Kerioth, the place from which he came. Others derive it from the Aramaic word for 'falsehood', because he was the false one. Yet others from the Greek word *sicarios,* 'assassin', after the *sica* or short curved dagger carried by the Zealots, an extremist Jewish sect to which Judas belonged. The Zealots believed that the kingdom of the Messiah would have to be established by force.

When his part was done Judas was said to have hanged himself. There were those who believed that Judas was a member of a secret cult, possibly established under the influence of the Stoics, who deemed it honourable to end one's life by suicide or have one's life terminated by another member of the sect. No stigma was attached either to the suicide, or the man carrying out his wishes and killing him.

The Greek term used in the Bible (Matt. 27:5) for the final act of Judas, comes from the word *apagcho,* which means not only 'to hang oneself', but also 'to strangle oneself'. Judas, it was said, was put into a trance and then strangled in a special rite, and though his body died he passed in a state of full psychic consciousness to heaven. Several gnostic sects, besides the Judasites, also advocated suicide, either direct or with the help of others.

Irenaeus mentions a *Gospel of Judas,* but this is now lost.

Lazarus

A man of Bethany, the brother of Mary and Martha, whose story is told only in the Gospel of John, chapters 11 and 12. Though Lazarus is not one of the disciples of Jesus, the closeness of their friendship is made evident when news of his illness is brought to Jesus: 'He whom thou lovest is sick.' In the gospel account Jesus did not immediately hurry to the scene, but remained for two days where he was, saying, 'This sickness is not unto death, but for the glory of God.' When he reached Bethany Lazarus was dead and it was the dead Lazarus whom Jesus raised.

The story of Lazarus and Jesus is given in no other New Testament account, but in the light of certain apocryphal evidence it has been suggested that a more intimate significance might be read into their relationship. It seems that some form of homosexual rite accompanied certain forms of gnostic initiation. In a report made by the gnostic Theodotus, and quoted by the Church Father Clement of Alexandria, Jesus taught his disciples, 'at first by examples and by stories with hidden meanings, then by parables and enigmas, but in the third stage, clearly and nakedly, in private.'

While 'nakedly' may simply mean 'plainly', it may be subject to a literal interpretation, and this would seem to be borne out from a handwritten copy of part of a letter from Clement of Alexandria to one Theodore. This letter was found in 1958 by Professor Morton Smith of Columbia University in the monastery library of Mar Saba in the Judean desert, and its discovery reported to the American Society of Biblical Literature and Exegesis. The manuscript refers to certain secret teachings of Jesus seemingly reserved for a special circle of followers, and to a secret gospel written by Mark.

It relates a different version of what is probably the Lazarus incident, which suggests a special kind of mystical rite. In this version Jesus was approached for help by a certain woman whose brother had died. Jesus entered the garden, and as he approached the tomb a loud cry was heard from within, making it obvious that the young man was not dead. Jesus then rolled away the stone from the entrance to the tomb, and stretching forth his hand raised the young man. 'And the youth looked upon him and loved him and began to beseech him that he might be with him.'

They went together to the house of the youth, and Jesus gave him instruction for six days. On the evening of the last day the youth remained with Jesus that night. The text includes a reference to 'naked [man] with naked [man]'. In the authorized version of the gospel of Mark there is an inexplicable reference to 'a certain young man having a loin cloth cast about his naked body', who followed Jesus after his arrest when all his other disciples had deserted him, and then fled naked when an attempt was made to seize him (Mark 14:52). He seems to be identified with the young man already mentioned (see Bruce, 1974, p. 166).

The incident related in the text would suggest that Jesus may have been the centre of what Professor Smith calls a 'libertine circle', and possibly admitted his chosen followers, singly and by night, to the mystery of the kingdom, by certain ceremonies derived from ancient erotic magic (Smith, 1974, p. 140). The single linen cloth worn by the candidate was removed and the naked body immersed in a form of water baptism. There were prayers and hymns, and some kind of rite of manipulation, accompanied by a technique for interfering with normal breathing. The disciple was possessed by the spirit of Jesus and so united with him. One with him, he participated, perhaps through hallucination, in the ascent to heaven, freed from the law of the lower plane. As Professor Smith says, 'Freedom from the law may have resulted in completion of the spiritual union by physical union' (Smith, 1974, p. 142).

Clement of Alexandria was aware that the sect of the Carpocratians used a secret gospel of Mark allegedly written when Mark was in Alexandria, but adds that these people 'polluted the spotless and holy words of scripture to accord with their blasphemous and carnal doctrine, and by doing so wandered from the narrow road into the abyss of darkness.'

Mary Magdalene

A prominent figure in gnostic and heretical literature. Some scholars believe that the name Magdalene is the Greek rendering of the Aramaic word *megadella* meaning 'hairdresser'. Women practising this profession were regarded among the Jews as ladies of easy virtue. Others think it more likely that she was named after the town of Magdala on the Sea of Galilee. She was a very wealthy woman and owned much property in the town.

There is a great deal of confusion about the various Marys mentioned in the Bible and the Apocrypha. Some have identified Mary Magdalene with the unnamed woman 'which was a sinner', who anointed the feet of Jesus with ointment (Luke 7:37), and some think she was the same as the woman of Bethany, also unnamed, who anointed his head (Mark 14:3), while yet others have attempted to identify both these anonymous women with Mary of Bethany who anointed his feet (John 12:3). This latter hypothesis would make Mary Magdalene the sister of Martha of Bethany and of Lazarus mentioned above.

In early and medieval lore Mary Magdalene is represented as a beautiful and meretricious woman, a witch and a whore. She repents and is led to Christ, who casts seven devils out of her (Mark 16:9). She washes the feet of Jesus and anoints his head with costly oils. In many gnostic texts she is the companion of Jesus and is with him on several important occasions. In one curious case, however, Mary is not present, and this is during an event of especial significance. Before the last supper Jesus called his disciples together and asked them for the bread and the cup to bless them. At that moment Mary Magdalene laughed, whereupon Jesus asked all the women to leave.

According to the gnostics, Jesus loved Mary Magdalene above all his disciples, and certain gnostic texts hint of an erotic relationship between them, as a result of which she becomes spiritually pregnant and perfect. According to the Nag Hammadi *Gospel of Philip* Jesus often kissed her on the mouth, a fact that offended the disciples so much that on one occasion Peter asked Jesus to make Mary leave their company. When the disciples asked Jesus, 'Why do you love her more than us?' he replied, 'Why do you suppose I do not love you as much as I love her?'

It has been suggested that Jesus and Mary Magdalene were united in a form of spiritual marriage permitted by the Essene sect to which Jesus is thought to have belonged, and also that she was his legal wife (Folliot, 1978, p. 39). She was the first to see a vision of the risen Christ after his death. He appeared to the other disciples only later, and when she spoke of her vision to the disciples Peter refused to believe her.

The Nag Hammadi text the *Dialogue of the Saviour* praises her as excelling all the disciples and being favoured with an insight far surpassing theirs. She is in fact the most spiritual of the disciples and is described as 'the woman who knew the All'. In the *Gospel of Mary* (Magdalene), she is the supreme initiate into Christ's mysteries and after the resurrection of Jesus the disciples say to her, 'Let us hear from you those words of his which you know and which we have not heard'. And she then discloses to them what Jesus said to her. Unfortunately, several pages of the script are badly damaged at this point, so no details of this teaching are preserved. But the narrative goes on to say that the disciples found the teaching unlike anything they remembered Jesus having taught.

Much of the medieval lore about Mary Magdalene is embodied in books like the *Golden Legend* by the Dominican priest Jacobus de Voragine (d. 1298), and her cult flourished for centuries in the south of France. In this tradition, Mary Magdalene, along with Martha her sister, Lazarus her brother, Mary the wife of Cleophas who was the half-sister of the Virgin Mary, Mary the mother of James and Joses, and Mary Salome, were all washed up on the shores of Provence in a rudderless boat, after they had fled persecution in the Holy Land.

The probability that Mary Magdalene was the wife of Jesus has recently been argued afresh by more than one writer. It has even been suggested that the title Notre Dame, 'Our Lady', conferred on many great French cathedrals, also refers to Mary Magdalene (Baigent, 1982, p. 73).

Salome

If there is confusion about the scriptural and apocryphal Marys, there is still greater confusion about the Salomes. A number of women named Salome (Heb. *shalom,* 'peace') figure in the texts.

One Salome appears in the infancy gospels as a midwife, or is otherwise present at or immediately after the birth of Jesus, and is the first to recognize him as the Christ. Sometimes she is said to be the sister of the Virgin Mary. Traditionally, Salome is the name given to the wife of Zebedee and mother of the apostles

James and John, although she is not so named in the Bible.

Another traditional Salome is the beautiful sixteen-year old daughter of Herodias (Mark 6:22) and step-daughter of Herod Antipas the tetrarch. According to the story John the Baptist denounced the marriage, incestuous in Mosaic law, of Herod and his sister-in-law Herodias. The latter conspired with her daughter to avenge herself on John the Baptist. During a palace feast Salome danced a voluptuous dance before Herod, which so pleased him that he promised to give her whatever she asked. She demanded, at the prompting of her mother, the head of the Baptist on a salver. John was duly beheaded and his head brought to her. According to the Jewish historian Josephus, this Salome later married her grand-uncle, Philip the tetrarch, and after his death, Aristobulus of Lesser Armenia.

In the apocryphal *Gospel of the Egyptians* a certain Salome appears as a disciple of Jesus. She asks him how long death would hold sway, and he says to her, 'So long as women bring forth, for I come to end the works of the female'. To this Salome replies, 'Then I have done well in not bringing forth.' It would appear from this text that Salome was childless, and apparently unmarried. Scholars who identify this gnostic Salome with Salome daughter of Herodias suggest that Josephus's statement about her twofold marriage may in fact refer to another member of Herod's household, perhaps Herod's own daughter of the same name.

Herod's household was thoroughly depraved, and Salome was part of a corrupt family, both on her mother's and step-father's side. In a popular tradition current at the time she, like her mother, had lusted after John the Baptist and had been spurned by him, for which reason she eagerly fell in with her mother's scheme to have him executed. Strange to say, medieval folklore does not condemn Salome for demanding the head of John the Baptist. It is her mother, 'the most damned and adulterous Herodias', who enters legend as the leader of the witches, and it is Herodias who is condemned to dance without respite till the day of judgment. This would lend support to the belief about the 'conversion' of Salome, after which she becomes a follower of Jesus. To add to the confusion, she is sometimes referred to as Mary Salome.

The only Salome actually mentioned in the Bible is described as watching the crucifixion from afar off, and coming after the entombment to anoint the body. In both contexts she is named with Mary Magdalene. The apocryphal Coptic *Book of the Resurrection of Christ,* attributed to the apostle Bartholomew, names the women who went to the tomb. Among them were: Mary Magdalene; Mary the mother of James whom Jesus delivered out of the hand of Satan; Mary who ministered to him; Martha her sister; Joanna (Susanna) who renounced the marriage bed; and 'Salome who tempted him.'

It would seem that some time after she had contrived the beheading of John the Baptist, Salome may have tried to use her wiles to tempt Jesus in some way, but was converted by him and became his follower, and like Mary Magdalene remained close to him thereafter. According to the *Gospel of Thomas,* Salome and Mary Magdalene became the disciples of Jesus when they transcended their human nature and 'became male'. Salome received certain secret teachings from Jesus, and these were said to have been communicated by her to a select group. The Carpocratians claimed to derive some of their tenets from Salome.

In the *Gospel of Thomas* there is a reference to Jesus sharing Salome's couch, and of Salome's strange questioning. 'Who are you sir,' she asks him, 'that you have taken your place on my couch and eaten from my table?' And Jesus says, 'I am he who is from the One, and the things that belong to the Father have been given to me.' Salome retorts, 'But I am your disciple.' And Jesus answers, 'When the disciple is united he will be filled with light, but if he is divided he will be filled with darkness.'

St Paul

Belonging to the tribe of Benjamin, a Hebrew of the Hebrews, born and bred a Pharisee, a pupil of Gamaliel, an eminent Jewish teacher of Jerusalem, Paul was foremost among the persecutors of the Christians. But in about AD 35 following a blinding vision on the road to Damascus he was converted to Christianity. Thereafter he became the greatest of the early missionaries, tirelessly propagating the gospel in Palestine, Syria, Asia Minor, Macedonia, Greece and Rome. He was martyred in Rome in AD 67.

Paul was not one of the apostles, and most of the biographical details we have about him, including the story of his conversion, are provided by Luke, author of one of the four New Testament gospels, who was not a disciple (apostle) either.

Most of the epistles of Paul were written before any of the canonical gospels had taken their present form. Paul does not preach the Jesus of the historical gospels, and is apparently not concerned with the acts and even sayings of Jesus in any form known to the gospel writers. In his epistles he makes no allusion to Bethlehem, to Nazareth, to the parents of Jesus, the virgin birth, John the Baptist, or Judas. There is no mention of the Sermon on the Mount, the Lord's Prayer, the miracles, the parables of the kingdom, no reference to a trial before a Roman official, to the denials of Peter, nor to many other significant events in the life and death of Jesus.

At some time in his career Paul was caught up to the third heaven and experienced an extraordinary vision, about which he remains silent (2 Cor. 12:4). In the *Panarion* Epiphanius says that the gnostics fabricated a book which they called the *Ascent of Paul* purporting to contain the record of the unspeakable things Paul is reported to have seen and heard when he ascended to the third heaven. If such a book ever existed, it is lost. There are, however, a number of extant apocryphal epistles, acts and apocalypses named after St Paul.

Close study of the biblical Acts and Pauline epistles shows that Paul was occasionally involved in bitter conflict with his opponents, including some of the original disciples of Jesus, who would have chosen to adapt Christianity to Judaism. According to some authorities Paul felt strongly drawn to a type of esoteric Christianity opposed to the ritualistic form favoured by the Judaisers. The gnostics believed that Paul was the chief of those to whom the risen Christ had revealed himself. He proclaims the doctrine of the mystic Christ, and speaks repeatedly of 'mysteries' and 'knowledge'. One of Paul's own disciples is said to have been Theodas, teacher of the great gnostic Valentinus. Another prominent gnostic, Marcion, claimed that only Paul understood the true nature of Christ's mission.

Yet Paul also warns against 'science (*gnosis*) falsely so called' (1 Tim. 6:20), and in a famous passage specifically proclaims the futility of both faith and knowledge without the right attitude of heart: 'Though I understand all mysteries, and all knowledge (*gnosis*); and though I have all faith so that I could remove mountains, and have not charity [love], I am nothing' (1 Cor. 13:2).

If Paul was a gnostic, he was a gnostic with a difference, for he preached not gnosis, but epignosis, not knowledge but transcendental wisdom – 'to know the love of Christ that passeth knowledge' (Eph. 3:19).

7.

THE PRACTICES

Basic to an appreciation of what the gnostics believed is of course their own understanding of the nature of knowledge itself, which was ultimately a secret knowledge of matters both divine and diabolical. From this flowed their beliefs regarding the human body and its interrelationship with the larger cosmos. Gnosticism in its application covered the extremes of sacramental praxis, ranging over the whole gamut, from the excesses of asceticism to the excesses of licentiousness, the latter descending to crude forms of anomalous ritualism that aroused the ire and indignation of the Church Fathers who wrote about them.

Knowledge

Gnostics spoke of two lines of tradition relating to the teachings of Christ: the public sayings, and the secret inner doctrines. This distinction, they believed, had biblical endorsement. Some things were told 'in darkness' and heard 'in the ear' (Matt. 10:27). They could thereafter be announced from the housetops but would not be understood by those not prepared to receive the teaching.

In the New Testament we read of Jesus saying to his disciples, 'To you has been given the secret of the kingdom of God; but for those outside, everything is in parables' (Mark 4:11). On another occasion he said, 'I have yet many things to say unto you, but ye cannot bear them now' (John 16:12). Paul likewise speaks of the wisdom of God as a mystery, being given to those who are 'perfect' (1 Cor. 2:6).

In the gnostic tradition the things that Jesus did not at first disclose were revealed by the risen Christ, and it is these revelations that form the subject of certain gnostic writings and of certain oral teachings never written down. In the words of a psalm discovered at Qumran, 'I will conceal knowledge, I will hedge wisdom about, to preserve fidelity'. The fact that a message is true does not mean it should become common property. According to the secret gospel of Mark, 'Not all true things are to be disclosed to all men'.

Gnosticism was essentially a mystery religion; gnostic sects were secret societies, and the final revelations were made only to the few. To all others such matters were 'sealed with seven seals'.

Because the surface trappings of religion and the outward observance of official worship were counted of small consequence, gnostics like Basilides asserted that there was no harm in apostasy, in denying the faith and submitting to the outward forms of another creed in times of persecution. The gnostic was not usually a man of martyrdom and rejected its necessity. Scriptural authority for this was found in the words of Jesus, 'Agree with thine adversary quickly' (Matt. 5:25).

The nature of the knowledge sought by the gnostic is a matter of central importance in gnosticism, and its full implications must therefore be clearly understood. One can encounter knowledge of a sort at many levels, so to begin with the different kinds of knowledge are first to be distinguished.

There is the practical skill (*episteme*) acquired through close involvement, such as knowledge of cookery and farming; or theoretical understanding through observation, like weather lore and astronomy. There is abstract knowledge (*mathesis*) acquired through logic and reason, like geometry. There is subjective or 'felt' experience (*pathesis*) acquired through suffering or strong emotion. A kind of knowledge may come to one obliquely, through xenophrenic or 'strange-minded' states, as in dreams, visions and trances. There is the judgment of ethics, pointing the way to a better moral life. There is the intellectual way of knowledge through philosophy. And a certain kind of unverifiable conviction that comes through faith (*pistis*). Yet all these fall short of the enlightenment sought by the gnostic.

Christ declared, 'The kingdom of God is within you' (Luke 17:21), and gnosis is essentially a quest for that kingdom. Important as faith is, the gnostic ideal is not a man of faith (*pistikos*) but a man of knowledge (*gnostikos*). It implies an awareness of self that leads to internal harmony, to unification within, and to union with the One.

The German philosopher Friedrich Nietzsche (d. 1900) wrote, 'There was only one Christian, and he died on the cross.' This may be taken as a paradoxical variation of the proposition expressed by St Paul, 'Christ lives in me' (Gal. 2:20). The gnostics laid great emphasis on the inner light. Professor R. M. Grant, an authority on the subject, characterizes gnosticism as 'a passionate subjectivity'. The wise Solon of Athens (d. 558 BC) said, 'Know thyself', and this was the aim of the gnostics too, and is repeatedly stressed in their works.

Gnosis cannot be taught, since it cannot be intellectually explained, only intuitively perceived. The *Discourse on the Eighth and Ninth,* referring to the higher eighth and ninth levels of cognition, emphasizes that a teacher can only set forth what is needful; understanding rests with the pupil. The Arabian gnostic teacher Monoimus (c. 180) wrote, 'Take yourself as the starting point in every search for the divine principle. Discover what abides within you and you will find all things'.

It must be borne in mind that to the gnostic the created cosmos is utterly alienated from the divine plane of being, and the higher mysteries of gnosis cannot be known from anything in this world. The soul within does not belong to the world, and the illumination of gnosis constitutes the original condition of the soul. When a candidate comes to this realization he is ready for the secret rite of 'release' (*apolytrosis*), when he formally addresses the demiurge and announces his independence of him, declaring himself now 'a son of the pre-existent Father'.

Gnosis cannot be communicated by words. All language is sequential and time-bound and therefore cannot express the mystery. Rather, the person who receives gnosis remembers (recognizes) it, and 'knows as soon as he hears'. It springs from the immediate perception of a transformed consciousness. It comes instantly, all at one stroke, as if a blindfold had been removed from the eyes.

Gnosis is not concerned with a moral life, but with mystical enlightenment and freedom from the bondage of creation. It is not a religion but a theosophy in the original meaning of the term, a cognizance of supramundane matters. It provides secret insight into the divine order of things, but also gives an insight into the snares of the demiurge as clearly revealed in scripture. It is knowledge not only of the 'deep things of God' (1 Cor. 2:10), but also of the 'deep things of Satan' (Rev. 2:24).

It comes by divine grace through the revelation of the Saviour. Whoever achieves gnosis, says the *Gospel of Philip,* becomes 'no longer Christian, but Christ'.

The Body

This is the creation of the demiurge, who took his model from the pattern limned on the heavenly curtain as it was reflected in distorted form in the murky waters below. Within the body (*soma*) is entombed the soul (*psyche*) and the light of the soul shining through the bodily shroud gives potency and significance to the human entity. The area of contact between psyche and soma is said to be a point that exists somewhere within the head. In the Naassene view this is the mustard seed (*sinapi*) mentioned in the Bible (Mark 4:31), an indivisible point within the cranium known only to the spiritually awakened.

In the gnostic belief the constellations exercise a powerful influence on the body. The signs of the zodiac are symbols of the archons who rule them. Because the body was put together part by part by the archons, each sign is said to govern and control one particular part. Such allocation of parts was called limb-placing (*melothesis*), and in later times diagrams were made, showing a man with the appropriate zodiacal signs superimposed. The association was as follows: head (Aries), neck (Taurus), arms (Gemini), breast (Cancer), stomach (Leo), loins (Virgo), back (Libra), sexual organs (Scorpio), thighs (Sagittarius), knees (Capricorn), calves (Aquarius), feet (Pisces).

In the school of Marcus, the letters of the Greek alphabet were also associated with the parts of the human anatomy. These were arranged in pairs; the first and last letters, the second and penultimate letters, the third and the antepenult, the fourth and fourth from the end, and so on, as follows: alpha and omega, governing the head; beta and psi, the neck; gamma and chi, the arms; delta and phi, the breast; epsilon and upsilon, the diaphragm; zeta and tau, the back; eta and sigma, the stomach; theta and rho, the hips; iota and pi, the genitals; kappa and omicron, the legs; lambda and xi, the ankles; mu and nu, the feet.

Certain philosophical treatises, such as the *Megale Apophasis,* allegorize texts from the Bible, Homer and others, to support speculations about the human embryo and the human brain, and the dynamic functioning of the human physiological system from birth to death. The topography of the Garden of

Eden is related to the veins, arteries and air ducts of the body. The fire that underlies and originates all things transforms blood into semen in the male, and into milk in the female.

According to the Peratics, there exists a sympathetic relationship between the stars and certain centres or plexuses situated in the brain and organs of the body, and the interconnections between them were traced by means of numbers and geometrical figures, especially the numbers one (represented by the circle), three (triangle) and twelve (dodecahedron).

Thus, there are two triangles in the head. An outer triangle links the top of the cerebrum with the frontal lobe (the front of the cerebrum) and the cerebellum (the back of the head). And an inner triangle links the third ventricle, the pineal gland and the thalamus. Yet another triangle links the blood stream (centred in the heart), the spinal marrow (centred in the medulla) and the semen (centred in the testicles). They devised special methods of 'crossing the Jordan' by exercises involving breathing rhythms, mystical syllables, and withholding and redirecting ejaculation.

Man is a replica of the cosmos, a minute universe, a microcosm of the greater world. In him are the seeds and symbols of all things. Whatever is elsewhere is in man: heaven and hell, good and evil, all elements, numbers, functions, dimensions.

In the system of Basilides, man has 365 bodily parts, and each part is under the control of a spiritual entity. To understand their interconnections is to know how to control all the limbs and organs of the body, both of earthly and archetypal man, and so bring the macrocosm above and the microcosm that is man into a magical relationship.

The Sacraments

Many cultic activities of the gnostics became ritualized as a result of usage and tradition, such as baptism, the eucharist, initiation, redemption and other transit rites, the bridal chamber, and prayers for the dying and the dead. Some of these corresponded with the rites of the Church and are thought to have had an influence on Christian forms of sacramental practice, although the precise extent and nature of the contribution is disputed. On the whole the gnostics regarded a multiplicity of sacraments, especially those involving the services of a hierarchy of priests, as a relic of paganism and a reversion to Jewish custom.

Circumcision was practiced by the Judeo-Christian gnostics but abandoned by the others. Jesus in the gospels never once enjoined circumcision. When in the *Gospel of Thomas* the disciples ask Jesus whether circumcision is necessary he replies, 'If it were necessary then every father would beget a circumcised male.' St Paul virtually rejected circumcision.

Baptism was undergone by most gnostics, usually only once. It was treated as a death rite because it marks the end of the old life; and also as a resurrection rite because it is a rebirth into a new life. However, in certain sects, such as the Mandaeans, baptism was a frequent occurrence. On the other hand some gnostics rejected baptism altogether, tracing it back to Jewish practice instituted by Jehovah. The prophet Elisha prescribed it as a means of purification for Naaman the Syrian captain who was cured of leprosy by washing seven times in the Jordan (2 Kings 5:10). It also had pagan precedents. On the analogy of the Mithraic candidate, who was cleansed by the blood of the bull, the Christian was cleansed by the blood of the Lamb.

Again, communal meals of a sacramental character were known to many pre-Christian communities, such as the worshippers of Dionysus and Mithra. The Greeks used to have a social meal (*eranos*) to which everyone who came made a contribution.

Christians trace the eucharist to the last passover supper in which Jesus broke bread and had wine with his disciples, and adjoined them to 'do this in remembrance of me'. The earliest form of this commemorative event was the feast of charity (*agape*), which was primarily an occasion for believers to meet and share a meal together, the rich paying for the poor. St Paul referred to it as the Lord's Supper. It was an occasion for remembrance and thanksgiving and not much more.

Gnostics held that Christ's injunction was in the nature of a charge to his followers to remember him at all meals, which was expressed in early times in the form of a prayer of thankfulness (*eucharistia*) at table. In the Lord's Prayer we are asked to say, 'Give us this day our daily bread'. Here the word for daily (*epiousios*) may also mean 'supersubstantial' (James, 1924, p. 4), thus transforming every meal into a kind of sacrament. The apocryphal gospels contain numerous references to the early Christians 'taking a communal meal and praising the Lord', so that each occasion was eucharistic.

Most gnostics regarded the whole idea of daily or weekly

until then is enough to last

'eating the body' as a pagan superstition. They saw it as a perpetuation of the 'sacrificed and suffering Jesus', who is constantly being made to experience the passion, and then being crucified, torn and 'served up in every dish'. They held that, like baptism, the eucharist as a sacrament, was unrepeatable for the person receiving it. It was to be taken only once in a lifetime.

Gnostics also opposed the growing supernaturalism of the rite. By the fourth century the Lord's Table had become an arcane mystery and was screened off with curtains. St Chrysostom spoke of it as 'a place of terror and shuddering'. By the eighth century the bread and wine were magically trans-substantiated into the 'holy body' and 'sacred blood' of Christ, a notion that was declared official Church dogma eight centuries later. In any event the Roman Church denied the cup ('the blood') to the laity.

It was also held that when eaten, these elements were not liable to the normal process of digestion and evacuation. By the ninth century the view that these elements were actually digested and expelled like any other edible substances was condemned as the heresy of stercoranism (Lat. *stercus,* 'dung').

The gnostics also had a death rite which was meant to pre-enact the soul's experience after death. Some think it was an actual astral or out-of-the-body experience during a xeno-phrenic or ecstatic state induced by vigils, fasting, chanting and possibly hypnosis. Some sects, under the influence of the pagan mysteries, taught the candidate the secret names of the archons who guard the gates of the various cosmic spheres, and the signs, seals, handgrips and passwords that would enable him to pass through these gates. Details are preserved in such books as the *Rulers of the Cities Up to the Ether,* which give the names of the archons ruling the different circles. The Alexandrian philosopher Celsus (d. 185) who wrote against Christians and gnostics alike, ridiculed the stupidities of these rituals and spoke caustically of those who learned by heart the names of the doorkeepers, as if it would do them any good.

Many gnostic sacraments were practiced in conjunction with magical formulas and cryptic gestures, and drew much from the symbolism of numbers, letters and drawings.

The fact that both in the Semitic and Greek languages numbers were designated by letters, facilitated their inter-change and the development of a numerological system by which their interrelationship was worked out. As already stated, special virtues were assigned to the hebdomad (seven), the ogdoad (eight), the decad (ten) and the dodecad (twelve). An elaboration was also made on the Pythagorean and Platonic notions about the higher symbolism of geometrical shapes and solids. Irenaeus said of the gnostics, 'They invent wonderful and unspeakable mysteries wherever they find in the scriptures that something is indicated by numbers and can be accommodated or adapted to their speculative fiction.'

Gnostics were also familiar with the reputed occult virtues of sound and the latent potency of sacred names, hermetic formulas and magical invocations. Some of the vocalizations they used were derived from very ancient sources, secretly handed down in the inner sanctuaries of the great religious and mystery cults of antiquity. Others were the hidden names of God, the Logos, the aeons and archons, and secret passwords and mystery titles, which are mentioned in several gnostic works, among them the *Books of Ieu* (or Ieou), named after an aeon, and *Allogenes,* meaning 'alien', referring sometimes to Christ, and sometimes to the spiritually advanced person who turns away from the world.

The most important of all sounds, they believed, is the phoneme, which is the smallest articulable sound unit, usually a monosyllable. The Greek phonemes, taken over by the gnostics, were the seven vowel sounds of the Greek alphabet – a (alpha), e (epsilon), ē (eta), i (iota), o (omicron), u (upsilon) and ō (omega). While intoning these vowels, variations could be made in their order, pitch, emphasis, length, and changes in the range of voice, all these bringing their own magical refinements.

From this there evolved in time the practice of singing each vowel in a single breath (*pneuma*) in a succession of rising and falling notes, which was the origin of the *neume* of early Christian plainsong. Further effects could be achieved by combining the vowels with certain consonants, especially those producing a buzzing and humming sound: Zeeza, Zezo, Zoza, Ozzi, Omazu, Nozama, Amenaz, Araraz. Such sounds, strung together, protracted to great length, and repeated for long periods, set up cerebral reverberations and led to ecstatic and trance states.

As far as possible these archaic syllables were used in unaltered form, even when their meaning, if they had any, was forgotten. This was in accordance with the hallowed principle embodied in the third-century theosophical miscellany known as the *Chaldean Oracles:* 'Change nothing in the barbarous names (*onomata barbara*) of evocation, for they are titles of divine things, energized by the devotion of multitudes, and their power is ineffable'.

Among other integral features of gnostic ritualism were the secret gestures, passgrips and hand-signs used by the different sects. The Phibionites, for example, recognized members of their community by a handshake, accompanied by a tickling of the palm. But there were also secret gestures of benediction, salutation, and a special resurrection handclasp where the candidate was held by the hand and raised up from the dead, as in the Mithraic rite. Some of these manusigns passed from gnostic practice to the Church and to certain secret societies, where they are used to this day.

Yet another rite was the ceremonial procession and dance of initiates on certain very special occasions. One of Christ's most important lessons was said to have been communicated through a choral dance. The *Acts of John*, a gnostic text discovered before Nag Hammadi, tells how before his arrest at Gethsemane, Jesus told his disciples to hold hands and circle around him. He then began to intone a mystical chant, to which his disciples responded by saying Amen as he directed. Several versions of the chant were apparently known to the gnostics.

Finally, we come to gnostic sacramental art. Some scholars have made a great deal of the gnostic illustrated papyri, wall and tomb paintings, and their decorated bowls and incised gems, depicting anthropomorphic and zoomorphic beings, cock-headed, snake-footed and fish-tailed creatures. But the gnostics themselves set little store by such representations.

On the whole they regarded any art form as a pagan attempt to leave a material trace intended to survive time. They felt that art, like history, nourishes time, and declined to give it prominence in their scheme of things. Within the broad outlines of the Christian gospel each person, if he so desired, could speculate and give expression to his views in any literary or artistic form he chose. But no great importance was placed on the outcome, no claim was made that it was true, complete or final, and no attempt was made to give it permanence.

They preferred the spoken word to the written. If something had to be set down they preferred writing on slate to books, because slate could be rubbed clean. Best of all, for those who were perfect, was writing on sand. The only record of Jesus ever writing anything was when he made marks on the ground (John 8:6). And no one can tell what mystery he inscribed on it.

Asceticism

In the gnostic view, the whole range of the social, ethical and moral commandments was the domain of the demiurge, the ruler of the universe and promulgator of the laws by which the world is governed. These imposed laws have little relevance to the upper world of God the Father.

The gnostic showed his contempt for the precepts of the demiurge by a kind of counter-existence, which was expressed in one of two ways: passively, through asceticism, or not making use of what the world has to offer; or actively, through licentiousness, or purposeful misuse and abuse of what is offered.

Privativism or voluntary self-deprivation is in opposition to the interests of the demiurge, who is frustrated if we abstain from what he has made or instituted in order to keep us bound to him. The gifts of the god of this world, and his vice-regents such as Mammon and Venus, and his earthly representatives like Caesar and his magistrates, cannot be accepted without involvement with the world and should therefore be rejected. We must, said Marcion, make the least possible use of worldly things.

Besides indicating one's opposition to the demiurge, privativism brings many incidental benefits that accrue from endurance and determination.

The gnostic practice of asceticism was undertaken for a wide variety of reasons. Behind most forms was the gnostic idea that pleasure, and even comfort, were evil. Asceticism hardens the will. Suffering, adversity and pain attenuate the flesh and strengthen the spirit, and for this reason must be sought and endured. Some turned to the life of renunciation to gain supernatural power. It had long been known that enforced wakefulness, vigils and fasts, thirst and starvation, extremes of heat and cold, flagellation and self-mortification, during which the body is put through a phase of heroic endurance to the point of exhaustion and collapse, can lead to lucid states of mind and spiritual exaltation.

Some renounced pleasure because they deemed it sinful;

because it was a degrading concession to human weakness; because it was transient and no permanent benefit ensued from its pursuit. It was also generally believed that if the body were not properly controlled, the physical appetites would take over and rule the individual. As one desert recluse said of his self-denials, 'I am killing the body because it is killing me'. Or as the ascetic Sarapion boasted to another of his group, 'I am deader than you are!'

Because the term ascetic originally signified the disciplined self-denial of contestants training for the athletic games, such religious ascetics were known as the 'athletes of God'. Even those gnostics who did not attempt the extreme forms, observed as best they could the simplist and quietist restraints of the reclusive life, as far as it concerned such matters as silence, fasting and sexual control.

The strict ascetics, however, were rigid in their discipline. They abandoned kindred and domestic ties, renounced their property and lived far from the haunts of men, devoting themselves to prayer and contemplation. Once set up in their environment they observed what was called *stability,* remaining in the same locality and never wandering away. A few, like the *cenobites,* lived in communities, but many, like the *eremites,* lived alone. In the *Gospel of Thomas,* Jesus says, 'Blessed are the solitary, for they will find the kingdom.'

Their practices took many strange forms. Some, like the *troglodytes,* lived in caves; the *hypogetes* lived in underground tombs; the *dendrites* lived on trees. One hermit named Maron spent eleven years in a hollowed tree-trunk; and another, Eusebius the *phrearite,* made his home at the bottom of a dried-up well. The *stylites* squatted on the tops of pillars, the most famous of these pillar hermits being Simon of Antioch (d. 459). The *ammonosites* burrowed in the sand like crabs; the *petrites* hacked out inaccessible niches in cliffs.

The *adamites* lived in primitive fashion, and practised nudity in imitation of the state of Adam and Eve before the Fall. The *saccophores* wore only sackcloth or old and tattered clothes. The *catenati* loaded themselves with chains so that they had to crawl about on all fours. Some slept on plaited reeds, or never slept in a normal reclining position, or indeed never lay down at all. The *flagellants* beat themselves with knotted cords and nettles. And all of them endured without complaint the scorching heat of summer and the intense cold of winter.

The diet of these recluses was meagre in the extreme. Some lived on coarse food unappetisingly prepared. Macarius the Younger often ate 'old shoes softened in a mess of palm leaves'. John of Egypt subsisted on seeds and water like a bird. Others like the *browsers,* subsisted on roots, leaves and grass, believing that if they followed the example of Nebuchadnezzar in his madness (Dan. 4:33) they would recover their lost likeness to God.

It was generally held that it is possible to support the body on incredibly small amounts of food, and that it was essential to reduce the importunate demands of eating and drinking to which nature has subjected all living creatures. Vegetarian foods were believed to contain the living spark, and when such foods were eaten uncooked the spark was retained, and in this manner a store of vital force could be built up within the body.

Many gnostic sects abstained not only from animal flesh, but also from fish, fowl and eggs. These products were regarded as dead substances in which the light had been extinguished, and eating them caused internal pollution. But all eating and drinking introduced impure and injurious influences into the body, so in addition to the normal régime of a sparse diet, the ascetic would undertake long fasts in order to allow what had already entered to be completely discharged, and so render the body pure again.

Wine was often regarded with dread and loathing. Severus, a disciple of Marcion, said that when Satan was cast out of heaven he mated with Earth as with a woman, and from his seed sprang the vine. Grapes are like gouts of poison. Wine is the source of many great evils; it confuses the mind, leads to enchantment and illusion, and fosters the fiery qualities of frenzy, wrath and passion.

Asceticism as a means of strengthening the spirit was advocated and practised from earliest times by many communities in the ancient middle east, such as the Egyptian hierophants in the wastes of Siwa, the Rechabites of ancient Israel, who dwelt in tents in the wilderness, and the religious recluses of the upper reaches of the Euphrates. The direct inspiration of gnostic asceticism may have been the institution of the recluse (*katoche*) dedicated to the Egyptian-Greek god Serapis, whose great temple was in Alexandria.

The most famous districts in which Christian and gnostic ascetics of both sexes practiced their austerities and endured their ordeals, were the Thebaid, the district around Thebes in Upper Egypt; the Nitriaid wilderness west of the Nile delta; and the desert areas of Syria and the Lebanon. In these barren regions the hermits dwelt, denied themselves the simplest pleasures of the flesh, and found themselves assailed by the most outrageous hallucinatory temptations, which in some cases brought on erotomania.

St Antony (d. 356) of Thebes was perhaps the most sorely tempted of all the saints whose record has survived. Scores of writers and artists right down to modern times have dwelled and enlarged upon the libidinous encounters of St Antony, which have never ceased to intrigue men.

Female hermits too were haunted by erotic fancies. Mary the Egyptian (c. 400), once very beautiful and given over to a life of pleasure, retired to the desert after her conversion to a gnostic form of Christianity, and was frequently tormented by 'raging, insistent and preposterous yearnings', when virile men, phallic demons and obscene animal shapes tempted her. This once beautiful woman was later described as barely human in appearance, her body blackened by exposure to the sun, her skin hard and thick from being battered by the fierce burning winds.

Other female recluses described nightmarish visions of flying phalluses that perched at the foot of the bed, slowly swelling, erecting and throbbing, then going through the motions of intercourse. Some assumed heads and spoke to them, promising untold delights. Phallic and female organs hovered in the air and performed the sexual act before them.

St Jerome (d. 420) tells of the assaults made upon him during a period of asceticism. 'Often while I was living in the desert amid the scorpions and wild beasts, I used to fancy myself amid the pleasures of Rome, with bevies of young women. My skin was dry and my frame gaunt from fasting and penance, my body was that of a corpse, yet my mind was aflame with the cravings of desire, and the fire of lust burned in my flesh.'

The ultimate goal of all forms of asceticism is to achieve a mental state of equanimity, of indifference (*apatheia*) and imperturbability (*ataraxia*), a dispassionate condition of the mind greatly esteemed by the Stoics of antiquity, as well as by the gnostics. It implied an attitude of philosophical calm in all circumstances, whether of pain or pleasure, adversity or triumph, joy or sorrow, success or failure. The true philosopher is neither elated by happiness, nor dejected by misfortune.

Wealth, social status, success, fame and honours are the stratagems of fate (*heimarmene*), and like the desire for progeny, represent a temporal ambition, staking a claim on a future that is as evanescent as the morning dew. The gnostic prefers anonymity, but does not avoid situations inviting odium and abuse.

Thus, the hermit Macarius the Elder (c. 290) falsely accused by a village girl of making her pregnant, remained silent and was almost killed by the irate villagers. Later when the truth came out and the villagers came to him with apologies and praise for his saintliness, he still remained silent. He cared as little for their adulation as for their hostility.

Castration

The most drastic form of religious asceticism involved rendering infertile or the excision of the organs of sexual intercourse and reproduction. Such an action usually followed divine precedent and had divine sanction.

Many gods of ancient mythology lost their virility in that way. The Egyptian sun-god Ra mutilated himself below. Osiris had his organs cut off after his death by Seth, and when he was restored to life by his wife she fashioned an artificial phallus for him. Seth himself was castrated by Horus, son of Osiris and Isis. The Phoenician god Eshmun, importuned by erotic advances from the goddess Astronae, castrated himself. In Greek legend Uranus had his genitals cut off by his son Cronos (Saturn), and Cronos in turn was castrated by his own son Zeus (Jupiter).

In many parts of the ancient middle east, the priests of the Great Goddess were celibates, since this deity, as a fertility guardian, was believed to utilize the conserved energy of her ministrants to ensure abundance for her worshippers. Both men and women were pledged to inviolable celibacy. This idea evolved into the ritual castration of males, the virile member being offered to the goddess as an act of sacrifice and dedication.

In legend, the Phrygian shepherd Attis, beloved of Cybele, was entrusted with the care of her temple on promising to remain celibate, and became a eunuch, and ever after Cybele's priests were eunuchs. Both the high priest (*archigallus*) and lesser priests (*galloi*) of Cybele would publicly castrate themselves during a wild corybantic rite, cutting off their genitals and flinging them on her altar. The priests of Artemis (Diana) of Ephesus, from the chief hierophant (*megavuzus*) down to the acolytes, all suffered similar emasculation. The servants of the goddess at Lagina were deprived of their masculinity in like manner.

After the operation all priests dedicated to the Great Goddess wore female attire. The obligatory celibacy, representing a token castration, of the Roman Catholic priesthood, and their wearing of long 'feminine' vestments, are said to be relics of dedication to the Great Goddess, in this case the Virgin Mary.

In spite of pagan precedent, the Church set its face against actual castration for its priesthood, and till the later Middle Ages no pope of the Roman Catholic church could be elected to papal office who lacked testicles, and his possession of these organs was first attested by a cardinal making a manual examination (A. Smith, 1968, p. 77).

The gnostics were in two minds about castration, particularly in view of the saying of Jesus, 'There are eunuchs who have made themselves eunuchs for the kingdom of heaven's sake' (Matt. 19:12). This was taken by some to mean that those dedicated to the service of God should remain celibate, and by others it was interpreted as an injunction for castration. Jesus, it was said, was sexless, and castration was a mark of Christhood.

Castration was sometimes undergone by certain individuals and groups as a means of suppressing sexual desire, and to preserve them from the sin of concupiscence. Leontius of Antioch (c. 240) had himself castrated for this reason, and had many devotees and imitators. The best known of the early Christian castrants was the great theologian Origen (d. 254), acknowledged to be the most learned of the early Church Fathers.

Origen's disciple, the Arab Valerius (c. 250) founded the castrant sect of the Valerians, who were probably the same as the Valesii sect mentioned by St Augustine. Origen's example was also followed by others, notably St Hilarion (d. 350) who founded a monastic order in the Palestinian desert between Gaza and Egypt.

In 325 the council of Nicaea issued a ruling against castration, but the Byzantine empire seems to have made a provision for the castration of those who desired the operation. Castrants like Eutropius (d. 370), Latin historian and secretary to the emperor Constantine, and Narses (d. 573) the great statesman and general of the emperor Justinian, were advanced to the highest dignities in the realm.

Some Christian castrant sects were persecuted and dispersed under the later Byzantine emperors, and became in time the spiritual forefathers of the Skoptsi, who first appeared in Russia at the end of the eleventh century.

Celibacy

Gnostics of an ascetic persuasion frequently remained unmarried and avoided sexual activity. St Paul was a strong advocate of celibacy, and gnostics often quoted him in support of it. The Abelites, gnostic heretics of Africa, abstained from women because Abel, to whom they paid reverence, died virginal.

Many of the Church Fathers also defended celibacy, although the early Church did not insist on it for their priests. The Church's subsequent attempt to impose celibacy on unwilling candidates led to iniquities that were the scandal of monkish life. Many monasteries and convents became hotbeds of vice and moral corruption.

For their own reasons, certain gnostic schools regarded sexual intercourse as an abomination. It involved the expenditure of man's precious seed. It propagated other human beings, thus endlessly multiplying suffering, and perpetuating the kingdom of wickedness. The pleasure accompanying sexual congress and climax touched the most sensuous reaches of the human being. Lust (*epithymia*) was the most formidable of Satan's contrivances, for with the whiplash of sexual desire he had wrought a wonderful weapon for gaining adherents to his rule of darkness.

Sexual desire is the domain of Saklas (Heb. *sakal,* 'fool'), the archon of fornication, so named because he reduces man to a state of imbecility. In the *Pistis Sophia* he is called Parhedron Typhon, the mighty ruler, with thirty-two demons under his command, whose business it is to arouse men and women and seduce them to lusting, adultery and the continual practice of fornication (*synousia*).

There was a strong element of sexophobia and misogyny in this attitude. Women were looked upon with fear, aversion, distrust and suspicion, and sexual contact with them was thought of as bestial. Halfway between men and beasts, women were natural deceivers, false, headstrong and vain. During the monthly production of their 'strengthless female fruit', their touch was tainted, their breath unclean, their body unholy. The

Nag Hammadi *Book of Thomas the Contender* warns, 'Woe to you who seek intimacy with women, and polluted intercourse with them'. In the *Dialogue of the Saviour,* also from Nag Hammadi, Jesus urges the faithful disciples to 'pray in the place where there is no woman...and destroy the works of feminity'.

Woman, it was held, is dangerous because of her beauty, which creates in man a raging torment of brutish passion. Her eyes are meant to entice, her feet swift to go wrong, her soft words to deceive. Her enchanting face, her soft breasts, her rounded buttocks, her seductive movements, are an invitation to voluptuous delights. She is the embodiment of temptation, leading men to their doom. The pathway to hell lies through the vagina, for the abyss of hell is the womb.

Woman is inherently impure, a snare of nature, a tool of the devil, used by Satan to possess the souls of men. It is best to stay away from them, but where their company is unavoidable they should be kept in subjection. The devil has given women so much power that it is right that men should give them little, so as to redress the balance.

The only hope for woman is transformation into malehood. She is otherwise unfitted for redemption. In the *Gospel of Thomas* Peter pleads, 'Let Mary [Magdalene] go away from among us because women are not worthy of the Life.' Jesus replies, 'See, I shall lead her, so that I will make her male that she too may become a living spirit, resembling you males. For every woman who makes herself a male will enter the kingdom of heaven.'

Encratism
The gnostic doctrine of love owed something to Plato's *Symposium.* Platonic love (*eros*), popularly though not quite accurately signifies love between the opposite sexes divested of all sexual passion. Actually Platonic love may imply a sexual association, but in its highest expression it is a relationship between the mortal and the divine. Such love leads a person to seek union, if need be through a human alliance, with the eternal principles of Beauty, Truth and Goodness, by means of which the soul becomes 'pregnant'.

The early Christians practiced a different kind of spiritual association. Here love (*agape*) was affirmed and fellowship strengthened during their communal meetings, when there would be prayers, talks on spiritual matters, the reading of letters from the 'saints' (Christians) in other places, hymn

a meal which was provided by a wealthy
of poor and needy Christians. This, some
en an early form of the eucharist. Such a
known as the agape or feast of charity.
he male and female 'saints' participating
saluting one another with a chaste kiss, as
hristian love. Such a salutation, known
y kiss (Rom. 16:16), the kiss of charity (1
eraphic kiss, was to be given without any
the heart.
developed the custom of the *agapetae,*
ere couples lived chastely in a 'spiritual
e praised by the Christian writer Hermas (c. 80-90
book entitled the *Shepherd.* This was treated
tual love', a companionship between the
lose association, with true spiritual under-
out physical intimacy.
referred to as Pauline marriage, because St
who lived and travelled about with him.
used some criticism, he replied, 'Have I no
tian wife [sister] about with me, like the rest
NEB, 1 Cor. 9:5).
andria (d. 215) wrote that St Paul would not
n on his journeys to lodge and live with him
vife. He classes Paul with Peter and Philip as
apostles. Clement himself held up total
continence as the ideal for all married couples, and felt that St
Paul may have had such a relationship. And indeed St Paul
states that a man does well who decides 'to preserve his partner
in her virginity' (NEB, 1 Cor. 7:37). In the fifth century the
Desert Father Amoun of Nitria is said to have spent the first
night of his honeymoon expounding to his bride the same
Pauline text, and lived with her as her brother for many years,
until they mutually agreed to live separately as hermits.

The Carthaginian theologian Tertullian (d. 230) discussed
the abuses likely to arise from such relationships, though so far
as Paul was concerned he thought that the woman who
accompanied him merely performed the necessary duties best
done by a woman, namely, cooking, mending and washing, and
that she was a spiritual sister to Paul rather than a wife. At the
same time he condemned all those communities 'whose charity
is expressed by men sleeping with their spiritual sisters.'

The Church Father Irenaeus wrote about people who make an impressive show of living with a woman as with a sister, until the 'sister' becomes pregnant by the 'brother' and their pretence is exposed. St Jerome voiced the same suspicion of those who shared the same room and sometimes slept in the same bed, and who expected no one to draw the obvious conclusion.

St Chrysostom spoke of another peculiar element in this type of relationship: 'Our fathers knew only two kinds of intimate association, marriage and fornication. Now a third kind has appeared. Men take young girls into their houses, maintaining a scrupulous regard for their virginity. The feeling aroused by such a situation must be ferocious, but is kept under control. That the pleasure from this kind of love can be more ardent and passionate than married union may at first seem surprising and appear unbelievable, but it is possible.'

Already from the end of the first century certain gnostic doctrines began to be propounded to justify these aspects of early Christian practice. Chief among the protagonists was Saturninus (d. 150), who advocated *encratism*, 'invigorism', a discipline of sexual restraint for the purpose of strengthening one's spiritual powers and attaining ecstatic states and gnosis. This soon developed into a kind of sexualized asceticism, where intimacy with the opposite sex was permitted, but not consummation. The purpose underlying encratism was to undergo temptations that offer the prospect of great pleasure, and to face the ensuing trials without succumbing to the climax.

One must defy the demiurge. Desire for the pleasures of the flesh is a sign of Satan's dominion over the individual and must at all costs be overcome. The heroic method was to enter boldly into the arena of sexuality, meet the enemy in the closest engagement and emerge victorious. A man could therefore put himself to the test by experiencing all the excitement of close contact with a woman but without touching her, or by raising tension still further by touching and caressing her without penetrating her, and finally by penetrating her but denying himself the relief of orgasm.

Confirmation for this point of view was found in certain passages in the apocryphal sayings of Jesus. For example, 'A man that is not tempted is not approved and shall not obtain the kingdom.'

Sexuality was the devil's lure, and the gnostic's resistance was to be tested in the furnace of temptation. He had to endure the ordeal in order to savour the triumph that follows resistance.

The Jordan Passage

This river takes its rise in the hills around Mount Hermon, flows south to the Sea of Galilee, and then continues its course downward, to vanish into the Dead Sea. The name Jordan is cognate with Jared, an ancestor of Noah, both names being derived from the same root word (Heb. *yarad,* 'descent').

Certain books of the apocrypha relate that the sin of sexual excess was the prevailing characteristic of the time of Jared, in whose days there were giants (Heb. *nefilim*) on the earth (Gen. 6:4). These giants lusted after the daughters of men and had intercourse with them.

By analogy, the Jordan came to symbolize lust, and acquired a special significance in the lore of certain encratic sects. As its name implies, descent is the natural course of the waters of the Jordan, and in taking its natural direction it represents the essence of sexual pleasure, the desire for carnal cohabitation (Jonas, 1963, p. 307) and descent into sexuality.

But in the gnostic view the river can be made to ascend. If the downflowing waters represent the expenditure of male energy, seminal emission and human generation; then the damming of the upward flow of the stream represents the conservation of semen during intercourse, and the generation of divinity.

Taking an illustration from the days of the Jewish captivity, the gnostics point out that as long as the Red Sea flowed down the children of Israel were prevented from coming out of Egypt. But when the sea was made to go back (Exod. 14:21), they were able to leave the land. Likewise, during the conquest of Canaan, so long as the river Jordan flowed down, the children of Israel could not cross over. But when Joshua (prefiguration of Jesus) checked it and made it flow upward so that its waters piled up (Josh. 3:16), they were able to cross (Foerster, 1974, p. 270).

The power of Moses and Joshua was derived from their continence. Checking the flow of the stream is therefore imperative at certain critical times, and the male seed should not be spilled even inadvertently since unsuspected consequences could ensue. According to Epiphanius, the gnostics relate that as Elijah was being taken up to heaven a female demon seized him saying, 'Where are you going? I have

children from you.' And when he replied, 'How can it be? I have
lived in purity', the succubus answered, 'When you discharged
semen during your dreams, I received the seed and bore you
sons.' And they quote the scriptures to confirm this story (Jude
8).

The third of the three secret words repeated by Jesus to
Thomas was said to have been *zeesar,* meaning, 'there a little',
and signifying, according to one curious commentary of the
Naassenes, the Jordan which flows upward (Bruce, 1974, p.
118).

According to the gnostics, the baptism given by John the
Baptist was the common or downflowing baptism, and John
himself was 'the archon of the multitude'. Hence too, John's
feeling that it would be inappropriate for Jesus to be baptized in
it (see Layton, 1980, p. 11). On his baptism Jesus 'went up
straightway out of the water' (Matt. 3:16), again, in the gnostic
interpretation, signifying the end of carnal begetting and the
retention of power.

Certain gnostic sects like the Peratae had a secret rite in
which they recapitulated the journey out of Egypt through the
Red Sea and the wilderness, and over the Jordan. They taught
that he who crossed this river when the waters were flowing
downward would have physical progeny, but he who could
make the waters flow up would receive divine progeny (Mead,
1960, p. 186).

The spunk or quintessential spark of the male seed originates
in the spiritual world, and, say the gnostics, is reflected and
condensed in the chambers of the brain. It is then disseminated
throughout the body and finally directed to the organs of
procreation. The conservation of sperm was seen as important
in restoring to man what is diffused, and could best be done
through *coitus reservatus,* the technique of holding back ejaculation during intercourse, and thus conserving the sperm-spark.

Here again, biblical support was claimed in the text, which
puts under condemnation the man 'whose seed goeth from
him' (Lev. 15:32). In the New Testament too, reference is made
to the sinlessness of the man whose 'seed (*sperma*) remaineth in
him' (I John 3:9), for it is through the seed that he is
regenerated.

This practice is related to what was known to certain
medieval sects as acclivity (Walker, 1977, p. 1), involving the
direction 'uphill' of the seminal fluids during coition.

Women

The misogyny that characterized certain ascetic groups was not a common feature of gnosticism. In many gnostic sects women were held in high esteem. They were eligible for important office, and their names were not excluded in the drawing of lots for the highest posts.

Women were believed to have more than mere administrative talent. They were thought to be endowed by nature to receive, understand and interpret profound mysteries. According to the gnostics, after Satan seduced Eve he communicated to her a revelation which in part was embodied in the *Gospel of Eve*. The work is now lost, except for fragments preserved in the writings of Epiphanius.

James the Just, the brother of Jesus, not the apostle, is said to have handed down certain secret teachings to a woman named Mariamne or Mary, from whom the Naassenes claimed to have inherited their hermetic tradition. The Carpocratians too claimed to have received their teachings from Mary, Salome and Martha. The disciple Helena played a major role in the career of Simon Magus; Priscilla and Maximilla in the life of Montanus; Lucilla in the life of the heretic Donatus; and Procula in the life of Priscillian.

Women were especially valued for their psychic and clairvoyant faculties and powers of mediumship. In the sects of Marcion and Carpocrates such women served as 'prophets', which does not necessarily mean they could foretell the future. Rather, they were seeresses, believed to be divinely inspired, and capable of being filled with supernatural power, so they could interpret dreams and portents.

The practice inevitably led to abuse. Marcus was accused of seducing many of his young female 'prophets'. Irenaeus writes that by various suggestions he makes his deluded victim believe she has the power of prophecy. Full of false pride, and excited by the expectation of using her gift, she ventures into oracular utterance. With pounding heart she articulates any ridiculous nonsense that enters her head. Henceforth, stimulated by vanity she audaciously considers herself a veritable sibyl.

Overcome by gratitude to Marcus she is prepared to be united with him in every way, and willingly repays him by permitting intimacy. Marcus, with the intention of degrading the bodies of his dupes, administers love potions and aphrodisiacs, and breathes upon them so that they pass into erotic convulsions and submit to him in any manner he desires. Often, says Irenaeus, have women confessed, after they had returned to the church, that they were moved by a violent passion and had been physically abused by him.

The male disciples of Marcus, emulating their leader's example, likewise deceived and led astray many female proselytes.

Progeny

The gnostic attitude to having children was based on their doctrine of souls. The soul is a particle of divine light, entrapped and put into corrupt flesh when a child is conceived, instead of being allowed to remain free in the spiritual realm.

Woman is the decoy. Unknown to her, the womb cries out to be filled, and that is like a cry from the tomb for yet another victim. Conception is not life, but a descent into death for some unhappy soul. The gnostics regarded a pregnant woman as having a devil in her.

Human reproduction was instituted by Satan and is an archonic device for the capture of souls and their enslavement in Satan's kingdom of darkness. Procreation indefinitely replenishes the world, and prolongs the captivity of the light, generation after generation. This renders difficult the work of salvation which will only be completed when every individual soul is awakened from its enforced sleep and freed (Jonas, 1963, p. 228).

As we have seen, one of the *logia*, or sayings attributed to Jesus, is prompted by Salome asking how long death would hold sway. To this Jesus replies, 'As long as women bear children. I have come to undo the works of women.' The behest to 'be fruitful and multiply' (Gen. 1:28) is the order of the god of the Jews and not a command from the supreme God. To breed unchecked, like the benighted heathen nations and as advocated by the Church, is to collaborate with the evil deity who governs this world.

If misogyny was advocated as a gnostic philosophy of life it was principally because women were potential mothers, and carnal intercourse with them could result in progeny. If the pathway to hell lay through the vagina, it was because it led to the womb, the abyss where the light of new souls is held captive. Masturbation, homosexuality, sodomy, sex with minors, were all preferable to intercourse with women because

these forms of sexuality did not result in the hateful imprisonment of more souls.

Androgyny

The underlying philosophy of most gnostic schools was based
on the concept of androgyny (*andros*, 'man'; *gyne*, 'woman').
This relates to the condition in which the characteristic
features of the two sexes are present in the same individual. In
certain religions androgyny symbolizes wholeness and unity
and is a sign of spirituality and sacred power.

Many ancient mythologies speak of male-female deities. The
Old Testament plural name Elohim, for God, implies a male-
female duality. In several gnostic systems the supreme being is
treated as androgynous. Simon Magus called the primordial
spirit Arsenothelys, 'male-female'. Hermetic writings such as
Asclepius and *Poimandres* contain references to the bisexual
nature of God. Other texts speak of the supreme being as
Mother-Father (*Metropator*).

In his *Symposium* Plato relates that originally men too were
male-female beings who were split in two by Zeus for their lofty
ambitions. The perfect human being is one who unifies within
himself the elements of both sexes. Sometimes the virgin is
regarded as a type of such perfection for the virgin is said to be
an androgyne. In folk etymology virgin means man-woman,
being derived from man (Lat. *vir*) and woman (Gk. *gyne*).

In gnosticism, Anthropos or Primal Man, like the other
aeons, was a hermaphrodite. His creation is described in terms
indicating this: 'Male and female created he them' (Gen. 1:27),
a passage which refers to Adam alone. Sex raised its head when
men and women were differentiated. The apocryphal *Gospel of
Philip* regards the separation of the sexes as the cause of death.
In this gospel we read: 'When Eve was in Adam there was no
death. But when she was separated from him, death came into
being.'

Like the virgin, the child too is an exemplar of the androgynous state. In the *Gospel of Thomas* Jesus says, 'Children are
like those who enter the kingdom. When like little children
you take off your clothes without shame, when you make the
two become one, when you make the male and female into a
single unity, then you shall enter the kingdom.'

In the fulness of time humanity will once again become
androgynous. Another of the apocryphal sayings of Jesus from

the *Gospel of the Egyptians* is prompted when Salome asks when the end of the world would come about, and Jesus answers, 'When you put off the garment of shame, when the two become one, and the male with the female is neither male nor female.'

Christ is the prototype of the male-female unity, the perfect androgyne. According to the Bible, by faith in Christ men become children, when all conflicting distinctions are overcome, and 'there is neither male nor female for ye are all one in Christ Jesus' (Gal. 3:28). It is to children rather than to the clever that revelations are made (Matt. 11:25).

In the gnostic view the discord inherent in gender has to be harmonized in a *coincidentia oppositorum* or 'union of opposites', wherein contraries and conflicts are resolved. Such a condition is periodically rehearsed in the sacrament of the bridal chamber when the original androgynous state is experienced. During this sacrament the disparate elements of the two sexes are transcended, man and woman cease to be separate, and achieve wholeness and unity. This calls for a union in virginal innocence, without opposition, combat, conquest, pleasure or personal satisfaction.

In a still more recondite interpretation, the essential male and female elements already reside within each individual, and every person is an actual androgyne. It is possible, say the gnostics, for anyone to unify the two opposites within himself in a kind of mystical *coincidentia oppositorum.* In his *Teachings* the sage Silvanus declares that the bisexual state is best for humanity. The earthly body, the sarkic element, which is the foundation of all assertive carnality, should be set aside, and the male *nous* and the female *psyche* harmonized, in anticipation of the final blessed state of wholeness.

Such a harmonizing of genders belongs to a larger reconciliation between opposite polarities that receives a much wider application in such texts as the *Gospel of Thomas,* the *Gospel of the Egyptians* and the *Martyrdom of Philip,* in which the macrocosm or divine world above and the microcosm (man) below, are identified. Thus, 'The Lord said in a mystery, "If you do not make the two become one, the male like the female, the inside like the outside, the left as the right, what is before like what is behind, and the things above as those that are below, you shall not see the kingdom".' This is reminiscent of the famous second principle enunciated in the hermetic text known as the *Emerald Tablet,* 'What is below is like what is above, and what is above is like what is below, for the understanding of the Unity.'

The Bridal Chamber

The aeons or primordial emanations of the Supreme Being were frequently thought of as being arranged in pairs, each pair (*syzygy*) consisting of complementary halves of a composite whole and functioning as a unity. At first their association was non-sexual, innocent and pure.

These unions included: Father (Pater) and Providence (Pronoia), Mind (Nous) and Truth (Aletheia), Saviour (Soter) and Wisdom (Sophia), Word (Logos) and Power (Dynamis), Abyss (Bythos) and Silence (Sige), Christ (Christos) and Church (Ecclesia), Man (Anthropos) and Faith (Pistis), Mercy (Eleos) and Deliberation (Enthymesis).

At some stage in the emanatory process the unions assumed a sexual character. The emergence of sex is one of the primal enigmas, about which there has been much gnostic speculation. The secrets concerning this activity are buried deep in the beginning of time, but they will be revealed in the end. The *Pistis Sophia* declares that at the dissolution of the world certain men will receive knowledge of various mysteries, among them 'the mystery of why sexual intercourse has arisen, and the mystery of adultery, fornication, continence and purity'.

Sexual differentiation or gender resulted in the separation of what had once been a unity. The gnostic fragments called the *Books of the Saviour* tell how the aeons turned from the mysteries of light, preferring the mystery of intercourse or sexual union, and began procreating archons and other lesser beings. Some gnostics held that the aeons emanated in androgynous form out of the divine unity, and then split as archons into sexual pairs.

The Valentinians found a sexual meaning and a reference to the wives of Jehovah himself, in the biblical text which speaks of the two harlot sisters, Aholah and Aholibah, of whom the Lord said, 'They were mine' (Ezek. 23:4). In some texts the distinctive functions of sexual gender were said to have been devised by Satan and taught to the lower aeons. Sophia too was said to have been responsible for the introduction of this mystery, although she later turned away from it.

In any event, for whatever reason and by whatever means, copulation became prevalent among the aeons. Thereafter the syzygies were accorded sexual significance. In the gnostic system the pairing couples produce other aeons and these in turn produce others and so on in ever proliferating generations of aeons. It was these 'endless genealogies' that were condemned by St Paul (1 Tim. 1:4).

One of the most important of all gnostic rites, known as the rite of the bridal chamber, is referred to in several gnostic texts. It consisted of the ceremonial re-enactment, from time to time, of the union of the male and female aeons. The Valentinians held that it was the duty of the elect to watch and be ever in readiness for the wedding feast to come (Matt. 25:13). They were required to imitate the union of the aeons in syzygy, on the principle that the sexual act ritually performed here below would sustain and reinvigorate the pairing aeons above.

It was in the bridal chamber, known by various names (*nymphon, thalamos, pastas*), that this mystical rite was carried out. As a result of this enactment, the primal male-female unity making for androgyny was said to be restored. The recreation of the original divine androgynous state reverses the process by which death has entered the world, and bestows upon the participants, wisdom, light and immortality.

According to the *Gospel of Philip,* a collection of Valentinian sayings, 'If any person becomes a son of the bridal chamber he will receive the light. If any person does not receive it while he is in this place, he will not receive it in any other place.'

The bridal chamber itself was an inner shrine where the congregation would witness the theogamy or divine marriage mimetically performed by the earthly representatives of the Redeemer (Soter) and Wisdom (Sophia), after which the faithful would unite with their angelic 'opposites', personified in the female members of the sect.

The Marcosians too prepared a bridal chamber and performed a similar rite with invocations, for those who were being consecrated. The woman was told, 'In thy chamber adorn thyself as a bride who expects her bridegroom. Accept his favour and receive from him the seed of light. And behold, grace will descend upon thee.' Marcosians claimed that what they were effecting was a spiritual marriage, after the image of the conjugations above. This was the mystic union of Christ and the Church (Eph. 5:32).

The rite of the bridal chamber was seen as a rehearsal for the time when the elect, as the children of the bridechamber (Matt. 9:15), would prepare for the messianic banquet and the nuptials of the Lamb, celebrating the great occasion with feasting and dancing. According to the Naassenes, all spiritual beings in the house of God, including those who were female, will become bridegrooms, women having been made male by the virginal Spirit. The wedding feast over, the elect themselves will receive angels as their spouses, for the elect have heavenly counterparts. Accompanied by his spouse each will enter into a bridal chamber of his own and be eternally united with her in the heavenly Beulah.

For the gnostic, the bridal chamber represented a temenos or sacred enclosure. It symbolized the place of reconciliation. Gnostics were obsessed with duality, the paradigm of which is the opposition of good and evil in the mind of man, which in turn reflects the dualism inherent in the cosmos. And this duality had to be resolved.

Whatever they might have felt towards Lucifer, gnostics were advised never to treat him with contempt, for he too has the divine spark in him. According to the gnostic formula, *Daemon est Deus inversus,* 'the Devil is the reverse side of God'. Lucifer, in one modern interpretation, is none other than the Holy Spirit (see Griffiths, 1966, p. 142). The Morning Star signifies Christ as well as the Devil (Jung, 1968, p. 72). In gnostic theology Satanel (Satan) is the elder brother of Jesuel (Jesus). The tree of knowledge is the tree of life. The Serpent represents the Saviour.

As Jesus was on earth, Satan is the wanderer and outcast. And like Jesus he has to be redeemed, and indeed, as Origen said, he will be redeemed. The return (*parousia*) of Christ will be preceded by the advent of his estranged brother, Antichrist, leading to a final conflict. Christ will be victorious and the two brothers will be reconciled. There will be a restoration of the lost unity, and all things will once more be as they were in the beginning.

The harmony of all opposites will be re-established in the divine mind. Extremes will meet in God. That is the message of the bridal chamber.

Libertinism

The restrictive philosophy of the ascetic was in sharp contrast to that of the libertine, though both were gnostics and both ultimately had the identical goal. But their attitude to the body, to sexuality, to marriage and many other matters differed considerably. Taken together, the gnostics were involved in a perpetual 'running between extremes' (*enantiodromia*), between the excesses of the castrant, and the excesses of the lecher.

The ascetic believes that love of the body (*philosomatia*) is a hateful evil, and he who cherishes the body and lusts after flesh lives in erotic error, remains wandering in the darkness, and suffers the things of death. The libertine on the other hand takes great care of the body, tends it night and day, washes and anoints himself, feasts on strengthening foods to make his body strong, so that he can devote himself to fornication, and be able to render its fruits whenever required.

Similar differences distinguished their attitude to marriage. Marcion, a champion of celibacy, deemed marriage 'a filthiness and an obscenity'. It was a diabolical institution that had upon it the seal of Antichrist and the mark of Satan. It did nothing more than sanction sexual indulgence, and elevate the coital act into a holy rite. The true gnostic, if he happens to be married, should live with his wife in perfect chastity. In the *Acts of Paul* it is written, 'Blessed are they that possess their wives as though they had them not.' For those who feel the need and cannot hold back, any willing woman may be used.

But even the libertine objected to marriage, because it involved one in family ties and responsibilities. Again, marriage can easily lead to uxoriousness (Lat. *uxor*, 'wife'), or an obsessive passion for one's wife, which makes it a form of legalized adultery. The uxorious husband insists on the exclusive enjoyment of his wife, instead of making her available to all the brethren. But above all, marriage results in the procreation of more human beings. Concubinage and prostitution were preferable to marriage, since these were not permanent and not generally productive.

In contrast to the ascetic's obligation to abstain from what the demiurge has to offer in the way of pleasure, the libertine's belief was that one should take note of the law (*nomos*) of the demiurge, and then by deliberate excess or perversion, undermine it. Such antinomianism, or opposition to the law, was common to several gnostic cults, upholding what has been variously called amoralism, immoralism, or moral nihilism. They held in reverence those scriptural characters who were condemned by conventional morality, such as Cain and Judas.

The antinomian alternative was open only to those with sufficient knowledge. There was danger in infringing the law because of ignorance or indifference, or from the wrong motives, or out of frivolity or foolhardy intransigence. The gnostic was to reflect carefully on the terrifying implications of what Jesus said to the man who was breaking a simple commandment (the fourth), and one that Jesus himself had broken: 'Man, if indeed you know what you are doing, you are blessed. But if you do not, you are cursed, and a transgressor of the law' (James, 1924, p. 33).

Gnostic antinomianism requires active participation in the world, but in a manner contrary to the intention of the law, and in defiance of the demiurge. Positive morality is 'legalistic', and confirms man's membership of a system set up by the demiurge. Thus, the libertine thwarts the designs of the dark powers, and paradoxically, contributes to the scheme of salvation.

The libertine believes in the free exercise of the will to satisfy one's desires, especially those commonly classed as sinful. As Christ said, 'Do not resist evil' (Matt. 5:39). Certain gnostics advocated the doctrine of peccatism (Lat. *peccatum,* 'sin'), the idea that one should indulge in sin. The demiurge, they said, has a stock of sins, and these only in limited variety, and one should 'make use' of illicit carnality and other unlawful activities in every form so as to exhaust and bring that stock to an end.

In any event, evil attaches only to the body and not to the pneuma. The true gnostic is a pneumic man and is therefore free from the yoke of Satan's moral law. He is 'saved by nature', and his divine spirit will remain unpolluted by any 'evil' act he might commit. That is why, writes Irenaeus, the 'perfect' among the gnostics, freely practise, unabashed and without fear, all that is interdicted by religion.

They eat things sacrificed to idols, which is forbidden to Christians. They do not avoid witnessing the murderous spectacle of fights with beasts, and single combat to the death, so hateful to God and man. They take potions to augment their lusts. Following Adam, whose nakedness before the Fall they try to emulate, they divest themselves of their clothing during their rites. After their banquets of feasting and drinking, the lights are extinguished and men and women enjoy one another indiscriminately.

Carnal appetites, they aver, belong to nature, and one must therefore repay to nature what is her due. Therefore, continues Irenaeus quoting their teachings, as they render to the spirit what belongs to the spirit, so they render to the flesh what belongs to the flesh, and serve intemperately their basest desires. They hold that sexual activity, being one of the features of society that has become institutionalized, must for that reason be fiercely attacked. They practise the mystery of conjugation, saying that whoever in this world has not possessed a woman will not attain the truth.

Epiphanius states that those among the Phibionites who strive for perfection perform intercourse in the name of their 365 invented archons, and, as though praying to each one in turn, say, 'To thee, O archon (naming it) I present my offering'. This is the so-called 'ascent', that they must make through 365 sexual acts, after which they make the 'descent' through 365 falls, and when they have completed a total of 730 immoral unions, the men declare, 'I am Christ' (Foerster, 1974, p. 322).

They sedulously avoid producing children. In complete disgust Epiphanius records that if by mischance a woman becomes pregnant as a result of their practices, 'listen to what further outrage these people dare to perform'. They abort the unborn foetus, the misborn infant, extract it from the womb, smash it in a pestle and mortar, and having mixed in honey, pepper and other condiments to avoid being sick, they assemble and each one with his fingers eats a morsel of the mangled child. In this way, they believe, they have harvested their brother's error and have performed the perfect mass (see Campbell, 1968, p. 166).

They commit adultery to nullify the commandment against adultery. They commit unnatural acts of a heinous nature and recommend that this be done by others of their persuasion, as a mark of contempt for the demiurge. Sexuality should not be confined to socially acceptable modes, but should be experimented with freely in all its varieties. Simon Magus advocated indiscriminate sex, saying, 'All soil is but soil, and it matters not where a man sows, provided he sows.'

Epiphanius remarks that some men are 'inflamed towards other men, and have intercourse with each other', a practice that also drew the wrath of St Paul (Rom. 1:27). The males of the gnostic Levitici sect did not have intercourse with women, but only with other men. Others in their sodomitic habits made use of the 'unmentionable vessels' of both sexes. According to Epiphanius, 'They designate as virgins those women, howso often they have copulated, who have not had natural intercourse.'

Members of other groups did not consort with women but 'corrupted themselves with their own hands', finding justification in a perverse interpretation of St Paul's statement to the Ephesian elders, 'You yourselves know that these hands have ministered to my necessities' (Acts 20:34). Others advocated fellatio, which was symbolized for them by the snake with its tail in its mouth. There were also those who encouraged incest between brother and sister or other near relations.

Intercourse with children was permissible, since it did not lead to procreation, and also with virgins. In both these cases too, it initiated the ignorant and innocent into ways that were essential for their gnostic liberation.

They practised every kind of abomination with the seminal fluid of men and the monthly flow of women. These they ingested along with drugs in order to attain ecstasy. When in a state of ecstatic frenzy, they stand up stark naked, take the semen in their hands, smear it everywhere, and pray that by this means 'they may obtain free access to the presence of God' (Lacarrière, 1977, p. 89).

Borborism

The principal sects of the Borborians will be mentioned later. According to Epiphanius this cult based their teachings on the idea that the divine light-spark exists not only in men and women, but in all living things, vegetables, plants, fruits, cereals, fish, serpents and beasts of every kind. The Borborian gnostic was required to collect these scattered soul-fragments and partake of them as a sacrament, for in this manner the plant or animal soul became absorbed into his own. They believed the gnostic was doing a kindness to the plants and animals, for by collecting their spiritual substance, he would in the end transmit it, along with his own, to the heavenly world.

Borborians found justification for their strange beliefs and practices in their own invented gospels, as well as in biblical texts which, like other extreme gnostic sects, they misinterpreted in their own perverse manner.

In the gnostic *Gospel of Eve*, fragments of which are preserved by Epiphanius, it is related how the voice of a mighty being declared, 'I am dispersed in all things, and in gathering me you gather yourself'. The Borborians took this to mean not only the soul-stuff in plants and animals, but in semen and menstrual blood as well.

There was, they believed, a deep mystery in the life-seed that lay concealed in men and women. The flesh of human beings belonged to the archons, and perished at death and was not raised up. But the power that resided in the life-seed contained the imperishable soul-spark. Semen and menses had therefore to be consumed as a sacrament, for these substances held the pure light.

The Bible directs, 'Drink waters out of thine own cistern, and running waters out of thine own well' (Prov. 5:15). Among the sayings of Jesus in the Nag Hammadi *Gospel of Thomas* is the following, 'If you bring forth what is within you, what you bring forth will save you. If you do not bring forth what is within you, what you do not bring forth will destroy you.' These texts were taken to refer to the male and female fluids, and Borborians accordingly enjoined their members to consume their own substance.

Further specific, if hidden, references were also quoted by them. Thus, it was said that the blood of the lamb (Exod. 12:7) that was used to mark the houses of the children of Israel so the angel of death would spare them, was actually menstrual blood. Also, that the scarlet cord fastened by Rahab to her window by which token she and her family were to be spared in the massacre at Jerico (Josh. 2:18) was a reference to a cloth stained with the blood of the female periods. The same meaning was read into the New Testament passage (Rev. 22:2) about the 'tree of life which bare twelve manner of fruits, and yielded her fruit every month.' At their ceremonies the Borborians would collect the blood of a woman's impurity and take communion with it saying, 'Here is the blood of Christ' (Lacarrière, 1977, p. 88).

For semen too they dreamed up their contrived corroboration. This from the Bible (Ps. 1.3): 'He shall be like a tree [the male member] planted by the rivers of water [testicles] that bringeth forth his fruit [semen] in his season [ejaculation]; his leaf also shall not wither [because he does not allow it to go to waste or into the vagina].'

If during intercourse semen does penetrate the womb and a child is conceived, the light-substance of the male and female partners passes over to form a new being, who becomes flesh-bound like other mortals. To prevent this happening, men should endeavour to spill the sperm outside, following Onan (Gen. 38:9), dedicating the act to the archon of the 'pestilence that walketh in darkness' (Ps. 91:6), who governs such external emissions. This was done to interrupt the accursed cycle of procreation, and also to provide material for their sacrament. They used the seed of masturbation, sodomy, or natural intercourse, believing it to be poured out of the 'horn of salvation', in support of which they found several allusions in the Bible.

Epiphanius describes the rite of spermepotation practiced by the Phibionites. At the moment of the man's ejaculation the woman lets her partner go, withdraws her body, and receives the emitted semen in her palm. She stands up naked throwing back her head, and pretends to pray, offering as an oblation to God the shameful product of their immorality. Then saying, 'This is the body of Christ', she consumes it (Campbell, 1968, p. 160).

St Augustine in his account of the Manichean (gnostic) system speaks of confessions made by certain women of Carthage about the scandals associated with their cult. On examination it was later confirmed that 'ground meal was sprinkled underneath the copulating pair to absorb the semen so that it could be mixed and consumed' (Allegro, 1979, p. 130).

There are two opposing gnostic views of what Jesus himself thought of these matters. At the end of the *Pistis Sophia* the disciple Thomas asks Jesus, 'We have heard that there are some people who take the male seed and female menses and make it into a porridge and eat it saying "We have faith in Esau and Jacob". Is this seemly or not?' And Jesus replies angrily that this sin is more heinous than any other.

But in one of the apocryphal texts, when Salome remarks that she has done well in not bearing children, Jesus replies, 'Eat of every pasture, but of that which has the bitterness [of death] eat not.' This signifies, according to the Borborians, that the woman should partake of semen that is not productive, in other words, receive it elsewhere than in the womb.

Again, according to the gnostic fragment from the *Great Questions of Mary* (Magdalene), quoted by Epiphanius, Christ was said to have taken Mary (Magdalene) up to a mountain to give her a revelation. From his side he produced a woman and began to have intercourse with her, *seminis sui defluxum assumpsisset* (Jung, 1968, p. 202), showing what was to be done that we might have life. Mary was so shocked that she collapsed to the ground and Jesus raised her up and reprimanded her for her lack of faith.

In quoting this passage Jung says it is understandable that its crude symbolism should offend our feelings today, but it also shocked the early Christians. The whole symbolism may have been based on some visionary experience that was misunderstood or perverted by certain gnostic teachers.

Epiphanius also relates another story taken from the gnostic texts, where the behest made by Jesus to his disciples to 'eat my flesh and drink my blood' (John 6:54) allegedly refers to the same indecency. Greatly perplexed the disciples exclaimed, 'Who can hear it?' (John 6:60), or in another version (NEB), 'This is more than we can stomach!' Jesus, aware that they were murmuring about it, said to them, 'Does this offend you? What if you were to see the Son of man ascending where he was before?' (John 6:62). This was interpreted to mean, 'When you see ejaculated semen restored to its Source' (Allegro, 1979, p. 132).

Many disciples were so dismayed that, as the text continues, almost sorrowfully (John 6:66), they 'went back, and walked no more with him' (see Foerster, 1974, p. 321).

8.

THE SECTS

As already stated, the gnostics in general tolerated a diversity of views and encouraged independent thought. This frequently led to extravagant speculation on religious and social matters and to a wild proliferation of sects. At the same time they vigorously defended their views against the rising tide of Christian orthodoxy. Irenaeus wrote that the gnostics 'sprout up like mushrooms and fight like hydras.'

Another Church Father stated that there were precisely eighty gnostic sects, corresponding to the 'fourscore concubines' mentioned in the Bible (Song of Solomon 6:8). In most cases little more is known about them than their names. We are not even sure whether these names were their own or were given to them by their opponents. Nor is the precise nature of their beliefs always clear either.

What is attempted here is a brief account outlining the basic tenets of some of the more important gnostic sects, as far as they are known to modern scholarship.

The Judaeo-Gnostics
Among the first-century gnostic sects were some that had emerged from a distinctively Jewish background and retained a number of Jewish features. Chief among them were the Ebionites and Elkesaites of Palestine and Syria. Scholars trace a relationship between these two sects and the Iessaei (Jewish-Christians), Nazareans, Sabians, Mandaeans, and other early Judaeo-Christian communities.

Both the sects rejected the Jewish sacrificial law, but otherwise held to the Torah, or law of Moses, adhered to the practice of circumcision, and kept the Jewish sabbath. Both denounced Paul as an apostate from the law of Jehovah, but differed somewhat in their views on Jesus.

Some early writers speak of a certain Ebion as the founder of the Ebionite sect, but there is no historical evidence of his existence, and scholars now derive their name from the Hebrew word *ebion,* meaning 'poor', because they followed a life of poverty. In the thirteenth heresy of his *Panarion,* Epiphanius says that according to the Ebionites, 'Two were begotten by God, one of them Christ, the other the Devil'. They held that Jesus was the human son of Joseph and Mary, and that the spirit of God (Christ) descended on him at his baptism, making him the greatest of the prophets, and the promised Messiah, but not the Son of God. It is not certain whether the so called *Gospel of the Ebionites* has any connection with the sect.

The Elkesaites are so named after an angelic being called Elkesai, 96 miles high, who was said to have given their founder a special revelation, embodied in the *Book of Elkesai.* They believed that Jesus was the Messiah and a reincarnation of Adam, and held a docetic view of his crucifixion. Still further reincarnations of Jesus are possible, so Christianity could not be looked upon as the final revelation. They practised purificatory ablutions and believed in the redemptive power of repeated baptisms. They were known to have influenced Mani of Ecbatana.

Nazarenes

A sect named after Nazareth, a town in Galilee. This town is mentioned in the New Testament as the place where Jesus was brought up, and after which his early followers came to be called Nazarenes (Acts 24:5).

Today this derivation is considered unproven. To begin with, religions or sects are not usually named after places. In any event no such town is mentioned either in the Old Testament or rabbinic literature, nor does any document before the Christian era speak of this place. It is not referred to in any of the epistles of St Paul.

The Jewish historian Josephus (d. AD 101) who was governor of Galilee and knew the area well, left a detailed record of all the places in the province, but never mentioned Nazareth. The present town of that name cannot be traced back with certainty to any time before the third century AD, when pilgrim traffic began.

The name Nazarene, and all names related to it, like Nazarite, Nazirite, Nazorean, Nazarean, all stem from the Hebrew word *nazar,* signifying one separated or consecrated. In ancient Israel the term was applied to those who were dedicated to God and observed certain taboos (Num. 6:2). For example, they abstained from wine, from ritually unclean food, and from contact with the dead, and usually left their hair uncut. Samson, Samuel and probably John the Baptist, were Nazarenes in this sense. It has been suggested that Jesus too was a Nazarene, perhaps the leader of the sect of Nazarenes, which in his day was probably of Essene affiliation. The Jews gave the name to the early followers of Jesus.

The present town of Nazareth seems to have been largely an outgrowth of immediate post-Christian times, because of the close association of the Nazarenes, especially Jesus, with that part of Galilee. By the fourth century, when the Emperor Constantine ordered the listing and identification of the holy sites associated with Christ, the village by then called Nazareth had become established as the Nazareth of the Gospels.

The term Nazarene was also applied to certain gnostic sects of Jewish race in Syria who claimed to obey the Mosaic law, though they were otherwise Christians. They reputedly used an Aramaic version of the gospel, known as the *Gospel of the Nazarenes.* They are not heard of after the fifth century.

Among the early sects spoken of as Nasoreans were the Mandaeans. In the Koran and in Muslim theological writings, Christians are referred to as Nasara.

Nicolaitanes

A gnostic sect erroneously said to have been founded by Nicolas, 'proselyte of Antioch' (Acts 6:5). Actually it was a pre-Christian sect that took on gnostic, perhaps Ophite, affiliations, after the Christian period, and advocated community of women, free sexuality and a return to pagan worship.

There is a reference in the New Testament to the 'doctrine of the Nicolaitanes, which thing I hate' (Rev. 2:15). The preceding verse speaks of 'the doctrine of Balaam', which caused a stumbling-block (*scandalon*) for the children of Israel. The word translated 'stumbling-block' also means something creating a scandal by its offensiveness.

The name Nicolas is the Greek equivalent of the Hebrew Balaam, both names meaning 'conqueror of the people'. The things for which the Nicolaitanes were anathematized by the early Church included eating food that had been sacrificed to idols and unrestrained fornication, but the unmentioned sins were sodomy and bestiality. In the second Epistle of Peter we read that Balaam 'was rebuked for his iniquity and the dumb ass speaking with man's voice forbad the madress of the prophet' (2:16).

The Hebrew *Zohar,* the chief kabalist text, relates that Balaam 'besmirched himself nightly by bestial intercourse with his ass' (Sperling and Simon, II, 1934, p. 11). The children of Israel slew Balaam in his thirty-third year, and his bones turned into serpents. And, adds the *Zohar,* 'If thou desirest to know more, ask his ass' (ibid. p. 72).

Simon Magus (15 BC-AD 53)

The son of a Jewish sorcerer, he was born in Samaria and educated in Alexandria, and was one of the patriarchs of the gnostic heresy.

He became the disciple of an Arab mystagogue, also of Samaria, named Dositheus (d. AD 29) who had been a follower of John the Baptist. Among the documents discovered at Nag Hammadi is a short text entitled the *Revelation of Dositheus* (also known as the *Three Steles of Seth*), but although it bears his name, it is not regarded as his work. Dositheus gave himself out to be the Messiah, affirming that his spirit was everlasting, and that his adherents too would become immortal through the baptism he gave them. Of his thirty disciples, twenty-nine were male and one female, named Helena. He acknowledged Simon Magus as an advanced spirit, and on his death the leadership of the Dositheans passed to Simon.

Simon Magus travelled widely, visiting Persia, Arabia, Egypt and other places, in search of magical lore. Wherever he went he was accompanied by a sorceress named Helena, by some said to be the same as the disciple of Dositheus, though Justin Martyr described her as a Greek prostitute, a slave taken from a brothel in Tyre.

Simon claimed that Helena was the incarnation of Helen of Troy, and that the famous beauty was never abducted by Paris. What Paris had taken from Troy was only an *eidolon*, an artificial dummy, and it was for this doll that the Greeks had fought the Trojans. Helena, said Simon, was an earthly embodiment of the aeon Pronoia, or 'first thought'; she was also Selene, the moon, the divine spouse, a manifestation of Sophia or divine wisdom, to be honoured with the title of Kuria, 'lady'.

For himself, he claimed to be 'the great power of God' (Acts 8:10), with the title of the Sun of Souls. Among his followers he was known as the Magus, and he also frequently used the cognomen Faustus, 'favoured one'. This fact, taken in conjunction with his female companion Helena, would suggest one of the sources of the medieval Faust legend (Grant, 1966, p. 70).

Many miracles became associated with his name. He healed the sick, raised the dead, walked through fire, flew through the air, turned stones into bread, created phantom banquets, caused trees to bear fruit out of season, made himself invisible, changed his own shape and that of others, animated statues, and commanded the demons to do his bidding.

He boasted, 'I once made the soul of a boy by my power, turning air into water, water into blood and flesh, and thus formed a new creature. This unsullied boy I violently slew and invoked him by my unutterable adjurations to assist me in my magical operations.'

Clement of Alexandria reported that Simon was called the 'Standing One', meaning that he was one who would not fall prey to destruction. Others suggested that he was so named because of the phallic rites in which he indulged. By means of erotic magic with Helena he was allegedly able to conjure up power for his miracles. According to Epiphanius, he made use of semen and menstrual blood in his sorcerous pursuits.

Simon held that fire was the basic principle of all things. From this primordial fire six aeons emerged in male and female pairs: Mind and Intelligence (heaven and earth), Voice and Name (sun and moon), Reason and Thought (air and water). He taught that the supreme deity did not create the world and in fact is not even aware of it. Creation was the work of a lesser being, the demiurge. The soul of man comes from the supreme being, and is thus superior to the creator. Jesus was not crucified except in appearance. Many of these ideas became the fundamental principles of later gnosticism.

The New Testament relates that Simon, curious to learn how the miracles of Philip the Evangelist were performed, agreed to be baptised. He was further amazed to see how the gift of the Holy Spirit was given to people by the laying on of hands, and desiring its power for himself, offered to buy it from Peter (hence the word *simony*), but was indignantly driven away (Acts 8:19).

Legend, partly embodied in the apocryphal *Acts of Peter and Paul* and partly in Origen, relates how Simon went to Rome while Peter was there and challenged him to a show of skill in magic before the Roman emperor. In the presence of all he levitated himself and remained hovering in the air. At the same time Peter (in some accounts Paul was with him) was on his knees praying, and so weakening the power of the demons who were supporting the mage. Suddenly Simon fell with a crash to the palace floor and broke his thigh. Still anxious to demonstrate his superior powers, he later allowed himself to be buried alive for three days, and so met his end, for he failed to be resurrected. It is said that Pope Paul I (d. 767) built a church on the site of Simon's defeat.

There is still some confusion about the true identity of Simon Magus. Some authorities doubt that Simon of the New Testament and Simon the heresiarch and mage are one and the same person. Simon Magus is sometimes confused with Simon of Gitta (c. AD 100), also a Samaritan and author of the *Megale Apophasis,* a semi-gnostic text. Again, it was long thought that the statue dedicated to Semoni found on an island on the Tiber was erected in honour of Simon Magus, whereas it was actually dedicated to the Sabine god Semo.

Simon's leading disciple was **Menander** (AD 35–117), another Samaritan, who taught at Antioch. According to him, redemption was not attained by faith alone but by the practice of transcendental magic. He invented a baptismal rite in the form of a 'bath of immortality', during which a visible fire descended into the water. This, it was said, rejuvenated the body, ensured indefinite longevity, and exempted one from old age and death. The pupils of Menander were known as Menandrists, two of whom, Saturninus and Basilides (see p. 141), eventually became leaders in their own right.

Saturninus (90–150), founder of Syrian gnosticism, also taught at Antioch. According to him there exist, besides the unknown Father God, seven creative angels under Jehovah, and several evil hierarchies under Satan. Jehovah is the demiurge who supervised the making of the world and created Adam and Eve. Because Eve took counsel of Satan and was seduced by him, sexual intercourse was introduced into the world, and with it, sin. The doctrine of Saturninus is world-denying and woman-denying. He rejected flesh-foods and wine and was a great exponent of encratism or sexual restraint for the purpose of acquiring spiritual power. The Logos (Christ) is the saviour who came to save the virtuous and destroy the evil-doer. Those who are good practice encratism and are saved, and the evil and self-indulgent are damned.

Cerinthus (c. AD 100)

Jewish-Christian gnostic, was born and educated in Alexandria and taught there and in Asia Minor. He was contemptuous of those Judaeo-Christians who clung to circumcision and the sabbath.

Like most gnostics he believed that the Supreme Father was unknown, and the world was created out of formless matter, not by this supreme being, but by an archon, the demiurge, who himself was ignorant of the supreme being. Jesus was an ordinary man, the son of Joseph and Mary. The Christ-force descended upon the body of Jesus at baptism and departed from it before the crucifixion. Since the Christ being is impassible, or incapable of suffering, only Jesus the man suffered.

The Church historian Eusebius of Caesarea (d. 340) stated that according to Cerinthus, Christ will return to Jerusalem and reign on earth for a thousand years, the period being marked by pleasures, banquets, nuptial festivities, limitless fornication and other sensual delights.

According to Polycarp (d. 155) the doctrines of Cerinthus so offended the aged apostle John that he refused to remain in the public baths with him, 'the enemy of the truth', for fear that the roof should fall upon them. In the opinion of Irenaeus, John wrote his gospel to refute Cerinthus.

Among the pupils of Cerinthus was Carpocrates (see below), also of Alexandria. Some authorities think it likely that Christianity first came to Egypt in a gnostic form, and teachers like Cerinthus and Carpocrates did much to strengthen the gnostic elements in the new religion.

Carpocrates (78–138)

A gnostic of Alexandria, and a disciple of Cerinthus. Influenced by the cult of Isis he adopted the paraphernalia of the Egyptian mystery religions, with an elaborate ritual of initiation that included passwords, mystic signs, grips, secret symbols and phonemes. Baptism also played an important part in the system. Certain members among the Carpocratians were branded with a seal (*sphragis*) behind the lobe of the right ear as a sign of dedication to the sect. Although some scholars suggest that he never existed, his name being merely a corruption of Harpocrates, the Greek name for the Egyptian god Horus son of Isis, it seems certain that he did indeed live and teach.

He had a female companion named Alexandria, and a son called Epiphanes, 'illustrious', who wrote a treatise, *On Justice*. On his death at the age of seventeen, Epiphanes was elevated to the rank of an aeon and received divine honours from the members of the sect. A temple and museum were built and consecrated to him. The teachings of the Carpocratians are attributed equally to father and son.

The sect paid reverence not only to the chief Egyptian deities but also to the great Greek philosophers, including Pythagoras, Plato and Aristotle, whose effigies they carried in procession from time to time. They revered Jesus and believed he had divine attributes but held that he was born by natural generation. They were said to possess images and paintings of Jesus made after a likeness drawn on the orders of Pilate himself. These images received special devotion and were likewise taken around in procession.

Carpocrates claimed to be in possession of certain secret teachings disclosed by Jesus to his apostles, which were made known only to the worthy and faithful. He also used a secret gospel allegedly written by St Mark, containing erotic rites. He rejected the Old Testament god and his law, and denounced the Mosaic injunctions against theft and against coveting one's neighbour's wife and property as ridiculous, for in the early and natural state of mankind there was neither property nor monogamy.

Concepts of 'mine' and 'thine' were introduced by the law in order to convert to private ownership what was meant to belong to all, and to prevent people from rightly sharing the fruits of the earth and from free intercourse between the sexes. The law deprives man of sexual freedom, which is denied to no animal. The Carpocratians held all things in common, including their property and their women.

Procreation was forbidden, but sex and sin encouraged, and the spermatic fluid divinized. Carpocrates taught that God had implanted in the human breast the biting itch of concupiscence for a special purpose, to make it obligatory to fornicate. By thus sinning, the divine light of God's grace was provided with a chance to operate, a fact eminently pleasing to God. Sin thus

became a way of salvation. The communal rites of the Carpocratians concluded with a feast of rich food and wine, after
which the lights were extinguished and the whole company
abandoned themselves enthusiastically to their singular pursuit
of God's grace, 'uniting as they desired and with whomsoever
they desired', says Clement of Alexandria.

The distinctions between good and evil exist only in the sight
of men, and whatever is considered good or evil should all be
experienced. Carpocrates believed in reincarnation, which he
said would only cease when the individual soul, through its
many incarnations, had gone through every kind of experience,
good and bad, pleasurable and painful, glorious and sordid, and
so tasted life in all its diversity, leaving nothing undone. Every
action has an angel overseer and should be performed while
invoking that angel, and in the angel's name, in order that all
deeds might be duly accomplished and recorded.

Among the disciples of Carpocrates was the female teacher
Marcellina (c. 145), who travelled to Rome to expound his
doctrine to converts there. Another was **Prodicus** (c. 180) of
Alexandria, a Persian, whose own followers spread as far as
Carthage. To the Carpocratian precepts about the sharing of
wives and possessions he added nudity and the need to return to
the simplist state of Adam and Eve before the fall. He also
taught the futility of making supplications to God. In his
Stromateis, Clement of Alexandria remarks that among the
teachings of the sect of Prodicus is the strange precept that one
must not pray.

Basilides (85-145)
He claimed to be the disciple of a certain Glaucias, who was an
'interpreter of Peter', and thus took his teaching back to the
apostles. Among his other teachers was said to have been the
mage Menander of Antioch. Basilides established his own
school in Alexandria.

A copious writer he composed a psalm book, several odes, a
biblical commentary (the *Exegetica*) in twenty-four books and a
short gospel, but only fragments of his work survive. He was
well versed in the Hebrew scriptures and familiar with some of
the Pauline letters.

Basilidean cosmology went something as follows. From the
supreme unborn Father, the 'non-existent' and wholly transcendent Godhead, had proceeded a series of emanations, namely,

Mind, Word, Understanding, Wisdom and Power, constituting the first heaven. These in turn produced, in descending order of emanation, the angels, archons and other beings of the cosmic host, grouped severally in 365 heavens.

The chief of the lowest orders in the hierarchy of emanations was Jehovah, who created the world and apportioned the nations to their respective areas on earth. His preferred people were the Jews, whom he helped in their subjugation of other nations. This was the origin of strife. The Mosaic law came from the god of the Jews, and the Old Testament prophecies from the other rulers concerned with governing the world, who were inspired by the Jewish God.

The most high God then sent his first-born son, the Logos aspect of Nous (Christ), to liberate those faithful to him from the bondage of the creator and his archons. Christ was incarnated as Jesus and worked many miracles. At the crucifixion the shape of Jesus was put upon Simon of Cyrene (Mark 15:21), who suffered instead of him.

Basilides held that not all the sins committed by a man are forgiven, but only those that are committed involuntarily or in ignorance. His other sins must be atoned for through suffering. The elect will ascend to the highest heaven and the rest of humanity will proceed to the heavens appropriate to their actions and exertions while on earth. He regarded his followers as the elect and as 'men', as compared with those who were ignorant of the doctrine and who were no better than pigs and dogs, and of whom Jesus had said, 'Cast not your pearls before swine' (Matt. 7:6).

Basilides laid great emphasis on secrecy, confining his teachings to a band of chosen disciples. He imposed a long period of silence on those who came to him for instruction, as was formerly the custom in the Pythagorean schools. He was an adept in numerology and magical phonemes, attaching particular importance to the number 365, and to the aeon Abraxas, the letters of whose name total 365. He himself practiced rigid encratism and lived an ascetic life, though Irenaeus accused him and his followers of idolatry, magic and libertinism.

Valentinus (see p. 147) may have been among his pupils. **Isidorus,** the son of Basilides, was also prominent in the cult and wrote gnostic works, with emphasis on ethics and allegorical exegesis. The Basilideans were numerous in Egypt and southern Europe, but died out by the fifth century.

Marcion (90-165)

The son of a bishop, Marcion was a wealthy shipowner of Sinope on the southern shores of the Pontus (Black Sea). He came to Rome in AD 140 and became prominent in Church affairs, but fell under the spell of a gnostic named Cerdo and was excommunicated in 144, ostensibly on grounds of immorality.

Cerdo (d. 143) a Syrian gnostic, had started his career as a Simonian (follower of Simon Magus) and then branched out on his own. He taught that God the Father was merciful and good. He was the Supreme Being, but unknown, until first made known to man by Jesus. The god proclaimed in the law and the prophets of the Old Testament was the creator of the world, and inferior to the supreme being. He was a god of justice who demanded obedience. Cerdo believed that only the soul and not the body shared in the resurrection.

From these basic elements Marcion developed his own theology. Here too the creator and ruler of the world is the Jewish god, the just, jealous and wrathful Jehovah, revealed in the Old Testament. God the Father had no hand in the work of creation. Biblical references to a divine providence active in the world referred to Jehovah's concern for the material welfare of the creatures in the world made by him, and in particular, concern for his chosen people.

In time the Jewish Messiah, the son of Jehovah, will come and establish his earthly kingdom, just as the prophets had foretold, but this has nothing to do with the salvation already brought by Christ, which is wholly spiritual in nature. The created universe of the Jewish God is left to itself, and will be destroyed in the end. Satan and his minions are separate characters within the domain of Jehovah.

God the Father is the supreme deity, the Absolute Other, remote from the cosmos, to whom men are entire strangers. He is a good God but has no concern with the world and is not even aware of the existence of human beings. It is only the Logos, his Son, who is aware of the predicament of mankind, and it is because of his concern that the Father became involved and chose to intervene on man's behalf. He therefore sent his Son to deliver man from the bondage of the material world and the domination of its god, the demiurge.

Salvation depends on faith in Jesus Christ the Redeemer as the emissary of the supreme God. Faith means trusting oneself to the mercy of the kind stranger God. As Adolf Harnack (d. 1930) expressed it: 'According to Marcion, Christ saved us from the world and its god in order to make us children of a new and alien God.'

The soul and not the body is the object of the redemptive mission of Christ. Man can be saved only by grace, and not by works or by obedience to the law. Marcion eliminated from the Christian message the need for fear and trembling. Christianity was a gospel of love and not the law.

Pointing out the pitfalls of having faith in Jehovah, Marcion said that Christ descended into hell to redeem, among others, Cain, Korah, Dathan, Abiram, Esau, the Sodomites, and all the nations who did not acknowledge the god of the Jews. Abel, Enoch, Noah, Abraham and the patriarchs and prophets who served the creator-god were deceived into remaining below. Aware from long experience that their god liked to put them to the test, they suspected Christ's mission to be just such a temptation, and refused to believe in him.

Marcion rejected the Old Testament since it was relevant only to the Jews. But he also rejected the New Testament, except for a version of St Luke's gospel and, with some changes, ten of the Pauline epistles. From these again he excluded all passages containing such phrases as 'in order that it might be fulfilled', which, he said, implied quite erroneously, that Christ came to fulfil the Old Testament prophecies. The birth story, with its Davidic references, was also removed.

According to him, St Luke gave the most reliable biography of Jesus, and St Paul correctly distinguished between law and grace. Alone among the followers of Jesus, Paul had an understanding of the true nature of Christ's redemptive mission. Marcion held a docetic view of Christ, stating that as the Logos and the Son of God he could not have taken on corrupt flesh, and therefore had a phantasmal and not a physical body.

Marcion made faith and not gnosis the vehicle of redemption. Salvation, he said, was available to all men, and did not involve secrets, secret revelations or knowledge of magical rituals. Moral conduct imposed from without was irrelevant. The saved are 'believers' and not 'knowers' or 'doers'. Love and mercy spring spontaneously from the heart of those who have faith in Jesus Christ. Because of this, scholars such as Harnack do not regard Marcion as a true gnostic, and point to the basically Christian character of many of his beliefs.

He gave women a prominent role in his church, and assigned many priestly offices to women and laymen. He discouraged marriage, and barred marriage after baptism, holding that marriage was an invention of the evil Old Testament god. The Marcionites abstained from flesh foods and wine, and used water instead of wine for the Eucharist.

All in all Marcion had a great influence on the developing Christian Church. It is to him that we owe the terms Old Testament and New Testament. By his study of these scriptures he forced on the Church the problem of establishing a canon, and was indeed the first to assemble a New Testament canon. His suggested emendations of the New Testament constituted the earliest textual criticism of the Bible. He composed his own psalms, which he used in preference to the Davidic ones, and was thus among the pioneers of Christian hymnology.

He also convened one of the earliest Church synods (Blackman, 1948, p. 1), and was the first of the 'Protestants'. According to the German theologian Ernst Barnikol, the first Christian Church in the proper sense of the term was the Marcionite Church.

Among the disciples of Marcion was **Apelles** (c. 180), who had great faith in the clairvoyant faculty of a certain woman named Philumene and based some of his teachings on the inspirational messages she received, as a result of which he separated from Marcion. He taught of four great beings: a supreme and good God; a creator god; a fiery lawgiver who spoke to Moses; and the devil or evil one. Serving the supreme God were angels, who sometimes tended to recalcitrance. Christ, said Apelles, came from the supreme God, took on real flesh, died in the flesh, rose again, gave back his flesh to matter and ascended to the Father. All sincere believers in Christ would ultimately be saved, irrespective of the religion they held.

Another of Marcion's disciples was **Severus** (d. 183), who spoke of an unnamed highest heaven ruled over by a good God, and a subordinate creator named Ialdabaoth who is the head of a host of still lesser powers controlling the material universe. Severus is notable for his pronouncement that marriage fulfils the work of the evil powers, and that wine is a Satanic product.

The philosopher **Numenius of Apamea** (150–209), a scholar of Pythagoras and Plato and exponent of Chaldean astrological teachings, is also associated with Marcionite doctrines. According to him matter is evil, for there exists a basic dualism in the world, shared between God and the demiurge. He was believed to have had a great influence on the neoplatonist philosopher Plotinus, who indeed was said to have plagiarized Numenius.

The Marcionite sect spread rapidly and established churches in Italy and all over the Roman empire, including Egypt, Palestine, Arabia, Syria, Asia Minor and Persia. It flourished till the eighth century, after which it was gradually absorbed by the Manicheans.

Montanus (110–172)

Born at Ardaban not far from Mount Ida in Phrygia, Asia Minor, Montanus was a pagan convert to Christianity. St Jerome speaks of him as a castrant, and he may have become one while serving as a priest of Cybele, the great goddess of Phrygia.

He was subject to sudden seizures, would fall into spontaneous trance, speak in tongues, and prophesy as one inspired. Claiming to be the Paraclete, the Spirit of Truth and the incarnation of the Holy Ghost, he founded an ecstatic and enthusiast sect in Phrygia, a region notorious in pagan times for its sensuous and orgiastic cults. The Church denounced him as the leader of what became known, in reference to its Phrygian origins, as the Cataphrygian heresy. He encouraged ecstatic states in his followers and what he called possession by the Holy Spirit, by means of which, it was believed, they received 'the Third Testament'. A Montanist verse goes, 'Behold, man is a lyre, and I play upon him as a plectrum.'

Although some Montanists were hostile to gnosticism, they themselves were commonly classed with the gnostics and may be considered representative of the ascetic branch of the gnostic movement. They stood against the officialdom of the Church, were puritanical, celibate, and strict in matters of diet. They were also adventist, predicting the imminent Second Coming of Christ and the establishment of the New Jerusalem in Pepuza, a tiny place in the heart of Phrygia. They believed in baptism for the dead, by which friends and relatives of believers could be baptized and so admitted to the community of the saved after their death, a practice that had been denounced by St Paul a century earlier (1 Cor. 15:29). Unlike most other gnostic sects, they forbade apostasy, or the denial of their faith, or flight during persecution.

The Montanists were strongly opposed to marriage and even

advocated the dissolution of the marriage tie where it existed. They considered childbearing improper and second marriage definitely adulterous. But in spite of this they came under suspicion and calumny, largely because so many women were attracted to their ranks and because their rites included sacred dances by virgins.

Many women left their husbands to join them, and Montanus always chose women as his chief ministrants and prophetesses. Some of the latter went into trance and experienced ecstasy, believing they were possessed by God. The most notable among the female converts to their fold were two wealthy women of noble family named **Maximilla** and **Priscilla** (or **Prisca**). Montanism won the allegiance of the great African theologian Tertullian, who joined the sect in AD 207 and remained a Montanist till his death.

During the sixth century the Church stepped up its opposition to the sect. In 550 the bishop of Ephesus dug up the corpses of Montanus and his chief prophetesses and burned them. A decade later, during their persecution by the Byzantine emperor, the Montanists barricaded themselves in their churches and set fire to them, preferring to perish rather than give up their beliefs. In the eighth century, after another such holocaust, the sect vanished from history.

Valentinus (110-175)

Egyptian poet and teacher of Alexandria, Valentinus was the most influential of the gnostics. He travelled from Egypt to teach in Rome (135-160), had hopes of being made Bishop of Rome, and failing to obtain a bishopric seceded from the church.

He claimed to have received St Paul's secret teaching from Theodas, one of Paul's disciples. Valentinus may have been a pupil of Basilides. He was well versed in Greek philosophy and the Christian writings of his day. To him has been attributed the poetic *Gospel of Truth,* discovered in Coptic translation in Nag Hammadi and mentioned by Irenaeus as *Evangelium Veritatis.* He also composed a number of psalms.

It is said that Valentinus himself led a blameless life, but his teachings were subjected to very liberal interpretation, and this led to the sect becoming one of the most libidinous of all gnostic sects, thereby arousing the hostility of many of the Church Fathers. Clement of Alexandria, Irenaeus, Tertullian and Hippolytus, all wrote against him.

A brilliant and eloquent man of immense personal magnetism, St Jerome said of him: 'No one can bring an influential heresy into being unless he is possessed, by nature, of an outstanding intellect and has gifts provided by God. Such a man was Valentinus.'

In Valentinian cosmology, the Glory of the Father gave rise to an ogdoad or eight-fold emanation, namely, Thought, Grace, Silence, Mind, Truth, Man, Church and Sophia (lists vary), from which in turn there emanated fifteen pairs, or thirty aeons, angelic beings constituting the pleroma or fullness of the upper realm. The paired aeons are wildly sexual in their activity, and Valentinians were enjoined to emulate them. An important Valentinian celebration began on the evening preceding 15 February, the day of the Roman Lupercalia, when cult members would witness and then imitate the divine nuptials enacted in the bridal chamber of their holy shrine.

Valentinians held that dualism pervades the universe. There is a dualistic rift between God and Satan; it is found in nature; it dwells in man. Achieving unity between these conflicting opposites is essential for salvation. The threefold distinction made by Valentinus, between noetic man with the soul predominant, psychic man with intelligence ruling, and hylic man with the carnal tendencies uppermost, played an important part in gnosticism.

When he first experienced gnosis, Valentinus said, he saw a vision of a new-born infant who declared, 'I am the Logos'. He added that once a man has received gnosis he can sin no longer, which was taken by some of his followers as a licence for self-indulgence.

The Valentinians were a prolific school in which independent speculation was encouraged, so we have numerous versions and elaborations of Valentinian doctrine. Irenaeus wrote, 'None of them is considered perfect unless he expounds something different in high-sounding phrases.' And according to Tertullian, the Valentinians 'have outgrown even the jungles of the gnostics in wildness.'

Chief among the pupils or followers of Valentinus were Theodotus, Ptolemaeus, Heracleon, Secundus, Marcus, Theotimus, Axionicus, Florinus and Bardesanes.

Theodotus (fl. 140–170) taught in Asia Minor. The valuable collection made by Clement of Alexandria of Greek excerpts from the writings of Theodotus, entitled *Excerpta ex Theodoto,* is actually a collection of sayings from several Valentinians. In an oft-quoted passage Theodotus describes the true gnostic as one who can understand, 'who we were, what we have become, where we were, into what we have been thrown, whither we are hastening, from what we are being redeemed, what birth is, and what rebirth.'

Ptolemaeus (c. 180) taught in Rome, and produced an Italic brand of Valentinianism. In his *Letter to Flora,* preserved by Epiphanius, he writes to a lady giving instruction about the sect and explaining the significance of the Mosaic law. Ptolemaeus believed that Christ had both a soul and a psychic body, so that not only the spiritual but also the rational man could be saved.

Heracleon (140–200) produced the first, and highly allegorized, commentary on the gospel of St John, in the prologue of which he describes the emanation of the aeons. He interpreted the gospel of St John as a Valentinian book.

Marcus (d. 175), an Egyptian, taught in Asia Minor and Gaul, laid great stress on ritualism, magic and numerology, and sought to adapt the Hebrew number system to the Greek alphabet. Irenaeus wrote that Marcus was 'knowledgeable in magical deceit', and accused him of charlatanry and debauchery, and the seduction of his female 'prophets'. His followers were known as Marcosians or Marcians.

Bardesanes (154–222), or Bar Daisan, lived at the court of Abgar VIII, the Great, of Edessa, where Syrian, Iranian and Hellenistic cultural trends intermingled. He was the father of Syriac hymnology. The famous 'Hymn of the Pearl' in the *Acts of Thomas,* if not by Bardesanes, came from circles close to him. Bardesanes has been called 'the last of the gnostics', but gnosticism continued to flourish long after him. His cosmology was emanationist, his Christology docetic. Because of his belief in the powerful sway of the stars he was criticized as a fatalist. His work and that of his son Harmonius had a great impact on the Manicheans.

The influence of Valentinianism was widely felt, spreading from Egypt eastwards to Syria, Asia Minor and Mesopotamia, and westwards to Rome, Spain and Gaul. The Church repeatedly tried to put a stop to the Valentinian heresy and the libertine practices associated with it, even going so far as to create a fictitious Christian martyr named St Valentine of Persia, who was supposed to have been beaten with clubs and then beheaded in the year 270 on 14 February. St Valentine has now been removed from the official catalogue of saints, but his day continues to be celebrated in the West by the exchange of sentimental missives, or 'valentines', between the sexes.

Several medieval cults were inspired by the Valentinians, and practices reminiscent of those of the sect continued in southern France until the twelfth century (Rutherford, 1861, p. 195). The modern revivals of gnosticism in southern France, notably Lyons, and in various other parts of the Western world, are largely of Valentinian provenance.

Cainites

Information about the so-called Cainite sect comes to us from Irenaeus, Tertullian and Epiphanius, who found Cainite leanings in the teachings of many gnostics, including Marcion and Valentinus.

Like other gnostics the Cainites were opposed to the Mosaic law, to Jehovah and the pretensions of the chosen people. They held that knowledge of the true God was attained by those figures in the Bible who are presented as wicked. In reality these persons derived their mission from a higher power, were bearers of a noetic message, and for this reason were persecuted by the god of this world. Jehovah's favourites, Abel, Isaac, Jacob, Moses and others, represented the unenlightened majority.

Cainites esteemed the serpent in paradise, who showed Adam and Eve the way to knowledge, far above Jehovah the god of this world who tried to withhold it from them. They exalted Cain above Abel, believing that some potent force operated in Cain, and that Abel was conceived and brought forth by an inferior entity. The god of this world did not accept Cain's offering of the first-fruits of the earth, but received instead the bloody sacrifice of Abel, proving that the god of this world delights in blood.

They preferred the raven sent forth by Noah (Gen. 8:7) to the dove, because the raven did not return to Noah; Lot to Abraham, because Lot chose the fertile plain of Jordan (Gen. 13:11) while Abraham chose Canaan; Ishmael to Isaac, because Ishmael was Abraham's first-born son and thus the natural heir to the inheritance; Esau to Jacob, because Esau was the eldest son of Isaac, and Jacob obtained his inheritance through deceit. They honoured Pharaoh rather than Moses, because Pharaoh did not acknowledge Jehovah (Exod. 5:2); likewise, Korah, Dathan and Abiram (Num. 16:1) rather than Moses and Aaron, because the latter wished to impose the law of Jehovah and so claim for themselves the exclusive privileges of the priesthood.

Among the New Testament characters, the Cainites preferred Judas to John, Mary Magdalene to the Virgin Mary, Simon Magus to Simon Peter, and glorified the role of Pontius Pilate. This Roman governor of Judea washed his hands and found nothing wrong with Jesus. In the apocryphal *Gospel of Peter* the Jews alone are blamed for the death of Jesus, and Pilate praised because he declared Jesus to be a just person (see Matt. 27:24). The Apostles' Creed says Jesus 'suffered under Pontius Pilate', but this only means that the 'suffering Saviour' suffered with Pilate. It is difficult otherwise to account for Pilate being mentioned at all in this context.

Pilate, along with his wife Procla, were honoured by some groups of early Christians too. In certain eastern churches he is regarded as a saint and a martyr. Even today the Coptic Church of both Egypt and Ethiopia revere his name and celebrate his feast day (25 June) every year. The Latin legend of his death tells of Pilate being arrested and brought before the emperor in Rome. He wears the seamless tunic of Jesus. He is stripped of his tunic and sent to prison where he meets his end either by being killed or committing suicide.

Peratae

Founded by Euphrates (d. 160) and further developed by his disciple Celbes, the Peratae or Peratic sect communicated their inner teachings in the greatest secrecy. Some information about them can be gleaned from Hippolytus.

The Peratics believed that nothing that emerges from physical generation can survive dissolution, and that salvation is only possible for those who can cross over from the sphere of creation and fatality and reach the 'other side' (*peratos*), and so transcend death.

They taught a mystical physiology interrelating the different parts of the body one with another and also with the stars and planets. Water symbolism figured prominently in their rites. They spoke of a male-female sea deity named Thossa (from *thalassa,* 'sea'), with five ministers bearing secret names, all of whom were given correspondences within the body.

Egypt was the symbol of mortality and corruption and in the

Peratic view, 'all ignorant ones [those outside the sect] are Egyptians'. They regarded the physical body as a miniature Egypt. By means of an interior discipline, while in a trance-like state achieved in the course of a sex rite, they went through a mystic re-enactment of the passage of the Israelites (the soul) out of Egypt (the body), through the Red Sea (the waters of corruption), into the desert (the torment of self-denial) to face attacks by serpents (the sins of concupiscence), until the final crossing of the Jordan into the Promised Land. The Jordan had to be crossed when the waters were flowing upward.

Barbelites
They gave honour to a primeval aeon named Barbelo, to whom the Supreme Being was said to have revealed himself. Irenaeus states that there were a multitude of Barbelo-Gnostics. Their centre was Alexandria.

Some scholars derive their name from the principle formed 'from four lights' (Heb. *be-arba-orim*) that shone forth from the Supreme Being, namely: Armozel, the great one, the father; Oroaiel, the light-mother (Barbelo herself); Davithe, the beloved son; and Eleleth, the other, namely, Anthropos or primal man.

In some texts Barbelo takes on the attributes of Sophia. She is the primeval never-ageing spirit, at once the virginal daughter of the Lord, cosmic consort, universal mother, and also Prunicus (*prouneikos*, 'lewd'), the whore.

The Barbelites practised borborism. Epiphanius writes that the power of Barbelo is dispersed among the archons and she therefore appears to them in seductive beauty, and gives them pleasure. She then appropriates the seed of their emission, thus taking back into herself her scattered power. Her followers do likewise, and say, 'We are collecting the power of Prunicus from bodies by their fluids', by which they mean semen and menses (Foerster, 1974, p. 317).

Nag Hammadi texts such as the *Apocryphon of John,* the *Hypostasis of the Archons,* and the *Origin of the World* are regarded as Barbelite.

Sethians
This sect was sometimes linked with the Ophites, Barbelites and other related groups. It established itself in Egypt and Asia Minor, and a branch called the Archontics was known in

Palestine. An Armenian named Eutactus (c. 340) visited Palestine where, says Epiphanius, he acquired the substance of their 'poisonous doctrine' from an old man named Peter of Capharbarica, a village near Hebron, and went back to his native land with 'this harmful stuff as if it were a valuable cargo'.

Their name was once traced to the Egyptian deity Seth, brother and murderer of Osiris, but scholars today derive it from Seth, the third son of Adam and Eve. In the Sethian view, Satan, the son of Sabaoth, god of the Jews, seduced Eve, and Cain and Abel were their children. The Flood was caused by the supreme deity, to exterminate the seed of Cain, but wicked angels smuggled Ham into the ark so that wickedness might continue.

After the murder of Abel, Adam and Eve came together and became the parents of Seth, who was appointed as 'another seed' (Gen. 4:25) in place of Abel. Because of this, Seth is spoken of as Allogenes, belonging to 'another race', and alien to the world. Through his sister-wife Norea, Seth became the progenitor of the elect race of human beings.

Adam on his deathbed communicated certain secrets to Seth, and these Seth was said to have inscribed on two columns, one of brick and one of stone, to secure them against the predicted calamities of flood and fire, and he hid them on the peak of Charaxio, 'the mountain of the worthy', to be found in due time. The inscriptions that survived the Flood have already been found, and the rest will be discovered after the universal conflagration still to come.

Among the Sethian writings found at Nag Hammadi are: the *Three Steles of Seth, Zostrianos,* the *Second Treatise of the Great Seth,* the *Paraphrase of Shem, Allogenes,* the *Trimorphic Protennoia,* and *Melchizedek.* In the last mentioned the high priest Melchizedek performs the work of salvation in the form of the crucified and risen Jesus.

The Sethians believed in intermittent revelation, and a continuous transmission of the 'secrets of Adam' through a Phoster or 'illuminator', who will appear from time to time. Each such earthly manifestation of the heavenly redeemer has been and will continue to be of the line of Seth: Melchizedek, Zoroaster, Jesus (Layton, 1981, p. 498).

It has been suggested that the title of the Sethian codex, *Zostrianos,* is a derivative of Zoroaster. In some gnostic works Melchizedek is the power behind the sun, and bears the alternative title of Zorokothoro, which also seems to be a clear variant of Zoroaster.

The Melchizedekians are sometimes treated as a separate sect, but they are a Sethian offshoot. They get their name from Melchizedek, King of Salem (old name of Jerusalem), who is mentioned in the Old Testament as the priest of the most high God and in the New Testament as 'having neither beginning of days nor end of life; but made like unto the Son of God'. St Paul refers to Jesus as 'called of God, an high priest after the order of Melchizedek' (Heb. 5:10).

According to the Sethians, Jesus is of the pure line of Seth, and in some texts is identified with Seth.

Ophites

So called, because the symbolism of the serpent (*ophis*) enters prominently into their faith. Some writers refer to them as a pre-Christian sect since snake worship and snake handling undoubtedly go back to very ancient times.

The Egyptian ram-headed god Khnemu became the Khnubis of the gnostics, who depicted him on their gems as a lion-headed and bearded serpent standing on human legs. Snake worship is also found in the mysteries associated with the Egyptian-Greek deity Serapis, with the Phrygian goddess Cybele, with Dionysus, and with many other ancient deities. Clement of Alexandria describes the Thracian cult of Sabazius whose rites included 'the deity gliding over the bosom'.

The serpent has a vast symbolism. It is associated with immortality and the conquest of death. It is also regarded as a phallic symbol and hence a deity of sexual pleasure. Being a chthonian (earth) creature and finding its home under the ground, it is also associated with darkness and the realms of death. Sometimes it is linked with the primordial egg from which all things emerged, and is shown entwined around an egg.

In gnosticism it was linked with the cosmos, whose ruler is the earth-encircling dragon, Satan. According to the *Pistis Sophia*, 'The outer darkness is a huge dragon whose tail is in its mouth.' The circular symbol of the serpent with its tail in its mouth was known as the *ouroboros,* 'tail-devouring'. This was the symbol of the Egyptian god Atum with his phallus in his hand, copulating with his fist. To the gnostic, however, the ouroboros represented the primal being who says, 'I am Alpha and Omega, the beginning and the end, the first and the last' (Rev. 22:13).

It is not known who founded the Ophite sect, if indeed it had any one founder. There were several branches of the sect. One branch seems to have been started by **Alexander the Paphlagonian** (d. 180), who came from the town of Abonuticus in Asia Minor. A pupil of the Neo-Pythagorean philosopher and wonder-worker Apollonius of Tyana, Alexander tamed a large serpent, called Glycon, covered its head with a mask of the human face, and through it manipulated an oracle and prescribed healing remedies. The Roman writer Lucian describes him as a charlatan.

Many gnostic sects had strong leanings towards Ophitism, notably the Sethians, the Peratics, the Justinians, and best known of all, the Naassenes (also known as the Nachaites or Nochaites). The Naassenes are mentioned by Hippolytus, the main part of his account being an extract called the 'Naassene Psalm'. The Hebrew word for serpent (*nachash*) is rendered in Greek as *naas,* which the Ophites connected with the eternal principle, *Nous,* 'mind', stating that the serpent in the garden of Eden was actually Nous in serpent form.

According to the Naassenes the demiurge, the Old Testament deity, tried to prevent Adam and Eve from acquiring knowledge, and it was the serpent who persuaded them to disobey the demiurge and taste of the fruit. This was the origin of gnosis. Because the serpent frustrated the designs of Jehovah, the 'accursed god of the Jews' (Grant, 1966, p. 117) cursed the serpent.

What appears to have been the cosmological scheme of the sect was set out in a mystical drawing known as the 'Diagram of the Ophites', varying descriptions of which have been preserved in the writings of the pagan Platonist Celsus, in the *Apocryphon of John,* in the Church Father Origen, and others.

The drawing depicted the seven circles ruled by the archons, enclosed within a large outer circle called Leviathan, the soul of the universe, representing the Ophite serpent. Within the innermost circle lay Behemoth, representing Hades, Tartarus, Gehenna, that is, the kingdom of evil. In some versions the rulers of the circles bore the names of the archangels, but more commonly they were the names of the archons, each symbolizing an aspect of the demiurge.

The first circle was ruled by Ialdabaoth, in the form of a lion; the second ruled by Sabaoth, in the form of a bull; the third by

Iaoth, in the form of a scorpion; the fourth by Eloaios, in the form of an eagle; the fifth by Thauthabaoth (perhaps representing Tohu and Bohu, the void and formlessness of Genesis 1:2), in the form of a bear; the sixth by Erathaoth, in the form of a dog or ape; the seventh by Thartharaoth (perhaps a Hebrew form of Tartarus), in the form of an ass.

Among the characteristic features of the Ophite rite was one in which a snake was made to glide from the bosom to the private parts of the believers, both men and women, as a result of which hysterical emotions were engendered. They uttered shrill cries, howled and wept, fell into convulsive fits, danced about, made prophecies, went into ecstasy. Also, serpents were allowed to crawl over loaves of bread, which, being thereby 'invigorated' and consecrated, the worshippers afterwards ate at a sacramental meal.

The intervention of the serpent at the Ophite ceremony was believed to have a purifying and healing effect. The Bible records (Num. 21:9) that Moses raised a brazen serpent (*nachash*) on a pole so that those bitten by poisonous snakes could look upon it and be healed. The Naassenes believed that Christ was the incarnation of the serpent of paradise, and of the serpent of Moses.

Sometimes a distinction is made between Christ the Saviour, and Jesus. Christ equated the serpent with the Son of man (John 3:14), whereas Jesus equated serpents with scorpions, and spoke of the serpent as the 'enemy' (Luke 10:19). For this reason some Ophite sects villified Jesus. In his *Contra Celsum* Origen records that 'they curse Jesus, and do not admit converts until they have cursed him too'. St Paul's reference to those who curse Jesus (1 Cor. 12:3) may point to the Ophites.

Justinus (c. 200)

The best known of the Ophite teachers was Justinus or Justin, author of the *Book of Baruch*, a fanciful mixture of Greek, Jewish and Christian myths.

According to this book there are three primal powers. The first, the Good, abides in the kingdom of light, above creation, and knows all things in advance. Curiously, this benign power is equated with Priapus, the god of procreative energy. He, however, plays little part in the scheme expounded by Justinus, whose chief protagonists are the two others, Elohim and Eden.

Elohim is a god of heaven, a demiurge, but without foreknowledge. He falls in love with Eden (or Israel), an earth-goddess who has the likeness of a serpent from the loins down. As a result of the cosmic marriage between Elohim and Eden, twenty-four angelic beings are begotten, allegorically referred to as the Trees of the Garden (Gen. 2:8), twelve favourable to Elohim, and twelve favourable to Eden.

Of those angels who are favourable to Elohim, the third is named Baruch; he is the Tree of Life. Of those who are favourable to Eden, the third is named Naas, and he is the Tree of the Knowledge of Good and Evil. The angels of Elohim create Adam and Eve as a seal and love-token of the marriage between Elohim and Eden. The angels of Eden bring famine, pestilence, affliction, lust and general unhappiness. Naas seduces and pours the poison of his lust into Eve, and thus brings adultery into the world; he then has impure relations with Adam, and so brings sodomy into the world.

Elohim sends Moses and the Prophets that they might prevail against the twelve Edenic angels and give succour to man, but they fail to help. Then he sends Hercules, a prophet of the heathen world, but he too is seduced by Omphale (or Babel), one of the daughters of Eden. Finally Elohim despatches Baruch to Jesus, the son of Joseph and Mary, and he alone remains faithful. Naas in his wrath causes Jesus to be crucified. After his death Jesus ascends to the Good One.

Hippolytus described *Baruch* as 'the most monstrous book he had ever set eyes on.'

The Borborians
Several gnostic sects of extreme libertine tendency combined their sex rites with the practice of eating revolting substances, for which reason they were called Borborians or 'filthy ones' (*borboros,* 'dirt'). Among them were sometimes included the Peratics, Barbelites and Ophites, but there were others, of whom little more is known than their often fanciful names, which were probably bestowed on them by their opponents.

The Borborians or Borborites included the Haimatitoi (*haima,* 'blood'), probably so called because they drank menstrual blood; the Entychites (*tyche,* 'chance'), because they had intercourse with partners selected by lot, whether such partners were their own sisters or other close relations; the Levitici (Heb. *levi,* 'joined') because of their sodomitic habits; the Phibionites, from a Greek word for 'fig', because they claimed to understand the sexual mystery of the tree that Jesus cursed (Matt. 21:19) and of the 'untimely figs' shaken by a mighty wind (Rev. 6:13); the Stratiotici (Lat. 'soldiers') of Egypt, because of their reputedly heroic sexual prowess; the Zacchaeans (Heb. *zak*, 'pure') the 'perfect ones', who could do no wrong; the Antitactae (*taktos*, 'fixed') or antinomians, who opposed the fixed or established order; the Coddians (Syriac, *codda*, 'dish') so named because they were served separately since no one would eat with them on account of their filthy life (Lacarrière, 1977, p. 92).

The outrages advocated and committed by these sects were known only to a few. With good reason their rites (already described) were performed in the greatest secrecy, and their meetings held at night in caves, or in some remote place, or in subterranean vaults (hypocausts) used for heating houses. Epiphanius (d. 403) was invited to join one of their groups, and in describing their practices in his *Panarion,* compares them to moles, who shun the light of day.

Priscillian (340-386)

A Spanish mystic who was converted to Christianity and subsequently ordained Bishop of Avila in Spain. He later took up a brand of gnosticism said to have been introduced to Spain in 370 by an Egyptian named Mark (or Marcus) of Memphis. In 380, following an enquiry, he was excommunicated by a synod at Saragossa, then reinstated, then tried again. In accordance with the Roman judicial procedure which the church inherited, he was tortured and eventually executed at Treves (Trier), being the first Christian to suffer martyrdom at the hands of other Christians for heretical beliefs. With him were executed six of his followers: two priests, the mother of his alleged mistress, a Christian poet, and two others. The Priscillian sect flourished in Spain till about the end of the fifth century, but for long after, Priscillian himself continued to be venerated as a martyr.

He had been condemned for a number of heretical doctrines. He was accused of dualism, holding that the devil was not a fallen angel but the principle of evil. He was charged with sorcery and maleficia. He admitted that he had studied the doctrines of magic, but denied that he ever put any of them into practice.

He was also accused of teaching theosophical mysteries

relating to the devil, whom he regarded as the one who created the body and governed its operations. The devil was also the ruler of thunder, lightning, drought, fire and other natural phenomena, and he and his underlings caused rain by urination and seminal ejaculation.

Besides the Bible, Priscillian used heretical apocrypha as a guide. He held a docetic view of Christ, denying the reality of a physical incarnation and of Christ's suffering on the cross.

He preached voluntary poverty and asceticism, and was well known for his austerity. He condemned the eating of animal foods, and stood for a strict vegetarian diet. He also advocated long periods of fasting. No wine was permitted, not even for the Eucharist.

He was opposed to marriage and procreation and encouraged celibacy. He even urged the separation of husbands and wives, and advised married couples for whom such a course was not feasible to confine sexual intercourse to the 'safe period' of the menstrual cycle.

He held that women could become vehicles of the Holy Spirit, and fostered their prophetic role in his sect. There were many women among his followers. He was alleged to have made pregnant the virgin Procula, and then aided her in disposing of the unwanted child by abortion.

He was also said to have presided at mixed gatherings of men and women who came together at night in the woods of the large estate belonging to the mother of Procula. There, after preliminary prayers in the nude, they conducted their intimate rites, which were of a magical and sexual nature.

Priscillian denied most of these charges, but his denial was dismissed since it was further alleged that he himself taught that strict truthfulness was obligatory only among sect members. Concealment of their teaching was essential, and they could swear and perjure themselves provided they did not betray the secrets. They could believe in one thing in private and say something else in public, and thus openly deny their deepest convictions.

Mandaeans

This sect, whose teachings reveal a syncretism of many faiths, is often confused or identified with the Sabians, Nazoreans, Johannites and others. They probably originated in an area east of the Jordan, then migrated to northern Mesopotamia and thence again to the region south of Baghdad, where they still survive, the only gnostic sect still in existence.

In their belief God, the 'great life', dwells in the realm of light. Under him are numerous intermediate beings called *uthras* or emanations from the divine source, who mediate between God and man. The most important of these beings is Hibil-Ziwa, or Manda (Aramaic for 'gnosis'), or Manda da Hayye, 'Gnosis of Life', who is the chief mediator and redeemer. He has made his appearance on earth in a series of incarnations, among them Abel, Seth, Enoch, and finally Yahya, or John the Baptist, the true prophet.

The chief of the evil beings is the demiurge who fashioned the world. He is known as Ptah-il, from the Egyptian deity Ptah and the Semitic *il*, 'god'; and sometimes as Adonai. Among the false teachers and prophets of the evil spirit are Abraham, Noah, Moses and also Jesus, who they said falsified the message of his master John the Baptist. Later, Muhammad too was included among the false prophets.

Their sacred books, such as the *Ginza* (c. AD 700), 'treasure', are replete with cosmological and magical lore. They repudiated most of the Jewish scriptures, and their own writings have a pronounced anti-Jewish bias. They disapproved of circumcision and rejected Sabbath observance. They also strongly attacked Christian monasticism, whose enforced celibacy they regarded as a form of infanticide. They had a high regard for marriage and encouraged procreation.

The Mandaeans practice baptism by total immersion in living, that is, running, water, and all such water is spoken of as the Jordan. They avoid stagnant water, as well as the troubled waters of the sea. Frequent baptisms are a feature of the Mandaen cult.

9.

THE GNOSTIC INFLUENCE

The history of gnosticism after the early Christian centuries is outside the scope of this book. What will be attempted here is a brief chronology that will roughly indicate the main areas of its expansion, its effect on other religions, and its influence on modern thought.

It is a historical fact that the new creed spread with remarkable rapidity. W. H. C. Frend writes that 'in the second century gnosticism was a world-wide movement' (1965, p. 62). There were gnostic sects in Asia Minor, Syria, Palestine, Rome, Egypt, Carthage, Spain and Gaul. In the latter province, Lyons became a focus of heresy and has remained so until recent times.

Its progress eastwards was equally rapid. Jacques Lacarrière says, 'No sooner was gnostic thought born than it began to be disseminated along the great routes of the Orient' (1977, p. 43). It is to be remembered that the flourishing outposts of Christian missionary activity that dotted the trade routes into Arabia, Parthia, Persia, Bactria, India, the western borders of Tibet, and still further east into Central Asia and China, propagated not so much orthodox Christianity as forms regarded by the Church as heretical, and largely gnostic.

Wherever it went gnosticism left a vast legacy, the full extent of which is only now coming to light. Orthodox Christianity itself, as well as the two other great monotheistic religions, Judaism and Islam, no less than Buddhism and Hinduism, received their portion of the gnostic bequest. It likewise gave an impetus to mystical schools like the Hermetics, philosophical schools like the Neoplatonists, and religious movements like the Manicheans. We shall briefly consider each of these in turn.

Judaism and Christianity

It has been established that a number of post-Christian messianic and apocalyptic Jewish texts were written under gnostic influence. And so were some of the mystical writings of the Jews. The great modern authority on the kabala, Gershom Scholem, refers to certain types of Hebrew mysticism as Jewish gnosticism.

The rabbinical texts speak out strongly against the *minim* or sectarians who flagrantly disregard the religious observances, feast days, the sabbath and circumcision, and give expression to theories based on some secret knowledge outside the Pentateuch. According to Professor M. Friedländer, the heretics against whom the rabbis directed their attacks in the first and second centuries were Jewish gnostics.

The rabbis warned, 'He who speculates on what is above and what is below, what was before and what comes after, and he who does not spare the honour of the Creator, would better not have been born.' These and related matters placed under rabbinic condemnation, were of obvious gnostic provenance. Already before the middle of the second century metaphysical speculation concerning the beginning (Heb. *bereshit*), the divine chariot (Heb. *merkaba*), and the heavenly mansions (Heb. *hekalot*) was well under way. During the same period Rabbi Akiba (d. AD 127) drew up the outlines of a treatise that was to become famous some centuries later, as the *Sefer Yetzira*. Other kabalists developed, in often fanciful ways, the symbolism of the gnostic decad (ten) in their elaborate scheme of the ten sefirot. The gnostic factor has never since been relinquished in kabalism.

Through the ages many Jewish and semi-Jewish reformist and mystical sects, who set out to purge the Hebrew religion of its rigid formalism, took on a gnostic tinge. Thus, the Magharians of Egypt and Mesopotamia, who are referred to as gnostic Jews, believed in the existence of a high God who is good and an angel-creator who is evil. Many parts of the Old Testament were attributed by them to the inspiration of this angel-creator and not to God (Yamauchi, 1973, p. 158). Again, the Karaites, who flourished in Mesopotamia from the eighth to twelfth centuries, opposed Hebrew phylacterism, talmudism and the inequality of women, and gave a great fillip to kabalist studies. They held that Jesus, among others, was a true prophet who brought an authentic message of redemption. And there were many others.

planet wheel

The Christian inheritance was even more abundant. There are few unorthodox, schismatic or heretical movements in Christian history that cannot be traced back to gnostic sources. There can be little doubt that gnosticism has a central place in the western religious tradition.

Gnostics were the first commentators on St John and St Paul. The early Church sharpened its critical weapons and strengthened its own defences as a result of controversy with rival groups, mainly gnostic. Under gnostic inspiration it drew up an authoritative list of scriptural texts (a canon), and an authoritative formula of faith (a creed). There grew up a Church hierarchy authorized to interpret the scriptures and so put a stop to the free interpretation encouraged by the gnostics and their congeners.

To lend support to their doctrines gnostic teachers were often concerned with tracing their authority through a succession of masters back to the apostles. By the second century the gnostic device of the apostolic succession was adopted by orthodox Christianity (Johnson, 1976, p. 52). The gnostics regarded the Church bishops as empty vessels and 'waterless canals', including the Bishop of Rome who to start with was a minor official first heard of in the second century, though later to claim supreme status and infallibility as the Pope.

It was in opposition to the gnostics that the Church emphasized the unity of the Bible, and the relevance of the Old Testament as a foreshadowing of the New and God's inspired word. In a number of other lesser matters, too, the gnostics left their mark on the church. For example, the gnostic custom of dedicating each day of the year to one of the archons was followed by the Church naming saints in the daily calendar.

Hinduism and Buddhism

Christian missionary activity in India began at the very commencement of the Christian era. Two of Christ's disciples, Thomas and Bartholomew carried the gospel to India. By the end of the second century Christian settlements extended along the western coast of the subcontinent (Walker, I, 1968, p. 238), and had already begun to have a formative influence on certain aspects of Hinduism and Buddhism. About that time too, Pantaenus (c. 189), who had converted Clement of Alexandria, brought a gnostic form of Christianity to India.

Only a single item need be mentioned in order to illustrate

Zurvanite - Mithras bridge

the impact of gnostic thought on Hinduism. This is from the *Bhagavad-Gita,* the famous Hindu text embodying a kind of Krishna gospel. Although it has sometimes been extravagantly dated to several millennia BC, it is well established that this work could not have received its first outlines before AD300, and was in fact little heard of till the ninth century. Here we find the first clear presentation in Hindu writings of the idea of the descent of a deity incarnate in human form and assuming the qualities of the saviour of all mankind, with faith (Sanskrit, *bhakti*) as an essential element in the redemptive scheme.

The claims made by Krishna about himself are very much like those found in the Christian gospels: All things are made by me. I am the way. I am the light. I am the first and the last. Those who worship me with devotion are in me, and I too am in them. Here also we find the characteristic gnostic imagery, when Krishna is transfigured and appears to his disciple Arjuna in a blaze of glory, brighter than the light of a thousand suns.

mithra The same motif is found in Mahayana Buddhism, where Buddha becomes the incarnation of a transcendent pre-existent Buddha. He becomes the Buddha of Boundless Light, and in a glorious transfiguration, a blinding effulgence surrounds him as he delivers his secret sermons to his disciples on the sacred mountain. Like Christ, Buddha becomes the Dharma (Truth) made flesh (Hick, 1977, p. 167). Humbling himself, he mixes with the lowest, with courtesans and outcasts. His birth, career and death are docetic, for Buddha has only an apparent and not a real body.

Although the historical Buddha died almost five centuries before the birth of Christ, the Buddha concept of Mahayana Buddhism only evolved during the first three centuries following the fourth Buddhist council convened by the Kushan king Kanishka in AD 120, and it was during this time that Mahayana took on its many gnostic features. The British scholar Edward Conze lists a large number of striking similarities between gnosticism and Mahayana Buddhism (see Bianchi, 1970, p. 651 et seq.).

In Mahayana we find many concepts not native to the Indian tradition, and new to the Buddhist faith. Ignorance or *agnosia* (Sanskrit, *avidya*) is the root of all evil. Salvation comes through gnosis (Sanskrit, *jnana*). Both gnosis and jnana are derived from the same Indoeuropean root. The idea of the 'soul' and its salvation are alien to pre-Mahayana Buddhism. Again, the notion of the soul being 'called' or 'awakened', and the comparison of the soul with untarnishable gold, are derived from gnosticism. There is a threefold division of mankind into those destined for salvation, those destined for perdition, and those whose destiny is not fixed either way. The eminent Buddhist authority Giuseppe Tucci assumed a gnostic influence in this respect, and, says Conze, 'I am prepared to agree with him' (Bianchi, 1970, p. 655).

While a claim for equally strong influences in the reverse direction, that is, from east to west, has frequently been put forward, the evidence is meagre by comparison. Gnostics revelled in the diversity of their views; they did not hesitate to reveal the sources of their doctrines, and such sources are acknowledged wherever known. Says Conze, 'It is indeed remarkable that gnostic texts often invoke Jewish, Babylonian, Iranian, Egyptian and other authorities, but very rarely Buddhist ones' (Bianchi, 1970, p. 665).

Islam

Islam like the other major religions received its share of the gnostic endowment. Long before the birth of Muhammad in AD 570, Christian communities had already been established in the Hejaz in the west by missionaries of the Abyssinian church, in the Yemen in the east and along the Persian Gulf by missionaries from India, and in the north on the borders of Iraq by missionaries from the Byzantine empire.

The kind of Christianity that was being propagated, however, was not that of western Christendom, but one or other of the many schismatic forms, especially those with a strong Nestorian or gnostic bias, and it was these that exercised their influence on the newly born faith of Islam. So when Islam spread to Iraq, for instance, it became coloured by various gnostic doctrines (Gibb, 1975, p. 73), clearly as a result of gnostic influences prevailing there.

Muhammad was familiar with the work and teachings of the missionaries. At the time of his persecution by fellow Arabs he received help and encouragement from them. He spoke appreciatively of Christian monks whose hermitages shone like lights in the desert (Parrinder, 1976, p. 130). One of his wives was a Christian, Mary the Copt, the mother of his son Ibrahim, who died young.

His knowledge about the birth, infancy, life and teachings of

Jesus were derived from apocryphal and gnostic sources. The death of Jesus was docetic or only apparent. As the Koran says, 'They crucified him not, but they only had his likeness' (4:156). In the Islamic tradition, Jesus was carried up alive, and is enthroned in heaven.

The influence of the gnostics is of course most conspicuously seen in Sufism. Islam itself was opposed to monasticism, and the Sufi orders were therefore not regarded as being in the true Islamic tradition, and were long proscribed by the orthodox theologians. One of the earliest Sufi mystics, **Ibrahim bin Adham** (d. 777) was instructed by a Christian anchorite, Father Simeon, in the means of acquiring gnosis (Arabic, *maarifa*). This opened another avenue for the Sufi mystics who followed, leading ultimately to the wholly un-Islamic Logos doctrine in which the Logos is made incarnate in Muhammad.

It is noteworthy that medieval Christian scholastics did not look upon Muslims as members of an alien or non-Christian faith, but rather as those who had broken away from a fundamentally Christian doctrine. They were regarded as heretics and seceders, and not as heathens. In denying the divinity of Christ, which Muslims did with consistent emphasis, they were not far from the position of many Christian theologians who were condemned on that score by the Church as schismatics.

Hermetics and Neoplatonists
The most important of the mystical schools with a gnostic affiliation is represented by a compendium of anonymous Greek writings from Egypt known as the *Hermetica* or Hermetic Corpus, preserved in manuscripts dating from the fourteenth century and later. For long the origin of these texts was uncertain, but they are now known to be 'the work of Gnosticizing Platonists probably contemporary with Valentinus and the Sethians' (Layton, 1981, p. xi).

The compendium is named after Hermes Trismegistus, 'Hermes the Thrice-Greatest', Hermes being the Greek name for the Egyptian god Thoth. It comprises a collection of astrological, magical and mystical material, the best known texts being the *Divine Pymander* (or Poimandres), *Asclepius,* the *Perfect Word,* and the *Secret Discourse on the Mount.* In broad terms, the hermetic writings tell of a God who is incorporeal, formless and invisible. The act of creation was mediated through a luminous

Logos or Word who is the Son of God. There also exist certain lesser divinities and rulers of the spheres as his agents. The soul of man was created in God's image but became enamoured of matter and was imprisoned in flesh and darkness. Man can free himself from despair through faith, from concupiscence through love, from greed through generosity, and above all, from ignorance through knowledge.

The last major school of pagan philosophy, **Neoplatonism**, originated in Alexandria in the third century AD. It was strongly eclectic, based to some extent on Pythagoras and Plato, with admixtures from Aristotle and the Stoics, and religious and mystical ideas from Judaism and the religions of the middle east.

Although some Neoplatonists were hostile to the gnostics they all had gnostic pupils, and in fact the whole movement was saturated with gnosticism. **Plotinus** (d. 268) was strongly opposed to certain gnostic beliefs and wrote a treatise against them, but his work reflects a number of gnostic ideas, and through him these ideas entered the mainstream of western religious philosophy.

The philosophy of Neoplatonism was one of divine revelation and unfolding. The creation of the world closely followed the gnostic theory of emanations. From the fullness of the Divine Unity emerged Nous or Pure Intelligence, and from Nous emerged the World Soul. All else emanated as an overflow from this heavenly triad. The human soul is of divine origin but clothed in a material vesture, and as a result is tainted, tarnished, gross and dark. It was the individual's duty to cleanse the soul of these gross accretions, so that it might return to God.

Asceticism, fasting and chastity were advocated in order to purge the soul of its many impurities. Plotinus was noted for his declaration that 'he blushed that he had a body'. Great value was attached to ecstatic experience and supernatural inspiration through the cultivation of the psychic faculties.

Neoplatonists like the Phoenician **Porphyry** (d. 304) and the Syrian **Iamblichus** (d. 333) together transformed Neoplatonism from a philosophical theory into a system of theurgy, magic and demonology. They laid emphasis on ritual procedures, the use of talismans, seals, spells, incantations and other appurtenances of ceremonial magic. They developed methods of inducing xenophrenic or strange-minded states, bringing about possession, pre-mortem experience, hypnotic sleep, and deep trance, very much like that of the modern spiritualist medium.

The Thracian **Proclus** (d. 485), besides a preoccupation with the occult, also reaffirmed the privative philosophy of the gnostics, stating that God is non-being, and can only be understood, if at all, by negatives. His disciple was said to have been the unidentified writer who took the name of St Paul's Athenian convert, **Dionysius the Areopagite** (Acts 17:34), but who is better known as the Pseudo-Dionysius (c. 500). His works introduced much of Neoplatonism and gnosticism into the Church, including such ideas as the unknowable God, the *via negativa,* and the angelic hierarchy.

Manicheism

This religion was named after its founder, the Persian sage Mani of Ecbatana (215–276). His father was a member of the Mughtasila, 'those who wash themselves', an ascetic baptismal sect of simple gnostic tendencies, perhaps related to the Mandaeans. Mani received an excellent education, took a special interest in religious studies, and had some acquaintance with gnosticism, having been influenced by the teachings of the Elkesaites.

The chief feature of Mani's creed was its dualism, inherited from the older established religion of Zoroaster. There were also the usual elements of gnosticism: God the ruler of light, Satan the ruler of darkness; the great struggle between the two principles; the creation of Adam; his imprisonment by Satan in a material body. Abraham and Moses were said to have been misled by Satan. The Pentateuch, being largely the work of the devil, was rejected.

Among the early biblical figures, Adam, Seth and Noah were regarded as prophets and messengers. In addition, God sent down two more prophets, Zoroaster and Buddha, so that other nations too might receive the message of light. But none of these was able to help man successfully to combat the forces of darkness. God therefore sent down a being created from his own substance, Christ, who preached the means by which men could claim their divine inheritance. The Jews were incited by Satan to put Christ to death, and he was finally, though only apparently, crucified. Jesus, the virtuous son of a widow took his place, while the true Christ, his mission accomplished, returned to the realms above.

Christ's objective, though successful, needed confirmation, so God sent the last in the line of messengers, Mani, the quintessence of all the prophets. Those who follow the path he set out will be liberated after death, and the light-particle of their being, their soul, will return to the habitation of light.

The Manicheans laid great emphasis on self-control and asceticism, and on the whole opposed marriage, sensual indulgence, the eating of animal food and the drinking of wine. The followers were divided into three orders. The first were the Perfect, the elect or true, who were the chosen priesthood, comprising celibate monks and nuns who lived apart from the world. The second were the Credenters or lay believers of long standing, who were allowed to marry but strictly regulated their sexual relations. The third group were the Auditors or hearers, who lived a normal life but avoided any form of killing and adhered to the principles of Manichean ethics.

While most other gnostic cults of the time were open only to approved initiates, Manicheism was a religion open to all. It therefore spread with extraordinary rapidity. Its missionaries moved westwards through Mesopotamia, Arabia and Egypt, carrying their creed to North Africa and the Roman empire, and gaining numbers of Christian converts. St Augustine (d. 430) was a Manichean 'hearer' for nine years before he was converted to the Christian faith of his mother Monica.

Eastwards, Manicheism spread through Iran, Afghanistan, India, Chinese Turkestan and Central Asia to China. It even took root in western Tibet and influenced the indigenous pre-Buddhist Bon and Lamaist religions of that country. In China it persisted from the seventh to the fourteenth centuries. The Uighur Turks were converted in the early eighth century and in 762 made it their state religion. Manicheans were extensively employed by the Muslims, who respected their zeal, their integrity, their knowledge of astronomy, medicine and mathematics, and their proficiency in the arts. Indeed, Manichean influence was felt in Christianity, Buddhism and Islam for over a thousand years.

The Cathars

The collective name, meaning 'the pure ones', assumed by or given to a number of heretical Christian sects that flourished between the third and eleventh centuries in Armenia, Syria, Asia Minor and the Balkans, and from there spread to western Europe.

Their beliefs varied from sect to sect, but they all shared certain features in common, mostly stemming from gnosticism. Like the gnostics they were dualist in theology and ascetic in practice. They believed in God the Father, the principle of all that is good, and in his son the Logos, or Christ the Saviour. The material world was the creation of Satan, and the Old Testament recorded the deceits practiced by Satan on Moses and the prophets.

The Cathars were uncompromising opponents of the whole ecclesiastical hierarchy, the liturgy and the sacraments. They rejected the worship of the Virgin Mary, and of icons and images, including the cross. In their eyes the established Church was the 'synagogue of Satan', and the altar the mouth of hell. The corrupt, luxury-loving, avaricious and immoral popes and clergy were the lackeys of the devil. In the same tradition of dissent, they opposed the pomps and vanities of the nobility and the whole state organization of magistrates and civil authorities because they upheld and supported the Church.

For their part, the ecclesiastical authorities accused the Cathars of celebrating a travesty of the Christian mass, of diabolism, sorcery, incest and sodomy. Unorthodox sects of any denomination who were subjected to persecution in later times were often conveniently accused of belonging to the congregation of the Cathars.

The central Cathar rite was the *consolamentum,* a kind of adult baptism of the spirit, which was administered only once. It was reserved as a rule for those who had attained the level of the Perfect, but it could be given to any Cathar prepared to make an irrevocable renunciation of the flesh and consecrate his or her life to God. The rite was preceded by a fast and imparted by the laying on of hands and placing on the head the gospel of St John.

If anyone sinned after being 'consoled', he was expelled from the Cathar communion. So strict were the requirements that many Cathars only underwent the rite at the point of death, so as to avoid any further chance of sinning. Because it was generally held that death through illness or old age only proved that Satan was still in control of the body, some Cathars hastened the end by what was called the *endura,* a ritual suicide or killing. It was thought best to be purified by the consolamentum and then face the endura, for then salvation was certain. The methods of endura included fasting to death or taking poison, or being smothered by one or more of the Perfect who held a pillow over the mouth of the endurist, or strangled him.

Almost thirty Cathar sects are listed in historical writings, of which only a few need be mentioned here. They were often pietist, mendicant and itinerant, but varied in their practices. In certain fundamental beliefs they were all united: that the material world was created by a god of evil, and that procreation advanced the work of Satan.

The **Paulicans** of Phrygia and Thrace rejected the church sacraments and were strongly iconoclastic. Associated with them were the Populani, Publicani and the Patarenes who spread to northern Italy. The last named sect originated in the Balkans where for a time their creed represented the state religion of Bosnia.

The **Messalians** or praying people, of Syria and Mesopotamia were named from the Aramaic word for prayer. They taught the importance of intoning the Lord's Prayer without ceasing, for in this way one became an enthusiast (God-imbued) and drove the devil out of the system. The Messalians of Asia Minor and Macedonia were called Euchites, from the Greek word for prayer. Their tendency to chant and do little else gave these sects a reputation for laziness. The Choreutes combined their prayer rhythms with certain mystic dances. These were performed to the accompaniment of rustic musical instruments played in the wild Phrygian mode, which in pagan times used to accompany the orgiastic mysteries of the goddess Cybele. They stamped on the ground, leapt high in the air, and boasted that they were trampling on demons. The dance ended in a bacchanalian debauch (Lacarrière, 1977, p. 111).

The **Athingani** ('non-touching') sect of Phrygia and Bulgaria were obsessed with avoiding defilement in any form, laid much stress on ritual purity, and kept strictly to themselves. In some places they acquired a sinister reputation and were commonly believed to be magicians and adepts in the occult arts. Their name, corrupted to Tsigane, was applied to the wandering gipsy tribes when they first appeared in the Byzantine empire in the middle of the ninth century (see Runciman, 1960, p. 183).

The **Bogomils** (Slav, 'God-beloved') of Bulgaria and the Balkans, preached the sinfulness of procreating, and the extreme branch encouraged homosexuality as an alternative to marriage. As a result their name passed into the slang vocabulary of the European vernaculars, where bogar, bougre, bugar and bugger became synonyms for sodomist.

These Cathar and quasi-Cathar sects spread via Bulgaria and the Balkans to Russia, to influence the various Russian heresies that will be considered later; and westwards to Italy and southern France to influence the Albigensians. With the Waldenses (Vaudois), Hussites, Wycliffites and Lollards, the Cathars, now greatly modified in their theological teachings, returned to the Christian fold, though in its Protestant form.

The **Albigensians**, the Cathar sect best known in Western Europe, are named after their headquarters in the Albi district northwest of Toulouse. Zealous, hardworking and skilful in many crafts, they prospered exceedingly and in time attracted the envious attention of the Church. Attempts to convert them having failed, they were subjected to violent persecution. Their rich lands were laid waste, their beautiful towns destroyed, and they themselves very nearly exterminated.

When in an attack against one of their unprotected towns, Beziers, in 1209, the monk-legate, the Abbot of Citeaux, was asked whether the followers of the True Church should be spared, and how they were to be distinguished from the heretics, he replied, 'Slay them all, the Lord will know his own'. The fall of the fortress-town of Montségur (the Mount Tabor of the Cathars) in the Pyrenees in 1244 marked the end of the Albigensians. When the fort was taken some 200 persons, mostly women, were captured. They refused to abjure their faith, were herded into a pallisade and burned alive.

The Cathars have been called the earliest precursors of the Reformation, for by their example they set a pattern for many changes the Church was obliged to adopt. The example of strict celibacy set by the Perfect finally imposed celibacy on the Roman Catholic priesthood. The sacrament of extreme unction was introduced after the Cathar rite of consolamentum. The constant polemic of the Cathar teachers against the cruelty, rapacity and irascibility of the 'Jewish tribal god', led the Roman Church to prohibit the circulation of the Old Testament among laymen. Scholars speak of their influence on the Catholic Church as enormous. J. A. MacCulloch refers to the Cathars as 'once formidable rivals to western Catholicism in southern France and other parts of Europe'.

At the same time there were many elements in Catharism that were open to a perverse interpretation, and during the

centuries of their persecution it was common to accuse anyone
who opposed the Church of being sympathetic to the Cathars,
for the term covered a multitude of heresies. The Templars, the
Witches, Diabolists, Luciferans, Satanists and similar secret
fraternities all in turn were charged, among other crimes, with
belonging to 'accursed sects' such as the gnostics, Manichees
and Cathars.

Troubadours

The literary wing, as it were, of the Cathar movement might be
said to be represented by the goliards and the troubadours. The
former were an impecunious version of the more courtly
troubadours, and for the most part were poor wandering
scholars, usually clerks in minor orders whose songs in praise of
wine, gaming and girls concealed a form of popular anti-clerical
Christianity, together with many features of the Albigensian
heresy.

The troubadours, on the other hand, emerged from the more
noble chivalric traditions of the twelfth and thirteenth centuries.
They were well represented in the Cathar-dominated regions of
Provence, and spread through France and beyond, to Italy,
Spain, England, Germany and Northern Europe. Both spiritual
and carnal elements were prominent in their beliefs, with
influences traceable to the pagan philosophers, to the gnostics,
and more directly to the Cathars.

What is known as troubadour love or courtly love was a form
of sexual morality that was a strange amalgam of gnostic
encratism or erotic restraint, of coitus reservatus and, at the
same time, of free love that permitted sodomy and adultery.
The verses addressed by the troubadour to the Virgin Mary
might implore her to sleep beside the husband whom the poet
wished to cuckold, so that the wife would be free to visit him at
night.

It was strongly woman-dominated and the so-called courts of
love that decided on issues of social and sexual behaviour were
made up largely of women, although the troubadours themselves were male. And here again their poems, songs and ballad-
chronicles, often veiled in double and treble meanings,
concealed religious tenets of dubious orthodoxy.

That the movement had a profoundly spiritual conscience
and expressed strong ascetic ideals is supported by the fact that
many people of deep religious sensitivity were drawn to its

ranks. St Francis of Assisi (d. 1226) has been called the greatest of the troubadours. He exchanged the rich dress of his pleasure-loving days for the rags of a beggar, dedicated his life to Dame Poverty, and to the subjugation of Brother Ass the body. He loved the Provençal poetry of the French troubadours and made use of Provençal as a nobler dialect than his native Umbrian. He is regarded as a 'genuine troubadour' in the sense that the troubadours were inspired by the Albigensian heresy. Throughout his ministry the Church treated him with some suspicion, and his successor Father Elias was eventually excommunicated for allegedly favouring schism.

The poet Dante Alighieri (d. 1321) was likewise thought in his time to be not of the orthodox persuasion. He was indeed a great fount of heresy, sympathetic both to the Templars (Roguemont, 1940, p. 120) and to the Albigensians (Bayley, 1909, p. 61). He knew Provençal well enough to write in it, ardently studied the writings of the troubadours, and was himself dubbed 'a late troubadour'.

10.

THE ELEUTHERIANS

This term, from the Greek word for 'free', is sometimes used to designate a number of sects and cults that rose to prominence in Europe from the middle ages, mainly carrying on the teachings and practices of the libertine branch of the gnostic religion.

They were dualistic, in the sense that they were extremely conscious of the rule of Satan in this world. The Evil One was behind all hatreds, all feelings of guilt and sin, all social distinctions, and all strife and violence. One could only be freed from his jurisdiction through the power of the Holy Spirit. They found biblical support for their beliefs in such verses as, 'Stand fast in the liberty wherewith Christ hath made us free, and be not entangled again with the yoke of bondage' (Gal. 5:1); and 'Where the Spirit of the Lord is, there is liberty' (2 Cor. 3:17).

At various times and places the Eleutherians were known by various names. Thus, they were the **Brethren of the Free Spirit,** because they believed they were free from the toils of Satan and free in the freedom of the Holy Spirit. They regarded themselves as **Homines Intelligentiae,** that is, men (and women) of knowledge (gnosis), filled with spiritual understanding. They were also called **Perfectionists,** because, following the injunction of Christ, 'Be ye perfect' (Matt. 5:48), they held that the state of perfection was open to all believers. Since they strove to emulate the blessed state of Adam and Eve before the Fall, they were known as **Adamites.** And since they stood in opposition to organized religious and social laws, they were branded as Antinomians.

Though generally against secular learning they were zealous students of Scripture, which they believed each person had the right to interpret in his own way. They were communistic in outlook, maintaining that except for small personal items, all things should be shared in common. People should give up the idea of *meum et tuum*, 'mine and thine', for this was a relic of the Mosaic law. Their economic creed was, 'Let us have one purse'. Staunch advocates of the simple life, they disdained riches. From time to time they would make a bonfire of their possessions, so following the example of those who 'take joyfully the despoiling of their goods' (Heb. 10:34).

In worship, they practised an ecstatic pentecostalism, encouraged xenophrenic ('strange-minded') states, spoke in tongues and publcly confessed their sins. They claimed to have visions and divine revelations under the inspiration of the Holy Spirit. This divine power, they believed, manifested itself especially during periods of silence and prayer.

Many were adventists, believing that the millennium was imminent, or had already begun. The New Jerusalem was to be established on earth, and the place of Christ's descent was to be Mount Tabor, the mount of the transfiguration, which could in fact be anywhere. The so-called Taborite branch of the Eleutherians was prominent in Bohemia.

Their views on sin and sinning were based on the gnostic idea of the perfect and the damned. Man, they said, is either in a state of sinlessness or sinfulness. Those who achieve perfection are in a state of grace and cannot sin, for they are incapable of sin. They have overcome Satan and are beyond good and evil. The sinful must learn that there can be no redemption without sin. Sinning is a means of salvation. God desires that the Holy Spirit shall work in the heart of man and yearns to forgive the repentant sinner. The self-righteous he plunges into the mire (Job 9:31). It is only through sinning, followed by true repentance that one becomes perfect. Thereafter one can yield without sin or remorse to the needs of the flesh. As regenerate Christians, sanctified by the Holy Spirit, the law is no longer operative, and they can sin no more.

Marriage was generally denounced as an imperfect state. It was held that the parties bound by the marriage contract are the prisoners of convention. Married love cannot lead to the ecstasy and bliss sought by the aspirants to the topmost spiritual heights. It is a selfish bond, and one that restricts the couple to a monotonous allowance sanctioned by law. Men and women are created to share in one another. Adultery possessed a symbolic value, as an affirmation of emancipation. Married men should make their wives available to all.

As nudity was the condition of Adam and Eve in the garden of Eden, many Eleutherians made it obligatory at their meetings. Nudity was a form of revelation and truth. In some sects the preacher preached naked to a naked congregation. Such occasions usually ended with a feast followed by indiscriminate sexuality. Uninhibited sexual intercourse was regarded as an expression of spiritual freedom raising one to 'the delight of Paradise'. Fornication has a mystical quality that can transform it into a sacrament. Approached in the right spirit it can be likened to a prayer in the sight of God.

The love experience between the 'perfect' was a sanctified love, and sanctification precludes sin. Like the gnostics the Eleutherians held that every kind of sexual activity should be permitted. Family relationships or the sex of the partner should not be a hindrance. A man could unite with his mother, sister or daughter. Again, if a man desired to commit sodomy with either sex he should be free to do so.

In normal heterosexual union, coitus reservatus or intercourse without orgasm was advocated. This form of pure forepleasure was meant to recapture the sublime eroticism of Adam and Eve before the Fall. Such spiritualized intercourse was known as acclivity, or the ascent to God in sexual union (Fränger, 1952, p. 21), and was related to the gnostic rite of the upward flowing Jordan.

One of the earliest proponents of the Eleutherian creed was **Amalric of Bena** (d. 1209), who believed it was the task of the free in spirit to inaugurate the era of love for all those in whom, as in themselves, the incarnation of the Holy Spirit had already taken place, and who were free. The sect was anti-clerical, practised free love, sex mysticism, incest and coitus reservatus. Amalric was condemned as a heretic and forced to make a public recantation.

In the beginning of the thirteenth century there arose in France, Holland and Germany, a mendicant organization known as the **Beghards** (the fraternity of men) and the **Beguines** (women) of definite Catharist sympathies. The word beggar is probably derived from their name (Cohn, 1970, p. 159). They advocated nudity and encratic love, or sexuality 'uncontaminated by the final degrading climax'. Condemned as heretics a number of them were burned at the stake. By the fourteenth century the Beghards were heard of no more, but the Beguines, after a reformation in their ranks, survived as a respected pietist group.

In about 1380 a 'Valentinian' sect known as the Society of the Poor, but dubbed the **Turlupins**, gained a following in Flanders, France and Savoy. They too lived in nudist camps in the woods and practised promiscuous sex. Several of their persuasion were caught and burned at the stake in Paris, along with their scriptures.

Another Adamite group were the **Picards**, a name derived either from Picardy in France, or from the Beghards. Their leader assumed the title of Picard the Prophet (c. 1415), took as his sexual partner a woman he addressed as the Mother of God. Together they preached nudity and sexual freedom, in anticipation of the second coming and the establishment of the New Jerusalem.

Martin Houska (d. 1421) planted the Free Spirit in Bohemia, probably brought from the west by the Picards. He envisaged a millenarian society, and spoke of the Second Coming as a wedding feast of the elect. After his triumphal return from heaven on Mount Tabor, now said to be in Bohemia, Christ would prepare a great Banquet of the Lamb as a nuptial feast for his Bride, the Church. Houska too was tried and condemned to be burned at the stake.

The end of the fifteenth century saw the rise of yet another flourishing Eleutherian sect in the Low Countries. The Dutch painter **Hieronymus Bosch** (d. 1516) was a member, and his famous triptych *The Garden of Earthly Delights,* now in the Prado, Madrid, is thought to be a portrayal of the Adamite vision of sexual emancipation preached by them.

From about 1520 the sect of the **Anabaptists** rose to prominence in Germany. It represented the extreme left of the Protestant party, and like the Eleutherians, advocated free love, polygamy and nudity. They were guilty of cruel excesses against those who opposed them, with the result that when their centres, notably at Münster, were captured, their leaders were put down with atrocious savagery.

The **Alumbrado** sect, named from a Spanish word for 'enlightened', first came into prominence in Spain in the fifteenth century, to reach its zenith in the following century. They were quietist, dispensed with holy images, opposed private property and the privileges of birth and title, and in the early years attracted many orthodox theologians. An extremist branch of the Alumbrados at Toledo, led by a 'sibylline woman' named Francisca Hernandez, practised a form of sexual mysticism. One disciple interrogated at his trial, declared that after intercourse with her, 'I learned more wisdom than if I had studied for twenty years in Paris. For not Paris, but only Paradise could teach that wisdom' (Fränger, 1952, p. 20). Many later sects are traced to the Alumbrados.

Heinrich Niclaes (d. 1581) of Amsterdam introduced an esoteric love rite which he celebrated in his mystical temple of love. According to him, Moses had entered only the forecourt of the temple, Christ the inner temple, but he, Niclaes, had penetrated the holy of holies. Under persecution Niclaes fled to England and here founded a society known as the **Familists,** or Family of Love, which survived till the following century. They were frequently attacked in popular broadsheets.

In 1645 the nickname **Ranters** was given to a fanatical antinomian and communistic sect that for a time gained prominence in England, to be suppressed during the Commonwealth. They were so called because they would 'rant', blasphemously and wildly rage, against established morals and religion. They held that the commandments of the Old Testament were wiped out by the crucifixion, and henceforward men and women were free to indulge in sexual activity in any manner and with whomsoever they chose.

One of their members, **Jacob Bauthumley** (or Bottomley) wrote a pantheistic book entitled *The Light and Dark Sides of God* (1650), for which he was punished by being burned through the tongue. He declared that all things exist in God, and that sin is the dark side of God and is divine. The sinner sins in God; sin therefore cannot separate him from God.

Bauthumley's treatise gave expression to a view held by many Eleutherian groups. Sin, specifically with regard to sex, is relevant only in the human situation here below. If treated as one of the many faces of God, no 'immorality' can be attached to it. This teaching was reiterated again and again by many groups over the years. Only one instance of it need be given.

In 1781 it was found that the nuns of the Dominican convent of St Catherine in Prato, Italy, led by the prioress, Sister Spighi, were preaching Catharist doctrines. They declared that since man's soul partakes of the supreme essence it is immortal and divine, and therefore sinless and free. The love of man for woman is the noblest example of divine law, and the sexual act the most perfect fulfilment of it. So also, any person, man or woman, who, lifting up his or her spirit to God, has physical enjoyment with a person of the same sex, or alone, also fulfils the divine law.

Asked by the members of the shocked commission sent to enquire into the matter, where they had received their teaching, they replied, 'From the deep and honest searchings of our natural inclinations and of those around us.'

11.

THE MODERNS

The abbreviated chronology of the Eleutherians compiled so far could perhaps best be concluded by listing, again in highly abridged form, some of the chief cults in France, Russia and America, that have a gnostic flavour. These cults cover both the puritanical and libertine extremes of the gnostic movement.

France

This country seems to have had a marked predilection for the more sinister side of the gnostic and Cathar doctrine, and the unsavoury activities of secret societies with such tendencies continued to be uncovered from time to time from the early medieval period, reaching a climax of notoriety in the seventeenth century. The ringleaders were almost invariably renegade priests, who in addition to practising Adamism, free love and aberrant sexuality, were found guilty of witchcraft, desecrating the host, and conducting the black mass.

Among the most notorious were the two groups associated with the names of **Father Louis Gaufridi** (d. 1611) and **Father Urbain Grandier** (d. 1634), who were charged with seduction, idolatry, witchcraft and sorcery. They were condemned, tortured and burned at the stake (Huxley, 1952).

An equally infamous case centred around **Pierre David**, another priest, the superintendent of the Franciscan convent of Louviers, Normandy. He made the convent the headquarters of a diabolist circle whose activities came to light in 1642. Along with his assistants, Father Thomas Boullé, Sister Madelaine Bavent (Summers, 1933), and other priests and nuns, he used to celebrate the black mass in the nude, 'using sacramental wafers soaked in clots of menstrual blood', ending in a rite of perverse intercourse.

Perhaps the most outrageous of all such cases was that of **Catherine Deshayes** (Madame Montvoisin), poisoner, abortionist and diabolist, whose clientele included many personages prominent in the French court. Among the dozen or so apostate priests in her employ was the **Abbé Etienne Guibourg** (d. 1683), who perfected the formulary of certain perverse religious services that are among the most macabre of their class: the foetus mass, the placenta mass, the semen mass and the faeces mass. The trial (1679–82) of the chief culprits remains the most celebrated case of black magic and diabolism in history (see Robbins, 1959; Mossiker, 1970).

After a lapse of nearly two centuries the sinistral sects rose to prominence once again with the French visionary and occultist, **Pierre-Michel Eugène Vintras** (d. 1875), originator of the Vintrasian masses, notably the Sacrifice of the Glory of Melchizedek, and the Provictimal Sacrifice of Mary, also performed in the nude and celebrated, it was alleged, with chalices brimming with blood and sacramental wafers steeped in menstrual blood, and ending as always with sexual intercourse in its proscribed forms.

One of Vintras's followers, the **Abbé Joseph-Antoine Boullan** (d. 1893) founded his own occult circle, centred at Lyons, devoted to sex magic reputedly involving intercourse with 'celestified organs' and with incubi and succubi. There were the usual blasphemies against God and the use of consecrated hosts mixed with defecated matter and urine. Boullan appears in the famous novel *La-Bas* (1891) by the French writer Joris Karl Huysmans, as Father Johannes. Another contemporary black magician, the Belgian abbé, **Louis Van Haecke** (d. 1912), apostate priest and devil worshipper, was the original model of the sinister Canon Docre in the same novel.

One of Boullan's followers was the Polish mystic, **Feliksa Maria Kozlowska** (d. 1921) who founded the Mariavite sect, dedicated to the Virgin Mary. After her death her work was carried on by the Roman Catholic priest, **John Kowalski** (d. 1940), who went in for erotic mysticism, polygamous 'mystical marriages', and sex rituals with young and immature girls.

Vintrasian circles continued to operate in Lyons after the second world war, and are probably still active there, and it is thought that a Vintrasian group may be operating in London as well (Griffiths, 1966, p. 145).

Russia

In the latter half of the seventeenth century, a schism occurred within the Russian Orthodox Church, leading to the formation of a new sect called the Raskolniks (Russian, *raskol*, 'split'). The result was that many Russian dissident factions took courage from this split to found communities of their own, giving vent to religious ideas that had long been simmering underground.

By the beginning of the eighteenth century, there was a great proliferation of such sects and sub-sects throughout Russia. When Archbishop Dmitri of Rostov wrote a book on the subject in 1720, he listed no less than 200 of them (Hare, 1901, p. 296). Most of these represented a Slavonic version of the Eleutherian groups we have already considered, and a few owed their origins to the Bogomils, who had established themselves in southern Russia in the fourteenth century.

All these sects operated under the constant threat of persecution, and whenever their more extreme activities came to light they were treated with the most stringent severity, being subjected to confiscation of property, exile to Siberia, knouting, torture, and occasionally beheading. For the most part, they lived simply and avoided getting entangled with the Church or state. Like other such sects they tended to treat marriage as an accursed bond.

The Russian schismatics included the **Khlysti** or flagellants, who used to knout themselves with whips and chains. Also, the **Stranniki** or wanderers, who would suddenly and without warning burn their identity papers, leave their homes and wander off to far-off places, never writing to their families. The Siberian hypnotist-healer, **Gregori Rasputin** (d. 1916) was for a time a member of both these sects.

Then there were the **Greshniki** or peccatists, who believed in the redemptive power of sin. Accordingly, they freely indulged in the sins of the flesh, and then revelled in public confession. The **Bezglovesniki** or 'voiceless ones', maintained long periods of silence, when they spoke to no one for months, sometimes for years on end.

The **Morelshchiki** or 'death-ers', believed in the virtue of taking one's own life, which was done either by committing suicide, or allowing others to kill one. The leader of one group, Igor Koweleff, under instruction from a prophetess of the sect, carried out a mass interment, burying alive twenty-five volunteers in the backyard of a house, among them his mother, wife and daughter.

Hundreds of men and women belonging to this and related sects slashed their throats, pierced their hearts with daggers, hanged themselves, or starved to death. The sect of the **Krasnye Krestinnye** or Fire Baptists, would make their exit from the world by assembling with their families and friends in a house and setting fire to it over their heads. In one such mass holocaust, over 2700 men, women and children burned themselves in the Paleostrovski monastery.

The **Dukhobors** or 'spirit wrestlers', miscalled the Quakers of Russia, were prominent in the province where Madame H. P. Blavatsky (d. 1891), founder of the Theosophical Society, was born. The Dukhobors would express their protest against Church or state interference in their mode of life, by burning their own homes, and by long, often suicidal marches in the nude, even in midwinter. Their continued persecution aroused the sympathy of Leo Tolstoy, who was said to have written his novel *Resurrection* to obtain funds for their exodus from Russia. At the beginning of the present century many of them migrated to Canada.

The **Skoptsi** or castrants voluntarily underwent an operation which, in the case of men, included the surgical excision of scrotum or penis or both; and the excision of nipples, breasts, or the removal of the ovaries, in the case of women. The Skoptsi had a following of many hundreds of thousands, most of whom were not castrated but were in sympathy with the Skoptsi ideal. Such adherents remained celibate or, if married, lived lives of great austerity.

Many others were ecstatic sects who sought by starvation, flagellation and other means of self-mortification to attain ecstatic trance. In their *radenya* or 'joy-making' ceremonies they would strip off their clothes, dance, sing, shout, stamp their feet and whirl around as if possessed by the Holy Spirit.

America

The end of the eighteenth century saw the emergence of the 'freedom' sects in America, which by the middle of the nineteenth century had multiplied unchecked. In most cases their members, male and female, lived apart from the world and followed a simple communal life style.

They adopted many strange names: the Altruist Community, the Alphadelphia Phalanx, the One Mentians (signifying that all the members were of one mind), the Universologists, the

Grand Pantarchy, the Abecedarians (from a sixteenth-century German sect, who held that all learning, even the ABC, was superfluous), the Philoprogenitive Familists, the Nothingarians (no church, no government, no marriage, no money), the Mount Taborians. The American poet R. W. Emerson wrote to Thomas Carlyle in 1840, 'We are all a little wild here. Not a reading man but has the draft of a new community in his waistcoat pocket.'

The middle of the nineteenth century saw the rise of the Kissing sects, started by **Lucina Umphreville** (d. 1855), who propagated her ideas among the women of her community in New York State (Dixon, 1868). The purpose was to permit men to indulge with them in the so-called seraphic kiss, giving them every opportunity of close contact, short of actual intercourse, which was a 'work of the flesh' and to be avoided. The female members of the sect described the 'electric thrills', 'waves of glory' and 'storms of rapture' that swept them into spiritual bliss during the osculatory embrace.

A number of these societies also practiced Adamism and free sex. Their exponents condemned modesty as a mark of hypocrisy and corruption, because no one in whom the sight of a nude person of the opposite sex excited feelings of lust, unease, shame, or modesty, could be called pure.

This curious philosophy reached its zenith with the Perfectionists, founded at Oneida Creek, New York State, by **John Humphrey Noyes** (d. 1886). He introduced a system of 'complex marriage', under which wedded members had to surrender the 'ownership' of their wives and husbands, and each could cohabit with anyone they pleased. He stressed the benefits of coitus reservatus in preventing conception, promoting male continence, conserving male energy, gratifying the woman's needs, and at the same time providing a wonderful spiritual experience.

The Cultural Stream

As we have seen, gnosticism has been the fountain-head of many heretical movements and many unusual religious and sectarian practices.

Modern secret societies, no less than the medieval guilds, have their 'mysteries', many of which retain vestiges of what is clearly a gnostic endowment. The Dutch scholar Gilles Quispel discerns gnostic types of religiosity in the Rosicrucians and

Freemasons (Yamauchi, 1973, p. 17). According to another writer, Kenneth Rexroth, 'Alchemy was gnostic through and through' (Mead, 1960, p. xx).

The history of magic and the occult is crowded with the names of exponents having a distinctively gnostic cast of thought. In contemporary terms this is perhaps best exemplified in the career of the English mage **Aleister Crowley** (Symonds, 1951). Under his aegis a number of occult organizations sprang up, whose membership made up a constellation of men and women distinguished in literature, the theatre and the arts.

But to return to the main current of the European cultural tradition. The names of the scholastics and other men of learning whose works were condemned as heretical during the middle ages would constitute a roll call of some of the most eminent figures in medieval thought. Later still, strong gnostic elements are found in the work of mystics like Jakob Boehme, himself accused of heresy, and George Fox, who suffered persecution and imprisonment for his teachings; in poets like John Milton, whose great sonnet beginning, 'Avenge, O Lord! Thy slaughtered saints', was written on the massacre of the Cathars (Vaudois) in 1655. His *Paradise Lost* is almost an apotheosis of Satan. According to Blake, Milton was a true poet of the Devil's party without knowing it.

For his part, William Blake gave vivid and rapturous expression to opinions that are nothing if not gnostic. He spoke frankly of interpreting the Bible 'in its infernal or diabolical sense.' Other well-known poets, like Gérard de Nerval, Rainer Maria Rilke and W. B. Yeats, as well as several leading composers have been named in a similar context. Quispel called Mozart 'a later gnostic.'

Among the novelists we have Novalis, Honoré de Balzac, Fyodor Dostoevsky, Victor Hugo, Herman Melville, Leo Tolstoy and Franz Kafka. The German novelist Thomas Mann speaks of gnosticism as 'Man's truest knowledge of himself'.

Many social, political, even psychological trends, like Puritanism, Marxism, Communism, Nihilism, Nazism and Psychoanalysis have been spoken of in conjunction with the gnostics (Layton, 1980, p. 38). Scientists like Wolfgang Pauli, and certain modern scientific theories, have likewise been drawn into the gnostic ambit.

Among the philosophers we have Blaise Pascal, G. W. F. Hegel, Soren Kierkegaard and Friedrich Nietzsche. Invoking the perennial gnostic riddle, Kierkegaard questioned the purpose of 'this thing called the world', and asked why he had been created and thus compelled to participate in existence. Existentialism, of which he was one of the founding fathers, is rife with gnostic ideas, as more than one authority has pointed out.

C. G. Jung, whose intuitive mind ranged over a wide field covering many of the obscure cultural byways of European thought, perhaps best summed up the full extent of the gnostic involvement in all the problems that had for so long preoccupied him, when he wrote, 'All my life I have been working and studying to find these things, and these people knew already' (Layton, 1980, p. 23).

12.

THE GNOSTIC PARADOX

The gnostic doctrine relating to sin, or spiritual evil, is the cornerstone of their theology.

Today the notion of sin tends to be dismissed as an offensive archaism. It is denounced as a sewer concept, a product of the salacious Puritan mind, breeding guilt and false contrition. Enlightened people prefer to believe in the essential goodness of man, despite his countless and continuing villainies.

Sin is not a Puritan invention. It is basic to every major religion. Perceptive individuals are aware of its constant presence in the human heart. The confessions of those we esteem saints, show that they did not regard themselves as saintly, and with good reason. In our own times, if we needed further evidence, the lewdness and violence lying dormant in our minds has been highlighted by psychoanalysis, and amply demonstrated by the Nazis.

Man is steeped in sin. This was the one tenet to which the gnostics adhered with fierce tenacity. They restored the doctrine of original sin to its original status. In this view even the new-born infant is contaminated with it. When Jesus said of little children, 'Of such is the kingdom of heaven' (Matt. 19:14), he was referring, according to the gnostics, to their androgynous state, and not to their innocence.

The taint of sin does not necessarily imply acts. It simply comes from being human. Man does not have to commit sin. He is sinful by nature. He is not just weak, but wicked in essence, evil in a Satanic sense, for he is Satan's creature.

From this follows the conviction that the sin of man cannot be wiped out by man. Man's good works do not expiate sin. In any event, man on his own can do no good works, for as the Bible states, without equivocation, 'All our righteous deeds are as filthy rags' (Isa. 64:6).

It is expedient for our own welfare to render 'good works' unto Caesar. Moral conduct is a social convenience, necessary in order to avoid a situation where the life of man would otherwise be 'solitary, poor, nasty, brutish and short'.

The moral qualities that make for a stable society, including the humanitarian and ethical traits we cherish as if they were religious principles, were recognized by the ancients for what they were, and classed by them as mere 'political virtues'. God, said the gnostic Marcion, is not concerned with them.

Man may give a good or bad account of himself in the contest of life, depending on the stars above, the environment around, and the hormones within. And all these, the Valentinians would say, are counters that are ultimately dealt out by the Prince of Darkness.

The law of Caesar is devoid of spiritual overtones. In Caesar's realm 'sin' can be legislated into or decreed out of existence. The gnostics saw with crystal clarity how easily the law of Caesar could be made to serve the ends of Satan.

In gnosticism the leading *dramatis personae* in the cosmic theatre are Christ and Lucifer. But in ultimate terms the gnostics were non-dualists, believing that God the Father is the Supreme Being, and is utterly transcendent to the world where the dualist conflict is taking place.

The material world is the preserve of Satan, and we might remain in bondage to him for all time – but for divine grace. St Augustine spoke of the happy fault (Lat. *felix culpa*), referring to the sin that caused the fall of our first parents, for it was because of this that the human race in time came to know Christ.

By himself, the human being is helpless, in a situation that is hopeless. His only hope lies in Christ. The second, and last, great Christian commandment – to love your neighbour – relates to Caesar's realm. It only becomes spiritually relevant when the first – to love God – is brought into operation.

And one can only love the transcendent God through a knowledge (*gnosis*) of Christ. When this understanding is attained, one's life assumes a new spiritual dimension, and the real virtues then begin to flow from a divine source.

In spite of their docetic views, most gnostics acknowledged the deeper significance of Christ's death on the cross. It is probably to a gnostic source that we must look for the famous remark attributed to Tertullian concerning the resurrection: is certain, because it is impossible.'

The gnostics were aware that to the rational mind the incarnation was a fantasy, the crucifixion an offence, and the resurrection an absurdity (see I Cor. 1:23).

All this lies outside the realm of common sense. But those who wish to avoid the absurdities of the Christian faith, and build up an image of Jesus as just another one of a long line of prophets preaching ethics and morals, find they can give no reason why anyone should follow Jesus in preference to another teacher.

Gnostic truth is heterodox, and presents alternative values. It is an allegory, since it speaks in another way. It is a paradox, which means something contrary to received opinion. It is not logical, rational, or even thinkable.

The existentialists, paraphrasing the gnostics, affirmed that Christianity involves the choice of the absurd alternative.

BIBLIOGRAPHY

Allegro, John. *The Sacred Mushroom and the Cross,* Sphere Books, London, 1973

Allegro, John. *The Dead Sea Scrolls and the Christian Myth,* Westbridge Books, London, 1979

Angus, Samuel. *The Religious Quests of the Graeco-Roman World,* Murray, London, 1929

Angus, Samuel. *The Mystery Religions and Christianity,* Murray, London, 1929; Dover, New York, 1966

Anonymous. *Ophiolatreia: An Account of Serpent Worship,* p.p., London, 1889

Anonymous. *The Divine Pymander of Hermes Trismegistus,* Shrine of Wisdom, London, 1923

Arberry, A. J. *The Ring of the Dove* (by Ibn Hazm), Luzac, London, 1953

Ashe, Geoffrey. *The Ancient Wisdom,* Macmillan, London, 1977

Baigent, M., Leigh, R., and Lincoln, H. *The Holy Blood and the Holy Grail,* Jonathan Cape, London, 1982

Baker, J. A. *The Foolishness of God,* Darton, Longman and Todd, London, 1970

Bamberger, Bernard. *Fallen Angels,* Jewish Publication Society of America, Philadelphia, 1952

Baring-Gould, Revd. S. *The Lost and Hostile Gospels,* Smith Elder, London, 1874

Barnard, L. W. *Studies in the Apostolic Fathers,* Oxford University Press, 1966

Barret, C. K. (ed.). *The New Testament Background: Selected Documents,* Macmillan, New York, 1957

Barrie, M. W. *Gnosticism,* Brahmavidya Library, Adyar, Madras, 1926

Bauer, Walter. *Orthodoxy and Heresy in Earliest Christianity,* Fortress Press, Philadelphia, 1971; SCM Press, London, 1972

Bayley, Harold, *A New Light on the Renaissance,* Dent, London, 1909

Baynes, Charlotte (ed.). *A Coptic Gnostic Treatise,* Cambridge University Press, 1933

Beare, F. W. *The Earliest Records of Jesus,* Oxford University Press, 1962

Bell, H. Idris. *Cults and Creeds of Graeco-Roman Egypt,* Liverpool University Press, 1953

Bell, H. I., and Skeat, T. C. (eds.). *Fragments of an Unknown Gospel,* British Museum, London, 1935

Bellinzoni, A. J. *The Sayings of Jesus in the Writings of Justin Martyr,* Brill, Leiden, 1967

Bernheimer, R. *Wild Men of the Middle Ages,* Harvard University Press, 1952

Bettenson, H. *The Early Christian Fathers,* Oxford University Press, 1956

Bevan, A. A. (ed.). *The Hymn of the Soul,* Cambridge University Press, 1897

Bevan, E. R. *Hellenism and Christianity,* Cambridge University Press, 1921

Bianchi, Ugo (ed.). *The Origins of Gnosticism. Colloquium of Messina, April, 1966. Texts and Discussions,* Brill, Leiden, 1970

Bigg, C. *The Christian Platonists of Alexandria,* Oxford University Press, 2nd ed., 1913

Bihalji-Merin, Oto, and Benac, Alojz. *The Bogomils,* Thames and Hudson, London, 1962

Black, Matthew. *The Scrolls and Christian Origins,* Nelson, London, 1961

Black, Matthew (ed.). *The Scrolls and Christianity,* SPCK, London, 1969

Blackman, Edwin Cyril. *Marcion and His Influence,* SPCK, London, 1948

Blumenthal, H. J., and Markus, R. A. (eds.). *Neoplatonism and Early Christian Thought,* Variorum Publications, London, 1982

Boas, G. *Essays on Primativism and Related Ideas in the Middle Ages,* Johns Hopkins Press, Baltimore, 1948

Böhlig, Alexander, and Wisse, Frederik. *The Gospel of the Egyptians,* Brill, Leiden; Eerdman, Grand Rapids, Michigan, 1975

Bond, F. B., and Lea, T. S. *Cabala Contained in the Coptic Gnostic*

Books, Oxford University Press, 1971

Bonner, Campbell. *Studies in Magical Amulets, Chiefly Graeco-Egyptian,* Michigan University Press, 1950

Borsch, F. H. *The Son of Man in Myth and History,* SCM Press, London, 1967

Borsch, F. H. *The Christian and Gnostic Son of Man,* SCM Press, London, 1970

Bosman, Leonard. *The Sacred Names of God,* Dharma Press, London, 1957

Boulluec, A. le. *Gnosis and Gnosticism,* Brill, Leiden, 1977

Bousset, Wilhelm. *The Antichrist Legend,* Murray, London, 1896

Boylan, P. *Thoth, the Hermes of Egypt,* Oxford University Press, 1922

Brandon, S. G. F. (ed.). *The Saviour God,* Manchester University Press, 1963

Brandon, S. G. F. *Religion in Ancient History,* Allen and Unwin, London, 1965

Bremer, Francis J. *The Puritan Experiment,* St James Press, London, 1976

Brend, W. A. *Sacrifice to Attis: A Study of Sex and Civilization,* Heinemann, London, 1936

Brooke, A. E. (ed.). *The Fragments of Heracleon,* Cambridge University Press, 1891

Brown, R. E. *The Virginal Conception and Bodily Resurrection of Jesus,* Geoffrey Chapman, London, 1973

Brown, S. K. *James: A Religio-Historical Study of the Relations Between Jewish, Gnostic and Catholic Christianity in the Early Period through an Investigation of the Traditions about James the Lord's Brother,* Brown University, Providence, 1972

Bruce, F. F. *The Teacher of Righteousness in the Qumran Texts,* Tyndale Press, London, 1957

Bruce, F. F. *Jesus and Christian Origins Outside the New Testament,* Hodder and Stoughton, London, 1974

Bruns, J. Edgar, *The Forbidden Gospel,* Harper and Row, New York and London, 1976

Budge, E. A. Wallis. *Osiris and the Egyptian Resurrection,* Dover, New York, 1911

Bultmann, Rudolf. *Theology of the New Testament,* 2 vols., SCM Press, London, 1952

Bultmann, Rudolf. *Primitive Christianity in Its Contemporary Setting,* Meridian Books, New York, 1956; Collins, London, 1960

Bultmann, Rudolf. *Jesus Christ and Mythology,* SCM Press, London, 1960

Buonaiuti, E. *Gnostic Fragments,* Williams and Norgate, London, 1924

Burkill, T. A. *Mysterious Revelation,* Ithaca, New York, 1963

Burkitt, F. C. *Jewish and Christian Apocalypses,* Cambridge University Press, 1914

Burkitt, F. C. *The Religion of the Manichees,* Cambridge University Press, 1925

Burkitt, F. C. *Church and Gnosis: Christian Thought in the Second Century,* Cambridge University Press, 1932

Burridge, K. O. L. *New Heaven, New Earth: A Study of Millenarian Activities,* Oxford University Press, 1968

Burton, E. *An Enquiry into the Heresies of the Apostolic Age,* Oxford University Press, 1829

Butler, E. M. *The Myth of the Magus,* Cambridge University Press, 1948

Butler, E. M. *The Fortunes of Faust,* Cambridge University Press, 1952

Cadbury, H. J. *The Peril of Modernizing Jesus,* SPCK, London, 1962

Caird, G. B. *Principalities and Powers,* Oxford University Press, 1967

Calverton, V. F. (ed.). *Sex in Civilization,* Allen and Unwin, London, 1929

Campbell, Joseph (ed.). *The Mysteries,* Routledge and Kegan Paul, London, 1955

Campbell, Joseph. *The Masks of God: Primitive Mythology,* Viking Press, New York; Secker and Warburg, London, 1960

Campbell, Joseph. *The Masks of God: Creative Mythology,* Viking Press, New York; Secker and Warburg, London, 1960

Capellanus, Andreas. *The Art of Courtly Love,* Columbia University Press, 1941

Casey, R. P. *The Excerpta ex Theodoto of Clement of Alexandria,* Christophers, London, 1934

Cavendish, Richard. *The Powers of Evil,* Routledge and Kegan Paul, London, 1975

Chadwick, H. (ed.). *Origen: Contra Celsum,* Cambridge University Press, 1953

Chadwick, H. *Early Christian Thought and the Classical Tradition,* Oxford University Press, 1966

Chadwick, H. *Priscillian of Avila. The Occult and Charismatic in the Early Church,* Oxford University Press, 1976

Chambers, John David (ed.). *Hermes Trismegistus,* George Redway, London, 1885

Charles, R. H. (ed.). *The Apocrypha and Pseudepigrapha of the Old Testament in English,* 2 vols., Oxford University Press, 1913; reprint, 1968

Charlesworth, J. H. (ed.). *John and Qumran,* Geoffrey Chapman, London, 1972

Charlesworth, J. H. *The Odes of Solomon,* Oxford University Press, 1976

Chaytor, H. J. *The Troubadours of Dante,* Oxford University Press, 1902

Christie-Murray, David. *A History of Heresy,* New English Library, 1976

Cohn, Norman. *The Pursuit of the Millennium,* Secker and Warburg, 1957; revised and expanded edition, Temple Smith, London, 1970

Cohn, Norman. *Europe's Inner Demons,* Chatto, Heinemann, London, 1975

Conybeare, F. C. *Russian Dissenters,* Harvard University Press, 1921

Conybeare, F. C. (ed.). *Philostratus: Life of Apollonius of Tyana,* Putnam, New York, 1927

Corbin, Henry. *The Man of Light in Iranian Sufism,* Shambhala, Boulder, Colorado; Routledge and Kegan Paul, London, 1978

Craddock, F. B. *The Pre-Existence of Christ in the New Testament,* Abingdon, Nashville, 1968

Cross, F. L. (ed.). *The Jung Codex,* Mowbray, London, 1955

Cross, F. L. (ed.). *Oxford Dictionary of the Christian Church,* 2nd ed., Oxford University Press, 1974

Cumont, Franz. *The Oriental Religions in Roman Paganism,* Chicago University Press, 1911; Dover, New York, 1956

Cumont, Franz. *The Mysteries of Mithra,* Kegan Paul, London, 1903

Cupitt, Don. *Jesus and the Gospel of God,* Lutterworth, London, 1979

Curtis, David. *Experimental Cinema,* Studio Vista, London, 1971

Cutner, H. *A Short History of Sex Worship,* Watts, London, 1940

Cutner, H. *Jesus: God or Myth?* Pioneer Press, New York, 1950

Daniélou, Alain. *A History of Early Christian Doctrine,* Darton, Longman, Todd, London, 1964

Daniélou, Jean. *The Dead Sea Scrolls and Primitive Christianity,* Burns and Oates, London, 1962

Daniélou, Jean. *The Theology of Jewish Christianity,* Darton, Longman, Todd, London, 1964

Dart, John. *The Laughing Saviour: the Discovery and Significance of the Nag Hammadi Gnostic Library,* Harper and Row, New York, 1976

Davidson, Gustav. *A Dictionary of Angels,* Free Press, New York, 1971

Davies, W. D. *Paul and Rabbinic Judaism,* 3rd ed., Hodder and Stoughton, London, 1970

Denomy, A. J. *The Heresy of Courtly Love,* D. X. McMullen, New York, 1947

De Vesme, Caesar. *Peoples of Antiquity,* Vol. II, Rider, London, 1931

Dixon, William Hepworth. *Spiritual Wives,* 2 vols., Hurst and Blackett, London, 1868

Dodd, C. H. *The Bible and the Greeks,* Hodder and Stoughton, London, 1964

Dodds, E. R. *The Greeks and the Irrational,* Cambridge University Press, 1951

Dodds, E. R. *Pagan and Christian in an Age of Anxiety,* Cambridge University Press, 1965

Doresse, Jean. *The Secret Books of the Egyptian Gnostics,* Hollis and Carter, London; Viking Press, New York, 1960

Drijvers, H. J. W. *Bardaisan of Edessa,* Netherlands Semitic Studies, Assen, 1966

Drower, Ethel Stefana. *The Mandaeans of Iraq: Their Cults, Customs, Magic, Legends and Folklore,* Oxford University Press, 1937

Drower, Ethel Stefana. *Water into Wine,* John Murray, London, 1956

Drower, Ethel Stefana. *The Secret Adam: A Study of Nasorean Gnosis,* Oxford University Press, 1960

Dupont-Somer, A. *The Essene Writings from Qumran,* Oxford University Press, 1961

Eels, Charles (trans.). *Life and Times of Apollonius of Tyana,* AMS Press, New York, 1923

Eisler, Robert. *Orpheus the Fisher,* Watkins, London, 1921

Eisler, Robert. *The Messiah Jesus and John the Baptist,* Krappe, London, 1931
Eliade, Mircea. *The Two and the One,* Harvill Press, London; Harper and Row, New York, 1965
Emerson, Richard K. *Antichrist in the Middle Ages: A Study of Medieval Apocalypticism, Art and Literature,* Washington University Press; Manchester University Press, 1981
Eusebius (Bishop of Caesarea, d. AD 337). *Ecclesiastical History,* Loeb Classical Library, London, 2 vols., 1957, 1959
Evans, C. F. *Resurrection in the New Testament,* SCM Press, London, 1970
Everard, D. R. *The Divine Pymander,* Weiser, New York, 1973

Faber-Kaiser, A. *Jesus Died in Kashmir,* Gordon and Cremonesi, London, 1977
Farrer, J. A. *Paganism and Christianity,* Redway, London, 1891
Fawcett, T. *Hebrew Myth and Christian Gospel,* SCM Press, London, 1973
Fern, Vergilius. *Forgotten Religions,* Philosophical Library, New York, 1950
Feucht, O. E., *et al. Sex and the Church,* Concordia Publishing House, St Louis, Missouri, 1961
Finegan, J. *Hidden Records of the Life of Christ,* Pilgrim Press, Philadelphia, 1969
Flaceliere, Robert. *Greek Oracles,* Elek, London, 1965
Foerster, Werner (ed.). *Gnosis: A Selection of Gnostic Texts,* Clarendon Press, Oxford, 1974
Folliot, Katherine. *Jesus Before He Was God* (printed by Hazell Watson and Viney, Aylesbury, Bucks.), Folliot, London, 1978
Forster, E. M. *Alexandria: A History and a Guide,* Michael Haag, London, 1982
Fränger, Wilhelm. *The Millennium of Hieronymus Bosch,* Faber, London, 1952
Frazer, J. G. *Adonis, Attis and Osiris,* Macmillan, London, 1919
Frend, W. H. C. *The Early Church,* Hodder and Stoughton, London, 1965

Garçon, Maurice, and Vinchon, Jean. *The Devil: An Historical and Critical Study,* Gollancz, London, 1929
Gardner, Percy. *The Origin of the Lord's Supper,* Mowbray, London, 1893

Gärtner, B. *The Theology of the Gospel According to Thomas,* Collins, London, 1961

Gaskell, G. A. *Gnostic Scriptures Interpreted,* Daniel, London, 1927

Gaster, Theodore H. *The Dead Sea Scriptures,* Doubleday, New York, 1964

Gibb, H. A. R. *Islam: A Historical Survey,* 2nd ed., Oxford University Press, 1975

Gibbons, J. A. *A Commentary on 'The Second Logos of the Great Seth',* Yale University Press, 1972

Godwin, Joscelyn. *Mystery Religions of the Ancient World,* Thames and Hudson, London, 1982

Goldberg, B. Z. *The Sacred Fire: The Story of Sex in Religion,* Jarrolds, London, 1931

Goldstein, Rabbi M. *Jesus in the Jewish Tradition,* Dutton, New York, 1950

Goodenough, E. R. *Light, Light: The Mystic Gospel of Hellenistic Judaism,* Oxford University Press; Yale University Press, 1935

Gore, Charles. *The Incarnation of the Son of God,* Murray, London, 1891

Gould, Thomas. *Platonic Love,* Routledge and Kegan Paul, London, 1963

Grant, F. C. *Hellenistic Religions: The Age of Syncretism,* Doubleday, New York, 1953

Grant, Robert McQueen. *Gnosticism: An Anthology. A Sourcebook of Heretical Writings from the Early Christian Period,* Collins, London, 1961

Grant, Robert McQueen. *The Earliest Lives of Jesus,* SPCK, London, 1964

Grant, Robert McQueen. *Gnosticism and Early Christianity,* 2nd ed., Columbia University Press, 1966

Grant, Robert McQueen. *Early Christianity and Society,* Collins, London, 1978

Grant, Robert McQueen, and Freedman, David Noel (eds.). *The Secret Sayings of Jesus,* Collins, London; Garden City, New York, 1960

Graves, Robert, and Podro, Joshua. *The Nazarene Gospel Restored,* Cassell, London, 1953

Graves, Robert, and Podro, Joshua. *Jesus in Rome: A Historical Conjecture,* Cassell, London, 1957

Gray, John. *The Canaanites,* Thames and Hudson, London, 1964

Greenslade, S. L. *Schism in the Early Church,* SCM Press, London, 1953

Grenfel, B. P., and Hunt, A. S. *Logia Jesou: Sayings of Our Lord from an Early Greek Papyrus,* Oxford University Press, 1897

Gresham, Machen J. *The Virgin Birth of Christ,* Collins, London, 1930

Griffiths, J. G. *The Conflict of Horus and Seth,* Liverpool University Press, 1960

Griffiths, Richard. *The Reactionary Revolution: The Catholic Revival in French Literature, 1870–1914,* Constable, London, 1966

Grobel, Kendrick (trans.). *The Gospel of Truth,* SCM Press, London, 1960

Groton, W. M. *The Christian Eucharist and the Pagan Cults,* Longmans Green, London, 1914

Gryson, R. *The Ministry of Women in the Early Church,* Minnesota University Press, 1976

Guillaumont, A., *et al. The Gospel According to Thomas,* Harper and Row, New York, 1959

Guthrie, W. K. C. *Orpheus and the Greek Religion,* Methuen, London, 1935

Haardt, Robert. *Gnosis: Character and Testimony,* Brill, Leiden, 1971

Hall, F. T. *The Pedigree of the Devil,* Trubner, London, 1883

Haller, William. *The Rise of Puritanism,* Columbia University Press, 1938

Halliday, W. R. *The Pagan Background of Early Christianity,* Hodder and Stoughton, London, 1925

Hamerton-Kelly, R. G. *Pre-Existence, Wisdom and the Son of Man,* Cambridge University Press, 1973

Hamilton, Bernard. *The Albigensian Crusade,* Historical Association, London, 1974

Hamilton, Bernard. *Monastic Reform: Catharism and the Crusades,* Variorum, London, 1979

Hardmann, O. *The Ideals of Asceticism,* SPCK, London, 1924

Hare, Augustus. *Studies in Russia,* George Allen, London, 1901

Harnack, Adolf. *The Sayings of Jesus,* Putnam, New York, 1908

Harris, J. Rendel. *Jesus and Osiris,* Cambridge University Press, 1927

Harris, J. Rendel, and Mingana, A. A. (eds.). *The Odes and Psalms of Solomon,* 2 vols., Manchester University Press, 1916, 1920

Harrison, Jane. *Prolegommena to the Study of Greek Religion,*

Cambridge University Press, 1903; Meridian Books, New York, 1955

Harrison, R. K. *The Dead Sea Scrolls,* English University Press, London, 1961

Hausdorff, David M. *A Book of Jewish Curiosities,* Crown, New York, 1955

Hays, H. R. *The Dangerous Sex: The Myth of Feminine Evil,* Methuen, London, 1966

Heilbrun, Carolyn. *Towards Androgyny,* Gollancz, London, 1973

Helmbold, A. *The Nag Hammadi Gnostic Texts and the Bible,* Baker Book House, Grand Rapids, 1967

Hengel, Martin. *Son of God,* SCM Press, London, 1976

Hennecke, E., and Schneemelcher, W. (eds.). *New Testament Apocrypha,* Lutterworth, London, 1963, 1965

Herford, R. T. *Christianity in Talmud and Midrash,* Williams and Norgate, 1903; Gregg International, New York, 1972

Hick, John (ed.). *The Myth of God Incarnate,* SCM Press, London, 1977

Higgins, A. J. B. *Jesus and the Son of Man,* Lutterworth, London, 1964

Hippolytus (see Legge)

Hitchcock, F. R. M. (ed.). *Against the Heresies (Adversus Haereses,* by Irenaeus), SPCK, London, 1916

Holmes, Edmond. *The Holy Heretics,* Thinkers Library, London, 1956

Horner, G. W. (ed.). *Pistis Sophia,* Watkins, London, 1924

Howlett, Duncan. *The Essenes and Christianity,* Harper, New York, 1957

Huehns, Gertrude. *Antinomianism in English History,* Cresset Press, London, 1951

Hull, John Martin. *Hellenistic Magic and the Synoptic Tradition,* SCM Press, London, 1974

Huxley, Aldous. *The Devils of Loudun,* Chatto and Windus, London, 1952

Irenaeus, Bishop of Lyons (d. AD 202), see Hitchcock, Richardson, Roberts.

Isser, S. J. *The Dositheans,* Brill, Leiden, 1976

James, E. O. *Origins of Sacrifice,* John Murray, London, 1937

James, E. O. *The Cult of the Mother Goddess,* Thames and Hudson, London, 1959

James, M. R. (trans. and ed.). *The Apocryphal New Testament,* Oxford University Press, 1924

Jennings, Hargrave. *Phallicism: Its Connection with the Rosicrucians and the Gnostics,* George Redway, London, 1886

Jeremias, Joachim. *Unknown Sayings of Jesus,* SPCK, 2nd ed., London, 1964

Jeremias, Joachim. *The Eucharistic Words of Jesus,* SCM Press, London, 1966

Johnson, Paul. *A History of Christianity,* Weidenfeld & Nicolson, London, 1976

Jonas, Hans. *The Gnostic Religion,* rev. ed., Beacon Press, Boston, 1963

Josephus (see Whiston)

Joyce, Donovan. *The Jesus Scroll,* Angus and Robertson, London, 1973

Jung, C. G. *Aion: Researches into the Phenomenology of the Self,* 1959; 2nd ed., Routledge and Kegan Paul, London, 1968

Kähler, Martin. *The So-called Historical Jesus and the Truly Historic Biblical Christ,* Fortress Press, London, 1964

Kaplan, Justin (ed.). *With Malice Towards Women: A Handbook for Women-Haters Drawn from the Best Minds of All Time,* W. H. Allen, London, 1953

Keating, J. F. *The Agape and the Eucharist in the Early Christian Church,* Methuen, London, 1901

Kee, Howard Clark. *The Origins of Christianity: Sources and Documents,* Prentice Hall, New York, 1973; SPCK, London, 1980

Kennedy, H. A. A. *St Paul and the Mystery Religions,* Methuen, London, 1913

Kerenyi, C. *Eleusis: Archetypal Image of Mother and Daughter,* Routledge and Kegan Paul, London, 1967

King, Charles William. *The Gnostics and Their Remains,* Nutt, London, 1887; Wizard Book Shelf, San Diego, Calif., 1973

Klausner, J. *Jesus of Nazareth. His Life, Times and Teachings,* Macmillan, London, 1925

Klijn, A. F. J. (ed.). *The Acts of Thomas,* Brill, Leiden, 1962

Klijn, A. F. J. *Seth in Jewish, Christian and Gnostic Literature,* Brill, Leiden, 1977

Knox, John. *Marcion and the New Testament,* Chicago University Press, 1942

Knox, R. A. *Enthusiasm: A Chapter in the History of Religion,* Clarendon Press, Oxford, 1950

Knox, W. L. *Some Hellenistic Elements in Primitive Christianity,* Collins, London, 1944

Koester, Helmut, and Robinson, J. M. *Trajectories Through Early Christianity,* Fortress Press, Philadelphia, 1971

Kraeling, C. H. *Anthropos and Son of Man: A Study in the Religious Syncretism of the Hellenistic Orient,* Doubleday, New York, 1927

Krause, Martin (ed.). *Essays on the Nag Hammadi Texts in Honour of Alexander Böhlig,* Brill, Leiden, 1972

Krause, Martin (ed.). *Gnosis and Gnosticism,* Brill, Leiden, 1977

Labib, Pahor. *Coptic Gnostic Papyri in the Coptic Museum of Old Cairo,* Coptic Museum, Cairo, 1956

Lacarrière, Jacques. *The God-Possessed,* Allen and Unwin, London, 1963

Lacarrière, Jacques. *The Gnostics,* Peter Owen, London, 1977

Lambert, Malcolm David. *Medieval Heresy: Popular Movements from Bogomil to Hus,* Edward Arnold, London, 1977

Lampe, G. W. H. *The Seal of the Spirit,* 2nd ed., SPCK, London, 1967

Langdon, S. H. *Tammuz and Ishtar,* Oxford University Press, 1914

Langdon-Davies, John. *Sex, Sin and Sanctity,* Watts, London, 1954

Langton, Edward. *Essentials of Demonology,* Epworth Press, London, 1949

Laver, James. *The First Decadent. The Strange Life of J. K. Huysmans,* Faber, London, 1954

Layton, Bentley (ed.). *The Gnostic Treatise on Resurrection from Nag Hammadi,* Scholars Press, Missoula, 1979

Layton, Bentley (ed.). *The Rediscovery of Gnosticism,* Vol. I (The School of Valentinus), Brill, Leiden, 1980

Layton, Bentley (ed.). *The Rediscovery of Gnosticism,* Vol. II, (Sethian Gnosticism), Brill, Leiden, 1981

Lea, Henry Charles. *A History of the Inquisition in the Middle Ages,* Vol. II, Harper, New York; Macmillan, London, 1888

Lea, Henry Charles. *A History of Sacerdotal Celibacy in the Christian Church,* Williams and Norgate, London, 1907

Leff, Gordon. *Heresy in the Later Middle Ages,* Manchester University Press, 2 vols., 1967

Legge, F. *Rivals and Forerunners of Christianity,* 2 vols., Cambridge University Press, 1915

Legge, F. (ed.). *Philosopheumena* (by Hippolytus), 2 vols., SPCK, London, 1921

Leroy, Jules. *Monks and Monasteries of the Near East,* Harrap, London, 1963

Lerner, Robert E. *The Heresy of the Free Spirit in the Later Middle Ages,* California University Press, 1972

Lewy, Hans. *Chaldean Oracles and Theurgy,* Institut Français, Cairo, 1956

Lilla, Salvatore R. C. *Clement of Alexandria: A Study in Christian Platonism and Gnosticism,* Oxford University Press, 1971

Ling, Trevor. *A History of Religion East and West,* Macmillan, London, 1968

Lohse, Eduard. *The New Testament Environment,* SCM Press, London, 1976

Longworth, T. C. *The Worship of Love,* Torchstream Books, London, 1954

Longworth, T. C. *The Devil a Monk Would Be,* Herbert Joseph, London, 1960

Lovejoy, A. O., *et al. A Documentary History of Primitivism and Related Ideas,* Johns Hopkins Press, Baltimore, 1935

Maccoby, H. *Revolution in Judea: Jesus and the Jewish Resistance,* Heinemann, London, 1973

MacCulloch, J. A. *The Harrowing of Hell,* T. Clark, Edinburgh, 1930

MacCulloch, J. A. *Medieval Faith and Fable,* Collins, London, 1932

McDonnell, E. W. *The Beguines and Beghards in Medieval Culture,* Rutgers University Press, 1954

McGinn, Bernard. *Visions of the End. Apocalyptic Traditions in the Middle Ages,* Columbia University Press, 1980

MacGregor, G. H. C. *Eucharistic Origins,* Macmillan, London, 1922

MacKean, W. H. *Christian Monasticism in Egypt,* Collins, London, 1920

Mansel, H. L. *The Gnostic Heretics of the First and Second Centuries,* Murray, London, 1875

Mead, G. R. S. *Simon Magus: An Essay,* Watkins, London, 1892

Mead, G. R. S. *The Mysteries of Mithra,* Watkins, London, 1907

Mead, G. R. S. *The Chaldaean Oracles,* 2 vols., Watkins, London 1908

Mead, G. R. S. *Pistis Sophia,* Watkins, London, 1921

Mead, G. R. S. *The Gnostic John the Baptizer: Selections from the Mandaean John-Book,* Watkins, London, 1924

Mead, G. R. S. *Fragments of a Faith Forgotten,* Watkins, London, 1932; University Books, New York, 1960

Mead, G. R. S. *Thrice-Greatest Hermes,* 3 vols., Watkins, 1906, 1964

Meily, Clarence. *Puritanism,* C. H. Kerr, Chicago, 1911

Mellinkoff, Ruth. *The Mark of Cain,* California University Press, 1981

Meutis, Georges. *The Mysteries of Eleusis,* Theosophical Society, Adyar, 1932

Mitchell, C. W. *St. Ephraim's Prose Refutations of Mani, Marcion and Bardaisan,* 2 vols., Faith Press, London, 1921

Mitchell, Walter (ed.). *Christian Asceticism and Modern Man,* Blackfriars Publications, London, 1955

Momigliano, A. D. (ed.). *The Conflict Between Paganism and Christianity in the Fourth Century,* Oxford University Press, 1963

Montefiore, C. G. *Rabbinic Literature and Gospel Teachings,* Macmillan, London, 1930

Moorsel, G. Van. *The Mysteries of Hermes Trismegistus,* Adrian, Utrecht, 1955

More, P. E. *Hellenistic Philosophy,* Princeton University Press, 1923

Morgenstern, J. *Some Significant Antecedents of Christianity,* Brill, Leiden, 1966

Mossiker, Frances. *The Affair of the Poisons,* Gollancz, London, 1970

Mowinckel, S. *He that Cometh,* Blackwell, Oxford, 1959

Mozley, J. K. *The Impassibility of God,* Collins, London, 1928

Murphy-O'Connor J. (ed.). *Paul and Qumran,* Runa, Dublin, 1968

Murray, Margaret. *The Witch Cult in Western Europe,* Oxford University Press, 1921

Murray, Robert. *Symbols of Church and Kingdom: A Study in Early Syriac Tradition,* Cambridge University Press, 1975

Mylonas, George E. *Eleusis and the Eleusinian Mysteries,* Princeton University Press, 1961

Neill, Stephan. *Christian Faith Today,* Penguin, London, 1956

Nelson, J. C. *The Renaissance Theory of Love,* Columbia University Press, 1958

Neumann, Erich. *The Great Mother: An Analysis of the Archetype,* Pantheon Books, New York, 1955

Nilsson, M. P. *The Dionysiac Mysteries of the Hellenistic and Roman Age,* Institute Publishers, Lund, 1957

Nock, Arthur Darby. *Conversion: the Old and the New in Religion from Alexander the Great to Augustine of Hippo,* Oxford University Press, 1933

Nock, Arthur Darby. *Early Gentile Christianity and Its Hellenistic Background,* Harper, New York, 1964

Norwood, G. *The Riddle of the Bacchae,* Manchester University Press, 1908

Nygren, Anders. *Agape and Eros,* Pennsylvania University Press; SPCK, London, 1953

Obolensky, Dmitri. *The Bogomils. A Study in Balkan Neo-Manichaeism,* Cambridge University Press, 1960

Origen (see Chadwick)

Osborn, Eric. *The Beginnings of Christianity,* Cambridge University Press, 1981

Otto, E. *Egyptian Arts and Cults of Osiris and Amon,* Thames and Hudson, London, 1967

Pagels, Elaine. *The Johannine Gospel in Gnostic Exegesis,* Abingdon, Nashville, 1973

Pagels, Elaine. *The Gnostic Paul: Gnostic Exegesis of the Pauline Letters,* Fortress Press, Philadelphia, 1975

Pagels, Elaine. *The Gnostic Gospels,* Random House, New York, 1979; Weidenfeld and Nicholson, London, 1980

Pallis, S. A. *Mandaean Studies,* Oxford University Press, 1926

Parrinder, Geoffrey. *Mysticism in the World's Religions,* Sheldon Press, London, 1976

Patterson, L. *Mithraism and Christianity,* Cambridge University Press, 1922

Perkins, P. *The Gnostic Dialogue,* Harper, New York, 1979

Peterkiewicz, Jerzy. *The Third Adam,* Oxford University Press, 1975

Phipps, William E. *Was Jesus Married? The Distortion of Sexuality in the Christian Tradition,* Harper and Row, New York, 1970

Pike, D. W. *Secret Societies: Their Origin, History and Ultimate Fate,* Oxford University Press, 1939

Pistorius, P. V. *Plotinus and Neoplatonism,* Cambridge University Press, 1952

Pitteuger, Norman. *The Word Incarnate,* Harper and Row, New York, 1959

Ploeg, J. van der. *The Excavations at Qumran. A Survey of the Judaean Brotherhood and its Ideas,* Longmans, London, 1956

Puech, Henri Charles. 'Gnosis and Time', in *Man and Time,* Papers from Eranos Yearbooks, ed. by J. Campbell, Routledge and Kegan Paul, London, 1958

Quispel, Gilles. *Gnostic Studies,* Netherlands Historical Institute, Istanbul, 1974

Rahner, H. *Greek Myths and Christian Mystery,* Burns and Oates, London, 1963

Reicke, B. *The New Testament Era: The World of the Bible from 500 BC to AD 100,* Fortress Press, Philadelphia, 1968

Rhodes, H. T. F. *The Satanic Mass,* Rider, London, 1954

Richards, Hubert J. *The First Christmas: What Really Happened?* Collins, London, 1977

Richardson, C. C. (ed.). *Against the Heresies* (Adversus Haereses by Irenaeus), Library of Christian Classics, London, 1921

Robbins, R. H. *Encyclopedia of Witchcraft and Demonology,* Peter Nevill, London, 1959

Roberts, A., and Rambaut, W. H. *Adversus Haereses* (Against Heresies by Irenaeus), Ante-Nicene Christian Library, Edinburgh, 2 vols, 1868–9

Roberts, C. H. *Manuscript, Society and Belief in Early Christian Egypt,* Collins, London, 1979

Robertson, A. *Jesus, Myth or History?* Watts, London, 1949

Robertson, J. M. *Christianity and Mythology,* Watts, London, 1910

Robertson, J. M. *Pagan Christs,* Thinkers Library, London, 1911

Robertson, J. M. *Jesus and Judas,* Watts, London, 1927

Robinson, J. A. T. *The Human Face of God,* SCM Press, London, 1973

Robinson, James M. (ed.). *The Nag Hammadi Library,* Harper and Row, New York, 1977

Robson, J. *Christ in Islam,* John Murray, London, 1929

Rogers, Katherine. *The Troublesome Helpmeet: A History of Misogyny in Literature,* Washington University Press, 1966

Roguement, Denis de. *Passion and Society,* Faber, London, 1940

Rowley, H. H. *The Qumran Sect and Christian Origins,* Manchester University Press, 1961

Runciman, Steven. *The Medieval Manichee,* Cambridge University Press, 1960; Reprint, 1982

Russell, D. S. *The Method and Message of Jewish Apocalyptic,* Westminster Press, Philadelphia, 1964

Russell, Jeffrey Burton. *Satan: the Early Christian Tradition,* Cornell University Press, 1981

Russell, Jeffrey Burton. *The Devil: Perceptions of Evil from Antiquity to Primitive Christianity,* Cornell University Press, 1982

Rutherford, John. *The Troubadours,* Vol. I, Smith Elder, London, 1861

Rylands, L. G. *The Beginnings of Gnostic Christianity,* Watts, London, 1940

Säve-Söderbergh T. *Studies in the Coptic-Manichaean Psalm-Books,* Uppsala University Press, 1949

Schmithals, Walter. *Gnosis in Corinth,* Brill, Leiden, 1971

Scholem, Gershom. *The Essenes,* Routledge and Kegan Paul, London, 1956

Scholem, Gershom. *Jewish Gnosticism, Merkaba Mysticism and Talmudic Tradition,* Jewish Theological Seminary, New York, 1960

Schneemelcher, W. *New Testament Apocrypha,* Westminster Press, London, 1965

Schonfield Hugh J. *After the Cross,* Barnes, New York; Tantivity Press, London, 1981

Schoukine, Ivan. *Collective Suicide Among the Russian Raskolniki,* Cambridge University Press, 1903

Schuré, Eduard. *Krishna and Orpheus,* Theosophical Publication Society, Adyar, 1919

Schuré, Eduard. *The Mysteries of Egypt,* Pennsylvania University Press, 1925

Schweitzer, A. *The Mysticism of Paul the Apostle,* Collins, London, 1931

Scobie, C. H. H. *John the Baptist,* SCM Press, London, 1964

Scott, W., and Ferguson, A. S. (eds.). *Hermetica,* Vols. 1–4, Oxford University Press, 1924–36

Scott-Moncrieff, P. D. *Paganism and Christianity in Egypt,* Oxford University Press, 1913

Segal, Alan. *Two Powers in Heaven: Early Rabbinic Reports about Christianity and Gnosticism,* Brill, Leiden, 1977

Seznec, Jean. *The Survival of the Pagan Gods,* Princeton University Press, 1972

Singer, Irving. *The Gods of Human Sexuality,* Wildwood House, London; Norton, New York, 1973

Smith, Anthony. *The Body,* Allen and Unwin, London, 1968

Smith, J. H. *The Troubadours at Home,* Putnam, New York, 1940

Smith, Morton. *Clement of Alexandria and a Secret Gospel of Mark,* Harvard University Press; Cambridge University Press, 1973

Smith, Morton. *The Secret Gospel: the Discovery and Interpretation of the Secret Gospel According to Mark,* Harper and Row, New York; Gollancz, London, 1974

Smith, Morton. *Jesus the Magician,* Harper, New York, 1978; Gollancz, London, 1980

Smith, P. *A Short History of Christian Theophagy,* Watts, London, 1922

Smythe, Barbara (ed.). *Trobador Poets,* Chatto and Windus, London, 1929

Speidel, Michael P. *Mithras-Orion,* Brill, Leiden, 1980

Spencer, S. *Mysticism in World Religion,* Penguin, Harmondsworth, 1963

Sperling, H., and Simon, M. (eds.). *The Zohar,* Vol. II, Socino Press, London & New York, 1934

Springett, Bernard H. *Secret Sects of Syria and the Lebanon,* Cambridge University Press, 1922

Stewart, Desmond. *The Foreigner: A Search for the First Century Jesus,* Hamish Hamilton, London, 1981

Stirling, William. *The Canon: An Exposition of the Pagan Mystery Perpetuated in the Cabala as the Rule of All the Arts,* Garnstone Press, London, 1974; Rilko, 1981

Stracey, Ray. *Religious Fanaticism: A Description of Some Curious Sects of America in the Nineteenth Century,* Faber, London, 1928

Streeter, B. H. *The Four Gospels: A Study of Origins,* Oxford University Press, 1924

Streeter, B. H. *The Buddha and the Christ,* Macmillan, London, 1932

Summers, Montague (ed.). *Confessions of Madeleine Bavent,* Fortune Press, London, 1933

Swiney, F. *The Esoteric Teachings of the Gnostics,* Yellon, Williams, London, 1909

Sykes, S., and Clayton, J. P. (eds.). *Christ, Faith and History,* Cambridge University Press, 1972

Symonds, John. *The Great Beast,* Rider, London, 1951

Tabori, Paul. *Secret and Forbidden,* New English Library, London, 1969

Talbert, C. H. *Luke and the Gnostics,* Collins, London, 1966

Taylor, C. *The Teachings of the Twelve Apostles, with Illustrations from the Talmud,* Cambridge University Press, 1886

Taylor, C. *The Oxyrhynchus Logia and the Apocryphal Gospels,* Oxford University Press, 1899

Taylor, G. Rattray. *Sex in History,* Thames and Hudson, London, 1959

Taylor, Thomas. *A Dissertation on the Eleusinian and Bacchic Mysteries,* Redway, London, 1891

Taylor, Thomas. *The Mystical Hymns of Orpheus,* Witthingham, Chiswick, 1896

Te Velde, H. *Seth, God of Confusion. A Study in his Role on Egyptian Mythology and Religion,* Brill, Leiden, 1967

Tiddeman, M. F. *A Short Life of Apollonius of Tyana,* Theosophical Publishing House, Adyar, 1929

Travers, Herford R. *Christianity in Talmud and Midrash,* Kegan Paul, London, 1903

Tredwell, Daniel. *Apollonius of Tyana,* George Redway, London, 1885

Trotter, R. *Gnosticism and Memar Marqah* (A Samaritan Document of the fourth century AD), Brill, Leiden, 1964

Tyler, Parker. *Underground Film,* Secker and Warburg, London, 1971

Unnik, W. C. van. *Newly Discovered Gnostic Writings: A Preliminary Survey of the Nag Hammadi Finds,* Allenson, Naperville, Illinois, 1960

Unwin, J. C. *Sex and Culture,* Oxford University Press, 1934

Vermaseren, Maarten. *Mithras the Secret God,* Barnes and Noble, New York, 1963

Vermaseren, Maarten. *Cybele and Attis: The Myth and the Cult,* Thames and Hudson, London, 1977

Vermes, Geza. *Jesus the Jew,* Collins, London, 1973

Voegelin, E. *Science, Politics and Gnosticism: Two Essays,* Regnery, Chicago, 1960

Waddell, Helen (ed.). *The Desert Fathers,* Constable, London, 1936

Waddell, Helen. *The Wandering Scholars,* Constable, London, 1966

Wagner, G. *Pauline Baptism and the Pagan Mysteries,* Oliver and Boyd, London, 1967

Waite, A. E. *Secret Doctrine in Israel,* Rider, London, 1913

Wake, C. Staniland. *Serpent Worship,* George Redway, London, 1886

Wakefield, Walter L. *Heresy, Crusade and Inquisition in Southern France, 1100–1250,* Allen and Unwin, London, 1974

Walker, Benjamin. *Hindu World: An Encyclopedia of Hinduism,* 2 vols., Allen and Unwin, London; Praeger, New York, 1968

Walker, Benjamin. *Sex and the Supernatural,* Macdonald, London, 1970; Harper and Row, New York, 1973

Walker, Benjamin. *Encyclopedia of Esoteric Man,* Routledge and Kegan Paul, London; Stein and Day, New York, 1977

Warner, H. J. *The Albigensian Heresy,* SPCK, London, 1922

Warner, Marina. *Alone of All Her Sex: The Myth and Cult of the Virgin Mary,* Weidenfeld and Nicolson, London, 1976

Wasson, R. G., Hofmann, A., and Ruck, C. A. P. *The Road to Eleusis: Unveiling the Secrets of the Mysteries,* Harcourt, New York, 1978

Weigall, Arthur. *Paganism in Our Christianity,* Hutchinson, London, 1916

Weightman, John. *The Concept of the Avant-Garde,* Alcove Press, London, 1973

Wells, G. A. *The Jesus of Early Christianity,* Pemberton, London, 1971

Wells, G. A. *Did Jesus Exist?* Elek, Pemberton, London, 1975

Whiston, William (trans.). *The Works of Flavius Josephus,* Broadman Press, Nashville, 1974

White, H. G. E. *The Sayings of Jesus from Oxyrhynchus,* Cambridge University Press, 1920

Whittaker, T. *The Neoplatonists,* 2nd ed., Cambridge University Press, 1918

Widengren, Geo. *Mesopotamian Elements in Manichaeism,* Uppsala University Press, 1946

Widengren, Geo. *King and Saviour: Studies in Manichaean, Mandaean, and Syrian-Gnostic Religion,* Uppsala University Press, 1947

Widengren, Geo. *Mani and Manichaeism,* Weidenfeld and Nicolson, London, 1965

Wilken, Robert L. *Aspects of Wisdom in Judaism and Early Christianity,* Notre Dame University Press, 1975

William, John Alden. *Islam,* Prentice Hall, London; Braziller, New York, 1961

Wilson, P. L. *Angels,* Thames and Hudson, London, 1980

Wilson, Robert McLachlan. *The Gnostic Problem*, Mowbray, London, 1958

Wilson, Robert McLachlan (ed.). *The Gospel of Philip*, Mowbray, London, 1962

Wilson, Robert McLachlan. *Gnosis and the New Testament*, Fortress Press, Philadelphia; Oxford University Press, 1968

Wilson, Robert McLachlan (ed.). *Nag Hammadi and Gnosis*, Brill, Leiden, 1978

Wilson, R. S. *Marcion: A Study of a Second Century Heretic*, Cambridge University Press, 1933

Wind, Edgar. *Pagan Mysteries in the Renaissance*, Faber, London, 1967

Wink, W. *John the Baptist in the Gospel Tradition*, Cambridge University Press, 1968

Witt, R. E. *Isis in the Graeco-Roman World*, Thames and Hudson, London, 1971

Woodcock, G., and Avakumovic, I. *The Dukhobors*, Faber, London, 1969

Wrede, H. *The Messianic Secret*, James Clarke, Cambridge University Press, 1971

Yadin, Y. *The Scroll of the War of the Sons of Light Against the Sons of Darkness*, Oxford University Press, 1962

Yamauchi, Edwin Masao. *Gnostic Ethics and Mandaean Origins*, Harvard University Press; Oxford University Press, 1971

Yamauchi, Edwin Masao. *Pre-Christian Gnosticism*, Eerdman, Grand Rapids, Michigan; Tyndale Press, London, 1973

Zacharias, Gerhard. *The Satanic Cult*, Allen and Unwin, London, 1980

GENERAL AND BIBLE INDEX

Aaron, 151
ab, 13
Abecedarians, 185
Abel, 62, 144, 150, 153
Abelarians or Abelites, 113
Abgar, 149
Abiram, 144, 151
abortion, 128, 159
above and below, 76, 102, 122, 162
Abraham, 43, 44, 80, 144, 150
Abram, 44
Abraxas or Abrasax, 142
absurd, 190
abyss, 39, 48, 84, 123
Abyssinian church, 165
acclivity, 118, 177
acēdia, 47
Acembes, (*see* Celbes)
Achamoth, 41
Achilles, 67
Acts of the Apostles, 86
  1:17, 89
  6:5, 135
  8:10, 137
  8:19, 137
  17:34, 168
  20:34, 129
  24:5, 134
Acts of John, 87, 106
Acts of Paul, 126
Acts of Peter, 86
Acts of Peter and Paul, 138
Acts of Pilate, 79
Acts of Prochorus, 87
Acts of Thomas, 58
Adam, 15, 22, 33, 42, 55, 81, 121, 127, 141
Adamas, 55
Adamel, Adamael, Adamiel, 33, 38, 55
Adamites, 108, 175, 185
Adam Kadmon, 55
Adembes, (*see* Celbes)

Adiabene, 23
Adōnaeus, 45
Adonis, 73
adoption, 81
adultery, 44, 47, 48, 83, 123, 128, 157, 173, 176
adventism, 146, 176, 178
Adversus haereses, (*see* Against Heresies)
aeon, 15, 32
Aeschylus, 18
Against Heresies, 24
agapē, 103, 114, 115
agapētae, 115
agathodaimōn, 58
agnōsia, 46, 164
agōn, 20, 73
agrapha, 71
Aholah and Aholibah, 123
Ahriman, 15, 50
air, 50, 63
aithēr, 50
Akhmim, 26
Akiba, Rabbi, 162
Albigensians, 172, 174
alchemy, 186
alef, 75
alētheia, 123
Alexander the Paphlagonian, 154
Alexandria, 11
Alexandria, disciple of Carpocrates, 140
allegory, 190
Allegro, John, 83, 131, 132
allogenēs, 81, 153
Allogenes, 105, 153
Alogoi, 31
Alpha, 28, 75, 154
alphabet, 75, 101
Alphadelphia Phalanx, 184
Altruist Community, 184
Alumbrado, 178
Amalric of Bena, 177
Ambrose, St., 72

America, 184
Ammonius Saccus, 23, 25
ammonosites, 108
Amoun of Nitria, 115
Anabaptists, 178
anakephalaiōsis, 72
anamnēsis, 60
anastasis, 20
androgyny, 55, 121, 124, 188
android, 56
angels, 12, 15, 33, 53, 58, 64, 141
anima bruta, 61
anima divina, 62
anima humana, 62
animism, 49
anodos, 20
anonymity, 111
anōthen, 81
Anthony, (*see* Antony)
Anthrōpos, 15, 55, 121, 123, 152
Antichrist, 66, 125
antimimos, 52
antinomianism, 126, 127, 158, 175
Antitactae, 158
antitheoi, 39
Antony, St., 110
apagchō, 90
apatheia, 110
apeitheia, 42
Apelles, 21, 56, 145
Apocalypse (*see* Revelation)
Apocalypse of Peter, 26, 77
apocalypticism, 12, 17
apocatastasis, 25
apocrypha, 22
Apocryphon of John, 31, 39, 45, 50, 53, 79, 87, 152
Apollonius of Tyana, 155
apolytrōsis, 100
aporia, 46
apostasy, 99, 146

apostles (*see* disciples)
Apostles' Creed, 79, 151
apostolic succession, 163
Aramaic, 71
archai, 33
archangels, 33
archē, 29, 31
archetypes, 34, 51, 52
archigallus, 111
archōn(s), 12, **38**
archontes, 33
Archontics or Archonites, 152
Areopagus, 19
Aristobulus, 94
Aristotle, 140, 167
Armageddon, 66
armour, 59, 60
Armozel, 152
arsēnothēlys, 121
art, 106
Artemis, (*see* Diana)
ascension, 73, 79
Ascent of Paul, 96
asceticism, 16, **107**
Asclepius, 121, 166
Ashtaroth, 14
ass, 45, 73, 136, 156, 174
Astaphaeus, 45
astral body, 13, 19, 62, 104
astrology, 12, 50, 51, 53
Astronae, 111
ataraxia, 110
Athingani, 171
Athos, Mount, 24
Atonement, 89
Attis, 73, 111
Atum, 154
auditors, 169
augai, 33
augēus, 60
Augustine, St., 112, 131, 169, 189
authadēs, 39
authorities, 33
avidya, 164
Axionicus, 148
axis mundi, 35
Aztecs, 11

ba, 13
Baal, 43
Babel, 157
Babylonia, 14, 53, 67
Bahrdt, K. F., 78
Baigent, M., *et al.,* 93
Balaam, 135-6
Balkans, 171-2
Balthasar, 75
Balzac, Honoré de, 186
baptism, 12, 14-17, 51, 77, 91, **103**, 118, 136, 138, 160, 168

baptism for the dead, 146
Barbelites, 152
Barbelo, 152
Bardesanes or Bar Daisan, 149
Barnikol, Ernst, 145
Bartholomew, St., 95, 163
Baruch, 157
Basilides, 29, 36, 38, 46, 47, 58, 63, 64, 76, 77, 99, 102, 141
bastard, 74, 83
bathos, 48
Bath-Sheba, 74
Bauthumley, Jacob, 179
Bavent, Madelaine, 181
Bayley, H., 174
beggar, 177
Beghards, 177
beginning, 31, 65, 162
Beguines, 177
Behemoth, 155
Benedict XIV, 24
Benjamin, 95
bereshit, 162
bestiality, 136
beta, 76
beth, 76
Bethany, 90, 92
Bethlehem, 75, 96
Beulah, 125
Bezglovesniki, 183
Beziers, 172
Bhagavad-Gita, 164
bhakti, 164
Bianchi, Ugo, 11, 13, 164, 165
Birth of Mary, 45
Blackman, E. C., 86, 145
Blake, William, 186
Blavatsky, H. P., 184
Bleeker, Jouco, 13
blood, 15, 102, 103, 150
body, 39, **61**, 76, **101**, 167
Boehme, Jakob, 186
Bogomils, 171, 183
Book of Baruch, 156
Book of the Dead, 13
Book of the Great Invisible Spirit (see Gospel of the Egyptians)
Book of Elkesai, 134
Book of Enoch, 26
Book of John the Evangelist, 45
Books of Ieu, 105
Book of the Resurrection of Christ, 95
Books of the Saviour, 123
Book of Thomas the Contender, 88, 114
Borborians, 74, **157**
borborism, 129

borboros, 157
Bosch, Hieronymus, 178
Bottomley, (*see* Bauthumley)
boulē, 30
Boullan, Abbé, 182
Boullé, Thomas, 181
boundary, (*see* horos)
Bousset, Wilhelm, 14
bowels of Christ, 76
brain, 101-2, 118
bread, 15
breathing, 91, 102
Brethren of the Free Spirit, 175
bridal chamber, 14, 41, 122, **123**, 148
browsers, 109
Bruce, F. F., 36, 91, 118
Bruce, James, 26
Bruns, J. E., 83, 87, 89
Buddhism, 163-4
bull, 15, 103
Bultmann, Rudolf, 87
Buñuel, Luis, 83
bythos, 39, 48, **123**
Byzantine, 112, 165, 171

cacodaimōn, 58
Caesar, 48, 107, 189
Cain, 61, 126, 144, 150, 153
Cainites, 89, 150
call, and the called, 59-62, 65
Cambyses, 16
Campbell, J., 128, 131
Cana, 87
Canaan and Canaanites, 74, 117, 150
cannibalism, 128
canon, 145, 163
canons of proportion, 16
Carlyle, Thomas, 185
Carpocrates, 91, 119, 139
Carthage, 24, 131, 141
Caspar, 75
castration, 25, 111, 146, 184
Cataphrygian heresy, 146
catenati, 108
Cathars, 169
Celbes, 151
celibacy, 87, 111-113, 172
Celsus, 25, 104, 151, 155
cenobites, 108
Cerdo, or Cerdon, 143
Cerinthus, 77, **139**
Cessation of the Oracles, 72
Chadwick, H., 87
chain of being, 32
Chaldea, 12, 14, 74
Chaldean Oracles, 105

change, (see flux)
chaos, 39, 48
charaktēr, 57
Charaxio, 153
chariot, (see merkaba)
Chenoboskion, 27
cherubim, 33
chi, 16, 35
child, as androgyne, 121, 122
children, (see progeny, and sex with minors)
China, 169
chitōn, 61
chivalry, 173
chokma, 41
choic, 61
choice, (see chosen)
Choreutes, 171
chosen, 65
chosen people, 44, 142-3
chous, 61
chrēstos, 80
Christ, 32-4, 41, 63, ch., 5, 80
Christ in hell, 79
Christianity, 17, 163
christos, 80
Christotokos, 75
chronos, 52
chthonian deity, 154
Chrysostom, St., 104, 116
church, 41, 65
circumcision, 44, 103
Clement of Alexandria, 23, 69, 72-3, 87, 90, 91, 115, 137, 141, 148
Clement of Rome, 80
Coddians, 156
Cohn, N., 177
coincidentia oppositorum, 122
coitus reservatus, 118, 173, 177
Colossians,
2:18, 33
communism, 140, 176, 186
concubinage, 126
Congress on the Origins of Gnosticism, 11
consolamentum, 170
Constantia, 25
Constantine, 112, 135
constellations, 53, 101
Contra Celsum, 156
Conze, Edward, 164-5
Coptic, 26
1 Corinthians,
1:23, 190
2:6, 98
2:9, 82
2:10, 100
7:37, 115

9:5, 115
9:22, 82
12:3, 156
13:2, 96
15:6, 78
15:29, 146
15:51-3, 20
15:55, 66
2 Corinthians,
3:17, 175
4:4, 42, 54
5:21, 84
8:9, 82
12:2, 33
12:4, 96
Cornelius, 82
Corpus Hermeticum, (see Hermetic corpus)
corybantes, 111
cosmology, ch.3
Cosmocrator, 42
courtly love, 173
creation, 48, 51
creator (see demiurge)
credenters, 169
creed, 163
Cronos (Saturn), 47, 57, 111
Cross, 16, 35, 77, 88
Crowley, Aleister, 186
crucifixion, 71, 75, 77, 190
Cupitt, Don, 83
curiosity, 40, 42
curse, 84
cursing the fig tree, 73
cursing of Jesus, 156
curtain or veil, 34, 56, 71
Cybele, 111, 146, 154, 171
Cyprus, 25

daimōn, 39
Damascus, 95
Damkina, 73
dance, 94, 106, 146, 171
Daniel, Book of,
4:33, 109
7:13, 81
Dante, 174
darkness, 15, 37, 43, 46, 47, 49, 154
Dathan, 144, 151
David, 74
David, Pierre, 181
Davithe, 152
Dead Sea, 17, 117
Dead Sea Scrolls, 17, 26
death, 15, 19, 41, 43, 63, 66, 68, 79
decans, 39
Delitzsch, F., 14
Demeter, 79

demiurge (demiourgos), 12, 37-9, 41, 52, 137
demon(s), 15
demoniarch, 43
dendrites, 108
descent into hell, 14, 16, 19, 144
descent through the spheres, 57
destiny, (see fate)
Deshayes, Catherine, 182
deus absconditus, 29
deus manifestus, 30
deuteros theos, 32
De Vesme, C., 72
devil, 43
dharma, 164
diabolism, 173
diabolos, 42
Dialogue of the Saviour, 93, 114
Diana of Artemis, 87, 111
dianoia, 61
diaphragmos, 35
didachē, 71
Didymus, 88
diet, 44, 108, 109
dikaios, 43
dinē, 48
Diodorus Siculus, 72
Dionysus, 103, 154
Dionysius the Areopagite, 168
disciples, ch. 6
Discourse on the Eighth and Ninth, 100
Divine Pymander, (see Poimandres)
Dixon, W. H., 185
Dmitri, Archbishop, 183
docetism, 33, 76
dokein, 76
dominions, 33
Donatus, 119
door, 35
Dositheus, 136
Dostoevsky, Fyodor, 186
dove, 150
dragon, 154
dualism, 12, 15, 125, 148, 189
Dukhobors, 184
dynamis, dynameis, 33, 123

Ea, 73
ear, 74, 98
earth, 50, 63
Ebionites, 133-4
ecclēsia, 41, 65, 123
Ecclesiastes,
4:3, 68
ecplexis, 46
ecstasy, (see xenophrenia)

Eden, a power, 156
Eden, Garden of, 102, 155, 157
egg, 154
ego, 64
Egypt, 12-14, 53, 66, 73, 117-8, 140, 151, 152
eidōlon, 51, 136
eikōn, 34
ejaculation, 102, 118
el, 38
elect, 64, 142, 153 (see also perfect)
Eleleth, 152
element(s), 50, 63
elemental spirits, 39, 51, 58
eleos, 123
Eleusinian mysteries, 16, 18, 72
Eleutherians, ch. 10
Elias, (see Elijah)
Elias, Father, 174
Elijah, 33, 43, 78, 117
Elilaeus, 45
Elisha, 43, 103
Elkesaites, 133-4
elleipsis, 52
Eloaios, 45, 156
Elohim, 45, 121, 156
El Shaddai, 45
Elysian Fields, 39, 66
emanations, 13, 32, 141, 167
Emerald Tablet, 122
Emerson, R. W., 185
enantiodromia, 126
encratism, 114, 138, 173, 177
Endor, 67
endura, 170
endurance, 107
Enkidu, 67
ennead, 13
Enneads, 54
ennoia, 13, 30-1, 41
Enoch, 22, 33, 144
entaphiosis, 20
enthusiasm, 146, 171
enthymēsis, 123
Entychites, 157
envy, 47
Ephesians,
2:2, 50
3:19, 36, 97
4:9, 79
5:12, 8
5:14, 60
5:32, 124
6:12, 39
Ephesus, 23, 87
Ephraem Syrus, 74
epignōsis, 97
epiousios, 103

Epiphanes, 140
Epiphanius, 8, 25, 45, 57, 87, 96, 117, 128, 129, 131, 134, 158
epistēmē, 99
Epistle to Flora, 25, 44, 149
Epistle of Peter to Philip, 79
Epistle to Rheginos on the Resurrection, (see Treatise on Resurrection)
epithymia, 42, 113
epoptēs, 20
eranos, 103
Erathaoth, 45, 156
erōs, 114
Esaldaeus, 45
Esau, 131, 144, 150
eschatology, 63
Eshmun, 111
Essenes, 17, 78, 92, 135
eternity, 52
ether, (see aither)
etheric body, 13, 61
ethics and morality, 12, 99, 100, 107, 189, 190
eucharist, 15, 17, 73, 89, 92, 103, 115
eucharistia, 103-4
Euchites, 171
eunuch, 83, 111, 112
Euphrates, 151
Eurydice, 16
Eusebius of Caesarea, 23, 139
Eusebius, hermit, 108
Eutactus, 153
Eutropius, 112
Evangelium, Veritatis, 147
Eve, 22, 55, 56, 58, 121, 141, 153
evil, 15, 37, 43, 46, 64
evolution, 33
Excerpta ex Theodoto, 149
Exegesis on the Soul, 40
Exegetica, 141
existence, 29, 66, 187
existentialism, 187, 190
Exodus,
3:14, 80
5:2, 151
12:7, 130
14:21, 117
20:5, 64
21:24, 44
32:28, 43
34:14, 52
exousiai, 33
Expositions of the Prophet Parchor, 59
extreme unction, 172
Ezekiel
23:4, 123

Faber-Kaiser, A., 78
faith, 12, 41, 47, 96, 99, 144
Fall, 36, 42, 57, 84
falsehood, 47
Familists or Family of Love, 179
fasting, 44, 109
fate, 13, 37, 50
Faust, Dr, 137
Fayum, 26
felix culpa, 189
fellatio, 129
female and male, 94, 114, 121-4
fertility rites, 18
figs, 73, 157-8
fire, 43, 50, 63, 66, 102, 137
flagellation, 108, 183
Flaming Walls, 35
Flood, 43, 72, 153
Flora, (see Epistle)
Florinus, 148
flux, 34, 36, 52
Foerster, W., 84, 117, 128, 132, 152
Folliot, K., 93
food, (see diet)
footprint, 87
Fortunate Isles, 39
forty days and nights, 79, 84
Fox, George, 186
France, 93, 150, 172, 181
Francis, St., 174
Fränger, W., 177, 179
Freemasons, 186
free will, 36-8, 65
Frend, W. H. C., 161
Friedländer, M., 162

Galatians,
2:20, 99
3:13, 84
3:28, 122
4:3, 39
5:1, 175
galgal, 48
Galilee, 134
galloi, 111
Gamaliel, 95
Gaufridi, Louis, 181
Gaul, 149
Gayomart, 15
Gehenna, 155
gems, 13, 106
Genesis
1:2, 48, 49, 156
1:3, 49
1:7, 50
1:26, 55

GENERAL AND BIBLE INDEX 217

1:27, 121
1:28, 120
2:8, 157
3:21, 56
4:25, 153
6:4, 42, 117
8:7, 150
13:11, 150
38:9, 130
geocentricity, 53
Gethsemane, 77, 106
giants, 42, 117
Gibb, H. A. R., 165
Gilgamish, 67
Ginza, 80, 160
Gipsy, 171
Glaucias, 141
Glycon, 155
gnōsis, 12, 96, **189**
gnōstikos, 99
God, 12, 30
Godhead, 12, 29, 141
gods, lesser, 33
Godspell, 83
gold in mud, 58
Golden Legend, 93
golem, 56
Goliards, 173
Gomorrah, 43
good, 15
Gospel of the Ebionites, 134
Gospel of the Egyptians, or The Sacred Book of the Invisible Great Spirit, 94, 122
Gospel of Eve, 60, 119, 129
Gospel of the Hebrews, 31, 83
Gospel of Judas, 90
Gospel of Mary (Magdalene), 26, 93
Gospel of the Nazarenes, 135
Gospel of Nicodemus, (see Acts of Pilate)
Gospel of Peter, 26, 45, 77, 151
Gospel of Philip, 81-2, 92, 101, 121, 124
Gospel of Thomas, 26, 34, 45, 49, 57, 65, 72, 74, 88, 95, 103, 108, 114, 121-2, 130
Gospel of Truth, 27, 37, 65, 147
grace, 48, 140, 144, 189
Grandier, Urbain, 181
Grand Pantarchy, 185
Grant, R. M., 17, 100, 137, 155
Graves, R., and Podro, J., 78
Great Announcement, or Great Exposition, (see

Megale Apophasis)
Great Goddess, 111-12
Great Questions of Mary, 131
greed, 47
Greeks, 15-17, 67-8, 72
Greshniki, 183
Griffiths, R., 125, 182
Guibourg, Abbé, 182
gynē, 121

Hades, 43, 155 (see also hell)
Haecke, Abbé, 182
haima, 157
Haimatitoi, 157
half-caste, 83
Ham and Hamites, 74-5, 153
hands and handgrips, 15, 41, 104, 106
hanging, 89, 90
Hare, A., 183
Harmonius, 149
Harmozel, (see Armozel)
Harnack, Adolf, 17, 144
Harpocrates (Horus), 140
harrowing of hell, (see hell)
Hathor, 13
Hausdorff, D., 68
heaven, 33
heavens, lesser, 33, 38, 66
hebdomad, 47, 53
Hebrews,
  5:10, 154
  10:34, 176
  13:8, 80
Hegel, G. W. F., 186
Hegesippus, 23
heimarmenē, 50-3, 64, 111
heka, 13
hekalot, 162
Helen, Helena, 119, 136
Heliopolis, 13
hell, 16, 43, 63, 66-7, 79, 144
Hellenistic period, 12
Heracleon, 44, 149
Heracleopolis, 13
Hercules, 79, 157
hermaphrodite, 121
Hermas, 115
Hermes, Hermetics, 19, 73, 166
Hermes Trismegistus, 13, 166
Hermetica or Hermetic Corpus, 49, 65, 121, 166
Hermon, Mount Hermon, 117
Hernandez, Francesca, 179

hero, 72, 73, 79
Herod, 22, 94
Herodians, 70
Herodias, 94
Herodotus, 16, 20
heterodoxy, 190
heuresis, 20
Hibil Ziwa, 160
Hick, J., 164
hierogamy, 14, 124
hierophant, 15, 73
Hilarion, St., 112
Hillel, Rabbi, 68
himation, 62
Hinduism, 163
Hippolytus, 16, 21, 24, 88, 157
history, 106
Hittites, 74
Holy Spirit, 30-1, 41, 72, 74, 77, 125, 137, 146, 175
Homer, 17, 101
Homines Intelligentiae, 175
homosexuality, 83, 90, 120, 128, 171, 180
horion, 35
horkos, 19
horn, 131
horos, 34
Horothetēs, 34
Horus, 13, 73, 79, 111, 140
Houska, Martin, 178
hu, 13
hubris, 47
Hugo, Victor, 186
Hussites, 172
Huxley, A., 181
Huysmans, J. K., 182
hylē, 48, 52, 61
hylic, 61
Hymn of the Apostle Judas Thomas in the Land of India, also known as the Hymn of the Pearl, the Hymn of the Robe of Glory, the Hymn of the Soul, 58, 149
hyperēphania, 42
hypocaust, 158
hypogetes, 108
Hypostasis of the Archons, 40, 53, 152
hystera, 48
hysterēma, 34

Ialdabaōth, 40, 45, 50-3, 155
Iamblichus, 167
Ian, 14
Iaō, 45

Iaoth, 45, 156
I am Thou, 60
Iblis, 43
Ibrahim, 165
Ibrahim bin Adham, 166
ichnos, 37
Ida, Mount, 146
ideas, Platonic, 34
Ieou, (*see* Ieu)
Iessaei, 133
Ieu, 105
ignorance, 46
il, 160
imitation, 52
immortality, 16
impassibility, 29, 76
incarnation, 71, 75, 77,
    190
incest, 129, 157, 177
incubi, 182
India, 23, 68, 78, 88, 163
infinity, 52
initiation, 17, 18, 20
Ion, 14
Iran, 14-15
Irenaeus, 21, 22, 24, 38,
    54, 90, 105, 116, 119,
    127, 133, 148
irrationality, 71
Isaac, 150
Isaiah,
    14:13, 42
    28:10, 88
    28:13, 36
    34:4, 39, 66
    34:11, 35
    45:5, 53
    53:2, 82
    64:6, 188
Iscariot, 89
Ishmael, 150
Ishtar, 14, 79
Isidorus (*or* Isidore), 59,
    142
Isis, 13, 18, 73, 79, 139
Islam, 68, 135, 165, 169
Israel and Israelites, (*see*
    Jews)
Jabal-al-Tarif, 26
Jacob, 44, 131, 150
James the apostle, son of
    Zebedee, 22, 78, 82,
    86, 94
James the Just, brother of
    Jesus, 86, 119
James, M. R., 46, 74, 103,
    127
Japheth and Japhetics,
    74-5
Jared, 117
Jehovah, 17, 21, 43, 52,
    123, 142-3
Jerico, 74, 130

Jerome, St., 22, 23, 62,
    83, 110, 116, 146, 148
Jerusalem, 40, 73, 139,
    154
Jesuel, 42, 125
Jesus, 17, 69, ch. 5, 77,
    125, 131-2, 140 (*see also*
    Christ)
Jesus Christ Superstar, 83
Jeu, (*see* Book of Ieu)
Jews and Judaism, 12, 17,
    67, 133, 152, 162
Jnana, 164
Joanna, 95
Job, 68
Job, Book of,
    3:3, 68
    9:31, 176
Johann, 14
Johannine, 86
Johannite, 86, 159
John, 14
John the apostle, 22, 78,
    82, 86, 94, 139, 151
John the Baptist, 17, 45,
    77, 87, 94, 118, 135-6,
    160
John of Egypt, 109
John, Gospel of, 90, 149
    1:14, 31, 80
    3:3, 81
    3:13, 81
    3:14, 73, 156
    4:12, 44
    6:54, 132
    6:60, 132
    6:62, 132
    6:66, 132
    8:6, 107
    8:44, 46
    8:58, 80
    8:59, 76
    10:9, 35
    10:30, 81
    12:3, 92
    12:31, 38, 42
    13:26, 89
    13:27, 89
    14:2, 33
    16:12, 98
    21:23, 87
    21:25, 70
1 John,
    3:9, 118
Johnson, P., 163
Jonah, 14
Jonas, H., 44, 117, 120
Jordan, 77, 88, 102-3,
    117, 150, 152, 160, 177
Joseph, husband of Mary,
    74, 75
Joseph of Arimathea, 78
Josephus, 70, 94, 134

Joshua, 117
Joshua, Book of,
    2:18, 130
    3:16, 117
Joyce, D., 78
Judah, 74
Judaism, (*see* Jews)
Judas, 77, 86, 89, 126,
    151
Judasites, 89
Jude, Epistle of,
    1:8, 118
Judeo-Gnostics, 133
Jung, C. G., 34, 125, 131,
    187
Jung Codex, 27
Jupiter, (*see* Zeus)
Justin (*see* Justinus)
Justin Martyr, 23, 73
Justinian, 112
Justinus, 156

ka, 13
Kabala and Kabalism, 48,
    55, 136, 162
Kafka, Franz, 186
kakia, 43, 48
Kanishka, 164
Karaites, 162
Karpistēs, 34
Kashmir, 78
katapetasma, 34, 71
kathodos, 19
katochē, 109
kaulakau, 36, 88
kau-tohu, 35
keiriai, 61
kenōma, 36-7, 52
kenōsis, 37, 82
kenos, 52
kenotēs, 48
Kerioth, 89
kērygma, 71
khaibit, 13
Khepera, 13
Khlysti, 183
Khnemu or Khnubis, 13,
    154
Kierkegaard, Soren, 186-
7
kingdom of heaven, 71,
    99
1 Kings,
    18:40, 43
2 Kings,
    2:24, 43
    5:10, 103
kismet, 68
kissing, 115, 185
klifot, 48, 53
knowledge, 12, 96, 98
kolpos, 48
Korah, 144, 151

Koran, 135, 166
koros, 42
Kowalski, John, 182
Koweleff, Igor, 183
Kozlowska, Feliksa
  Maria, 182
Krasnya Krestinnye, 184
Krishna, 164
Kuria, 137
kuriotētes, 33
Kyrios, 80

Labib, Pahor, 14
Lacarrière, J., 69, 129,
  130, 158, 161, 171
L'Age d'Or, 83
lamb, 41, 103, 125
Lanczkowski, Dr Günter,
  11
language, 100
last days, 66
last judgment, 66
last supper, (see eucharist)
laughter, 77, 92
law, 37 (see also Mosaic
  law)
Laws, 39
Layton, B., 89, 118, 153,
  166, 186-7
Lazarus, 86, 90, 92-3
left and right, 41, 61-3,
  122
leitourgi, 39
Leontius, 112
letters, (see epistles)
Leucius, 87
levi, 157
Leviathan, 155
Levitici sect, 128, 157
Leviticus, Book of
  15:32, 118
libertinism, 16, 107, 125,
  141
life, physical, 61
light, 15, 37, 49
lila, 68
liturgists, 39
logia, 71, 88
logoi, 33
Logos, 12, 23, 30-4, 55,
  80, 123, 143
Lollards, 172
Lord's Prayer, 81, 171
Lord's Supper, (see
  eucharist)
Lot, 74, 150
lots, 51, 119, 157
Louviers, 181
love, 30, 36-7, 114
Loves of Jesus Christ, 84
Lucian, 155
Lucifer, 42, 125, 189
Luciferans, 173

Lucilla, 119
Lugdunum, (see Lyons)
Luke, St., 86, 95
Luke, Gospel of, 144
  1:28, 74
  2:47, 75
  3:22, 77
  4:6, 42
  7:37, 92
  8:29, 61
  10:18, 42
  10:19, 156
  12:8, 65
  12:49, 66
  16:26, 63
  17:21, 99
  17:34, 83
  19:41, 40
Lupercalia, 148
lust, 42, 47, 48, 113
Lutrōtēs, 34
Lyons, 24, 150, 161, 182

maarifa, 166
Macarius the Elder, 111
Macarius the Younger,
  109
MacCulloch, J. A., 172
macrocosm, 102, 122
magi, 75
Magharians, 162
Magus, 173
Mahayana, 164
makom, 45
male, (see female)
Mammon, 47, 107
mamzer, 74
man, 12, ch. 4
Manda da Hayye, 160
Mandaeans, 26, 50, 103,
  133, 135, 159
Mani (or Manes),
  Manicheans, 26, 131,
  134, 149, 168
Mann, Thomas, 186
mansions, 33, 162
Marcellina, 141
Marcion, 23, 61, 69, 86,
  96, 107, 119, 126, 143,
  189
Marcus, the Marcians and
  Marcosians, 101, 119,
  124, 149
Marduk, 73
Mareotis, 18
Mariamme or Mariamne,
  119
Mariavites, 182
Mark, St., 86
Mark, Gospel of,
  4:11, 98
  4:31, 101
  6:22, 94

  7:15-19, 83
  14:3, 93
  14:52, 91
  15:21, 77, 142
  16:9, 92
Mark, secret gospel, 24,
  90-1, 99, 140
Mark of Memphis, 158
Maron, 108
marriage, 126, 145, 176
marriage, mystical, 14, 41,
  123, 148
Mars, 47, 57
Mar Saba, 90
Martha of Bethany, 90,
  92, 93, 95, 119
martyrdom, 99, 158
Martyrdom of Philip, 122
Marxism, 186
Mary, 92, 95, 119
Mary of Bethany, 90, 92
Mary, wife of Cleophas,
  93
Mary the Copt, 165
Mary the Egyptian, 110
Mary, mother of James
  and Joses, 93
Mary Magdalene, 22, 86,
  92, 95, 114, 131-2, 151
Mary, mother of Jesus,
  73-5, 87, 112, 151, 173
Masada, 78
mask, 57
masturbation, 120, 129,
  131, 154, 180
mathēsis, 99
matrix, 48
matter, 37, 48, 52
Matthew, St., 86
Matthew, Gospel of
  3:16, 118
  4:1, 84
  5:25, 99
  5:39, 127
  5:40, 62
  5:48, 175
  7:6, 142
  9:15, 124
  10:27, 98
  11:19, 83
  11:25, 122
  11:29, 35
  13:3, 61
  13:25, 62
  13:35, 82
  19:12, 112
  19:14, 188
  21:19, 158
  21:31, 47
  22:14, 65
  25:3, 63
  25:13, 124
  27:5, 90

27:24, 151
Maximilla, 119, 147
Mead, G. R. S., 28, 118, 186
Megale Apophasis, 31, 50, 60, 101, 138
megavusus, 112
Melchior, 75
Melchizedek, Melchizedekians, 78, 153, 154, 182
Melchizedek, 153
melothesia, 101
Melville, Herman, 186
Menander, 138
menses, menstruation, 113, 129, 130, 137, 152, 181
Mercury, 47
mercy, 41
merkaba, 27, 33, 162
Mesopotamia, 14, 67
mesos, 62
Messalians, 59, 171
Messiah, 17, 143
Metagōgeus, 34
metanoia, 41, 60
Mētropatōr, 121
meum et tuum, 140, 176
microcosm, 102, 122
millennium, 176, 178
Milton, John, 186
mimēsis, 52
minim, 162
Mishna, 67
misogyny, 113, 119, 120
Mithra and Mithraism, 15, 103
Moab, 74
Monica, 169
monogenēs, 31
Monoimus, 100
Montanus and Montanists, 24, 146
Montségur, 172
Montvoison, Madame, 182
moon, 47
morality, (*see* ethics)
Morelshchiki, 183
Moses and Mosaic Law, 17, 43, 44-5, 67, 78, 84, 88, 117, 133, 140, 150
Mossiker, F., 182
moth, 41
mother, 31, 74
Mother Goddess, (*see* Great Goddess)
Mozart, W. A., 186
Mughtasila, 168
Muhammad, 160, 165
murder, 47, 48
Muslim, (*see* Islam)
mustard seed, 101

myein, 19
mystagogue, 19
mysteries, 18, 72, 98
mystēs, 19
mythology, 72

Naaman, 103
Naas, 155, 157
Naassene(s), 17, 30, 48, 80, 88, 101, 118, 119, 125, 155
Nachaites, 155
nachash, 155-6
Nag Hammadi, 12, 14, 25
nakedness, (*see* nudity)
name, 13
Narses, 112
Nasseni (*see* Naassenes)
nature, 52, 61
nazar, 135
Nazarenes, Nazareans, Nazoreans, Nazarites, Nasoreans, Nasara, 133, 134, 135, 159
Nazareth, 96, 134, 135
Nazism, 186, 188
Nebuchadnezzar, 109
nefilim, 42, 117
neighbour, 189
neophyte, 15, 20
Neoplatonism, 23, 54, 146, 166, 167
Nerval, Gérard de, 186
Nestorius and Nestorianism, 74, 165
neume, 105
New Jerusalem, 146, 176
New Testament, 21, 145
Nicaea, 112
Niclaes, Heinrich, 179
Nicodemus, 78, 86
Nicolaitanes, 135
Nicolas, 135
Nietzsche, Friedrich, 100, 186
Nihilism, 186
Nitriaid, 110
Noah, 144, 150
nochaite, 155
Nock, A. D., 17
noēsis, 63
noetic, 62, 64-5, 148
nomos, 126
Norea, 153
Nothingarians, 185
nothingness, 29
Notre Dame, 93
noumenal world, 34, 36
Nous, 30, 62, 122-3, 155, 167
Novalis, 186
Noyes, J. H., 185

nudity, 91, 108, 127, 141, 177
numbers, 14, 102, 104, 142, 149
Numbers, Book of, 6:2, 135
16:1, 151
21:8, 73
21:9, 156
Numenius of Apamea, 145
Nun, 113
nymphōn, 124

Oannes, 14
Odes of Solomon, 81
Odyssey, 67
ogdoad, 53, 148
okhēma, 62
Old Testament, 7, 17, 21, 43-4, 72, 144-5
Olives, Mount of, 79
Olympus, 68
Omega, 28, 154
omniarch, 42
Omphale, 157
omphalos, 48
Onan, 130
One Hundred and Twenty Days of Sodom, 83
One Mentians, 184
Oneida Creek, 185
onomata barbara, 106
ontological world, 34
ophiomorphus, 42
ophis, 154
Ophites, 154
opposites, 122-3, 125
oracles, 72
Oreus, 45
Origen, 20, 25, 112, 125, 138, 156
Origin of the World, 152
Ormazd, 15
Oroaiel, 152
Orpheus, 16, 73, 79
Orphism, 16
Osiris, 13, 20, 73, 79, 111
ouroboros, 53, 154
ousia, 62
Oxyrhynchus, 26

paganism, 12, 71
Pagels, E., 88
Pan, 39, 73
Panarion, 25, 96, 134, 156
panoplia, 59
Pantaenus, 23, 163
Panthera, 74
parables, 98
paraclētos, 31, 146
paradeigmata, 34

paradise, (*see* heavens, lesser)
Paradise Lost, 186
paradox, 100, 190
Paraphrase of Shem, 153
Parchor, 59
paredros, 58
Parhedron Typhon, 113
parousia, 125
Parrinder, G., 165
Pascal, Blaise, 186
Pasolini, P. P., 83
passgrips, 106
pastas (*or pastos*), 124
Patarenes, 171
patēr, 123
pathēsis, 99
Patmos, 87
Paul, St., 20, 33, 86, 95, 113, 115, 138, 144
Paul I, Pope, 138
Pauli, Wolfgang, 186
Paulicans, 171
Pauline marriage, 115
pearl, 58
peccatism, 127, 176, 183
Pentateuch, (*see* Mosaic Law)
pentecostalism, 176
Pepuza, 146
Peratae or Peratic sect, 102, 118, 151
Perfect or Perfecti, 64, 98, 127, 158, 169, 170, 176 (*see* elect)
Perfectionists, 175, 185
Perfect Word, 166
Peripatetics, 23
Perry, W. J., 14
persecution, 99
Persephone, 73
Persia (*see* Iran)
persona, 57
personality, 64
Peter, St., 22, 77-8, 82, 86, 92-3, 114-15, 138, 141, 151
1 Peter
3:19, 79
4:6, 79
5:14, 115
2 Peter
2:16, 136
Peter of Capharbarica, 153
petrites, 108
phallus, 16, 110
phantasia, 59
Pharaoh, 150
Pharez, 74
Pharisees, 70, 89
phenomena, 34, 36, 37
Phibionites, 106, 128, 157

Philip the apostle, 115
Philip the evangelist, 83, 137
Philip the tetrarch, 94
Philippians, Epistle to,
2:7, 82
3:20, 60
Philistines, 14
Philius, 16
Philo of Alexandria, 17-8, 31, 55, 72, 80
Philoprogenitive Familists, 185
philosōmatia, 126
Philosopheumena, 24
philosophy, 99
Philumēnē, 145
phoneme, 13, 105, 142
phōs, 60
Phōstēr, 153
phragmos, 35
phrearites, 108
Phrygia, 12, 111, 146, 171
Phrygian mode, 171
phylacterism, 44, 162
physis, 52, 61
Picards, 178
Pilate, 22, 140, 151
pillar hermits, 108
pistikos, 99
pistis, 41, 99, 123
Pistis Sophia, 26, 40, 49, 79, 113, 123, 131, 154
Place, 36, 45, 82
plainsong, 105
planē, 46
planets, 47, 53, 57, 64
plasm, 56
Plato, 17, 23, 27, 34-5, 39, 49, 52, 114, 121, 140, 167
pleasure, 107
plērōma, 32, 34, 36, 41, 52
plexus, 102
Plotinus, 54, 146, 167
Plutarch, 13, 19, 20, 39, 72
pneuma, 62, 105
pneumatikos, 62, 127
Poimandres (*or* Pymander), 49, 121, 166
Polycarp, 24, 139
ponēria, 43
Pope, 163
Populani, 171
Porphyry, 58, 167
powers, 13, 33, 39
practices, ch. 7
Prato Nuns, 179
prayer, 33, 60, 81, 141, 171
prayers for the dead, 102

prefiguration, 72-3, 79
pride, 42, 47
Priapus, 156
principalities, 33, 39
Priscilla (*or* Prisca), 119, 147
Priscillian, 87, 158
privativism, 107
proasteion, 35
probolē, 32
Prochorus, 87-8
Procla, 151
Proclus, 168
procreation, (*see* progeny)
Procula, 119, 159
Prodicus, 141
prodigal son, 60
progeny, 94, 120, 128, 131, 140, 147
promiscuity, (*see* libertinism)
Promised Lane, 44, 152
pronoia, 50, 123, 136
Prophets, 43-4, 72
prosartēmata, 47
prostitution, 126
Protestants, 145, 172
prouneikos, 40, 152
Provence, 93, 173
Provençal, 174
Proverbs, Book of
5:15, 130
providence, 37, 50
Prunicus, 152
Psalms, 44
1:3, 130
91:6, 131
Pseudo-Clementines, 80
Pseudo-Dionysius, 168
psychē, 61, 62, 101, 122
psychikos, 62
psychoanalysis, 186, 188
psychopompos, 19
Ptah, 13, 160
Ptah-il, 160
Ptolemaeus, 25, 44, 149
puberty rites, 18
Publicani, 71
Publicanism, 171
Puritanism, 186, 188
pyknōsis, 37
Pymander, (*see* Poimandres)
Pythagoras, 17, 23, 140, 142, 167

Quakers, 184
Quietists, 108
Quispel, Gilles, 185, 186
Qumran, 17, 26, 78

Ra, 13, 111
races, 56, 74, 75, 142

radenya, 184
Rahab, 74, 130
Ranters, 179
Raskolniks, 183
Rasputin, G., 183
raven, 150
real world, 34, 36
reason, 13
Rechabites, 109
redeemed Redeemer, 79, 84
Redeemer, 34, 36
Red Sea, 117-18, 152
Reformation, 172
Refutation of All Heresies, 24, 88
reincarnation, 36, 63-4, 141
ren, 13
Renaissance, 16
resurrection, 15, 65, 67, 71, 75, **78,** 189-90
Revelation, 87
  2:11, 66
  2:15, 135
  2:24, 100
  6:8, 43
  6:13, 158
  10:6, 66
  12:9, 42
  20:14, 66
  21:5, 66
  21:9, 41
  22:2, 130
  22:13, 29, 155
Revelation of Adam to His Son Seth, 53
Revelation of Dositheus (see Three Steles of Seth)
Rexroth, K., 186
Rheginos, 59
rheos, 52
Richards, H. J., 46
right, (*see* left)
Rilke, R. M., 186
Ring-pass-not, 35
ritualism, 102
Robbins, R. H., 182
Robertson, J. M., 73
Roguemont, D., 174
Romans, 17, 78, 82
Romans, Epistle to,
  1:27, 128
  5:20, 45
  8:3, 83
  10:4, 84
  13:12, 60
  16:16, 115
Rope of the Angels, 35
Rosicrucians, 185
Rulers of the Cities up to the Ether, 104
Runciman, S., 171

Russia, 172, **183**
Ruth, 74
Rutherford, J., 150

Sabaōth, 45, 64, 153, 155
Sabaeans, (*see* Sabians)
Sabazius, 154
Sabbath, 44
Sabians, 133, 159
saccophores, 108
sacraments, 102
sacramentum, 19
Sacred Book of the Invisible Great Spirit (see Gospel of the Egyptians)
sacrifices, animal and human, 44, 73
Sadducees, 67, 70
Sade, Marquis de, 83
saints, 163, 188
Sais, 13, 20
Saklas, 113
Salamis, 25
Salem, 154
Salome, 86, **93,** 119, 120, 122, 131
salvation, 12, 47, 65-6, 68
Samael, 53
Samaria, 23, 136
Samaritans, 44, 67, 82, 138
Samothrace, 16
Samson, 135
Samuel, 67, 135
1 Samuel,
  28:13, 67
Sarapion, 108
sarkic, 61
sarkikos, 61
sarkos, 61
Satan, 55, 81, 125
Satanel, Satanael, Sataniel, 38, 41, 125
Satanists, 173
satiety, 42
Satornilus, (*see* Saturninus)
Saturn, (*see* Cronos)
Saturninus, 56, 116, **138**
saulasau, 45, **88**
scandalon, 135
Scholem, Gershom, 162
Schonfield, H. J., 78, 83
scotos, 46
seals, 57, 81-2, 104, 139
second death, 66
Second Treatise of the Great Seth, 40, 153
secrecy, 19, 22, 82, 98, 99, 142
Secret Discourse on the Mount, 166
sects., ch. 8
Secundus, 148

Sefer Yetzira, 162
sefirot, 162
Selēnē, 136
sēma, 16
semen, (*see* sperm)
Semo or Semoni, 138
seraphim, 33
Serapis, 109, 154
serpent, 42, 73, 125, 150, 152, **154**
Seth, Egyptian god, 111, 153
Seth, son of Adam, 22, 63, 153
Sethians, 49, 58, **152**
Severus, 24, 58, 109, **145**
sex, 113, 116, 121, 123, 128
sex with minors, 120, 129
sex mysticism, 27, 177, 182
sexophobia, 113
Shammai, Rabbi, 68
Shekina, 41
Shem, 75
sheol, 67
Shepherd, 115
shoy, 13
sia, 13
sicarios, 89
sigē, 29, 123
silence, 29, 87, 108, 142, 183
Silvanus, 80, 122
Simeon, Father, 166
simia Dei, 52
Simon of Cyrene, 77, 142
Simon of Gitta, 138
Simon Magus and Simonians, 17, 23, 121, 128, **136,** 151
Simon Stylites, 108
simony, 137
sin, 47, 84, 127, 140, 176, 179, **188,** 189 (*see* peccatism)
sinapi, 101
Siwa, 109
Skoptsi, 113, 184
sloth, 47
Smith, A., 112
Smith, Grafton Elliot, 14
Smith, Morton, 22, 90, 91
Socrates, 59
Sodom, 43, 144
sodomy, 120, 128, 131, 136, 157, 172, 173, 177
solitude, 108
Solon of Athens, 100
sōma, 16, 101
Son of God, 12, 30-32, 80, 154
Son of Man, 53, 81, 156

Song of Solomon,
  6:8, 133
Sophia, 38, 39, 53, 81,
  123-4, 137, 152
Sōtēr, 123-4
soul, 13, 56, 57, 62
sound, 105
space, 37, 39, 48, 52
Spain, 149, 158
Sperling, H., and Simon,
  M., 136
sperm, 102, 117-8, 137,
  140, 152
sperma, 118
spermepotation, 129-31
sphragis, 57, 139
Spighi, Sister, 179
spinthēr, 56
spiral, 35-6
spiritual love, spiritual
  marriage, 115
stand, 31, 137
stability, 108
Star of the Nativity, 75
stars and star lore, 14, 49,
  50-3, 57
Stauros, 35, 52, 88
stenochoria, 46
stercoranism, 104
Stewart, D., 71, 78
Stoic(s), 17, 23, 54, 89,
  110, 167
stoicheia, 39, 51
Stranniki, 183
Stratiotici, 158
Streeter, B. H., 70
Stromateis, 23, 141
stylites, 108
subtle body, (*see* astral
  body)
succubus, 18, 182
suffering, 35, 77, 78, 106
Sufism, 166
suicide, 89, 90, 147, 151,
  170, 183
Summers, Montague, 181
sun, 47
Susanna, 95
Symonds, J., 186
Symposium, 114, 121
syndexi, 15
synoptic gospels, 86-7
synousia, 113
Syntagma, 24
Syria, 133, 135, 138, 143,
  146, 149
syzygy, 13, 123

Tabor, Mount, 78, 172,
  176, 178
Taborites, 176, 185
taktos, 158
Talmud, 52, 162

Tamar, 74
Tammuz, 14, 73
Tartarus, 155-6
Tatian, 23
tau, 16, 35
Teacher of Righteous-
  ness, 17
Teachings of Silvanus, 80,
  122
teletē, 19
teleutē, 19, 20
telos, 29
temenos, 125
Templars, 173-4
Temple, 44-5
temptation, 73, 79, 84,
  116
Tarah, 74
Tertullian, 24, 38, 60, 63,
  82, 115-6, 147, 189
texts., ch. 2
thalamos, 124
thalassa, 48, 151
Thales, 49
thanatos, 43
Thartharaoth, 45, 156
Thauthabaoth, 45, 156
Thebaid, 18, 110
Thebes, 13
thelēma, 37
Theodas, 96, 147
Theodore, 90
Theodotus, 65, 82, 90,
  148
theogamy, (*see* bridal
  chamber)
theoi, 33
Theophilus of Antioch, 24
Theorem, 83
Theosophy, 56, 100
Theotimus, 148
Theotokos, 75
Therapeutae, 18
Theseus, 79
2 Thessalonians,
  2:7, 48
Theudas (*see* Theodas)
theurgy, 167
Third Testament, 146
Thomas, St., 36, 45, 86,
  88, 131, 163
Thorsen, J. J., 84
Thossa, 151
Thoth, 13, 166
Thrace and Thracians, 16,
  154, 171
Three Steles of Seth, 136,
  153
thronoi, 33
thuella, 48
Thunder, Perfect Mind, 41
thura, 35
Tiberius, 73

Tibet, 169
Timaeus, 35, 49, 52
time, 15, 34, 37, 39, 48,
  51-2, 59, 66, 106
1 Timothy,
  1:4, 124
  6:20, 96
Titanic, 16
tohu-bohu, 48, 156
tolma, 40, 42
Tolstoy, Leo, 184, 186
toparch, 39
topos, 37, 39, 45
Torah, (*see* Mosaic law)
Torchbearer, 73
trance, (*see* xenophrenia)
transfiguration, 76-78,
  164
transit, 35, 102
transubstantiation, 104
Treatise on Resurrection, 59
Trees of Eden, 125, 157
triad, 13
triangles, 102
Trimorphic Protennoia, 153
Trinity, 13, 30-1, 73
Tripartite Tractate, 38
troglodytes, 108
troubadours, 173
Troy, 136
Tsigane, 171
Tucci, Giuseppe, 165
Turfan, 26
Turlupins, 178
twin, 88
tychē, 157
Tyler, P., 83

ugliness, 82
Uighurs, 26, 169
Ulysses, 67
Umphreville, Lucina, 185
universals, 34
Universologists, 184
Uranian, 16
Uranus, 111
uthras, 160
uxoriousness, 126

Valentine, St., 149-50
Valentinus, 38, 45-6,
  50-1, 58, 63, 68, 76,
  123, 124, 147, 189
Valerius, Valerians,
  Valesii, 112
Valhalla, 66
Van Haecke, Abbé, 182
Vaudois, 172, 186
Vaughan, Thomas, 35
vegetarianism, 109
veil, (*see* curtain)
Venus, 47, 57, 107
via negativa, 29, 168

vine, 109
Vintras, Eugène, 182
Virgil, 72
virgin, 74-5, 121, 129
virgin birth, 73
Virgin Mary, (see Mary)
Vitruvius, 16
Voragine, Jacobus de, 93
Vorago, 48
vortex, 48
vowels, 105

Waldenses, 172
Walker, B., 118, 163
Warner, M., 84
water, 14, 50, 63
Weightman, J., 84
wheel, 48
whirlwind, 48
widow, 75
wilderness, 70, 73, 79, 84
will, 30, 37 (see free will)
Wilson, R. M., 14
Winckler, Hugo, 14
wine, 15, 109, 135, 145

wisdom, 13
Wisdom of Jesus Christ, 79
witches, 94, 173
womb, 120
women, 113-4, 119, 145, 147
word, 13, 73
works, good, 12, 144, 188, 189
worm, 56
wrath, 47
writing, 106
Wycliffites, 172

xenophrenia, 19, 99, 104, 146, 152, 156, 167, 176

Yahveh, 45, 50
Yahyah, 160
Yamauchi, E. M., 162, 186
yarad, 117
Yeats, W. B., 186
yoke, 35

Zacchaeans, 158
Zacchaeus, 75-6
Zacharias, 45
Zagreus, 73
Zahner, R. C., 50
Zealots, 70, 89
Zebedee, 86, 93
Zechariah,
4:10, 50
zeesar, 88, 118
zētēsis, 20
Zeus (Jupiter), 47, 73, 111, 121
zodiac, 39, 53, 101
zōe, 61
Zohar, 136
zophos, 46
Zoroaster, 15, 17, 153-4, 168
Zoroastrianism, 12, 50
Zorokothoro, 154
Zostrianos, 153
Zurvan, 15
zygos, 35